Comics Art in Korea

University Press of Mississippi / Jackson

Comics Art in Korea

John A. Lent

The University Press of Mississippi is the scholarly publishing agency of the Mississippi Institutions of Higher Learning: Alcorn State University, Delta State University, Jackson State University, Mississippi State University, Mississippi University for Women, Mississippi Valley State University, University of Mississippi, and University of Southern Mississippi.

www.upress.state.ms.us

The University Press of Mississippi is a member of the Association of University Presses.

Manufactured in the United States of America
∞

Library of Congress Control Number: 2024948959

ISBN 9781496854711 (hardback)
ISBN 9781496854674 (trade paperback)
ISBN 9781496854681 (EPUB single)
ISBN 9781496854698 (EPUB institutional)
ISBN 9781496854704 (PDF single)
ISBN 9781496854667 (PDF institutional)

British Library Cataloging-in-Publication Data available

Collaborators:

Kwon Jae-woong
Suh HaeLim
Yu Kie-un

Let me tell you about "Crazy Nick."

In the 1940s, in the tiny, worked-out Pennsylvania coal mining town where I was growing up, on regular occasions, hoboes would appear at my family's home, offering to do chores in exchange for a meal. My mother and grandmother would always feed them.

"Crazy Nick" was a regular "guest."

Though we never knew his real name, Crazy Nick was a memorable character, primarily because of how he unwittingly sought retribution from the coal operators who had enslaved miners and their families, forcing them to live in towns where the company owned everything, using a currency (scrip) spendable only in highly priced company-owned facilities, sending men into an unsafe, unhealthy underground, and polluting and destroying the land, air, and water, for many decades.

To make ends meet, every day, my mother, brother, and I went to the tracks and picked coal that had fallen from loaded railroad cars passing by on their way to the steel mills near Pittsburgh. This coal was our only source of fuel.

This is where Crazy Nick comes in. Every once in a while, riding the rails north, Crazy Nick would be standing atop a loaded coal car, calling attention to himself while feverishly tossing the largest lumps overboard for us to pick up later.

Crazy Nick was repaying the generous townsfolk who had given him a meal, with coal "provided" by the companies that had made them suffer for generations. A noble (though illegal) gesture, indeed.

To all the "Crazy Nicks" of the world who exacted a bit of justice and payback from those parts of capitalism and corporatism that put their selfish gains far ahead of the basic needs of the people.

—John A. Lent

Contents

Acknowledgments

First off, I would like to explain my dedication page in this book, though I feel no need to justify or defend my choice. Why would I dedicate a book to a nameless, willing-to-work-for-food hobo of the 1940s? one may ask. Because, over my long life, I have lived among or otherwise associated with many downtrodden, derogatorily nicknamed, and otherwise simple people, and found them to be sincere, helpful, respectful, and still able to quip or crack a joke under very dire circumstances. They were or could be in league with the "Crazy Nicks."

For this book, there are a number of people to whom I am very grateful. During my college/university teaching career (1960–2011) in various parts of the United States, Canada, different universities in China, the Philippines, and Malaysia, I have been fortunate to teach and/or supervise many excellent students. In my thirty-seven years at Temple University (1974–2011), I supervised many dozens of graduate students seeking PhDs, MAs, and MJs, the majority coming from abroad, predominantly from Asia, but also the other continents to a lesser extent. Most were exceptional, and a number went on to become professors, researchers, and administrators. Their high-quality scholarship was greatly appreciated and welcomed, especially during the ending years of my teaching stint, when undergraduate study had dipped, in some cases, below secondary school levels, when Temple University and some other academic institutions absorbed "more-is-best" standards of admission and the approach that "students-are-all-knowing-customers" once in the classroom.

Top of the list of those I wish to acknowledge are Korean graduate students who studied under my supervision and sparked my interest in authoring this volume, and, early on, had key roles in conceptualizing it, namely Dr. Yu Kie-un and Dr. Kwon Jae-woong, followed shortly after by Dr. Noh Sueen and Dr. Kim Chunhyo. They were joined by other advisees such as Dr. Kim Hoon-soon, Dr. Kim Myung-jun, and Lee Sang-kil in helping set up interviews and serving as interpreters while I was in Korea. Dr. Noh Kwang-woo, Roh Byung-sung, and Park Jae-dong were very helpful in the same regard. Also helpful and to whom I am thankful is Dr. Suh HaeLim, for checking for inaccuracies and proper spelling of Korean names; my assistant, Denise Gray, for typing the manuscript multiple times and eagle-eyeing it for typos and inconsistencies, and Xu Ying for her encouragement and love.

The many cartoonists who met with me and provided vital information and anecdotes deserve a hearty thank you; some gave me their time on multiple occasions, such as Park Jae-dong, Shin Dong-hun, Nelson Shin, and Ahn Hyun-dong.

I have been privileged to work with the excellent staff at the University Press of Mississippi, the grandfather of comic art publishing. In fact, my association with the press goes back more than thirty years, actually to the beginning of its interest in comic art, which was spurred on by my friend Tom Inge and the press's director, Seetha Srinivasan. Over the years, I worked, to my extreme satisfaction, with others, particularly Vijay Shah and Lisa McMurtray. My deepest gratitude to University Press of Mississippi and its staff for advancing comic art scholarship and for having faith in my work.

Historical Timeline of Korea—Including Comics Art

37 BC–68 AD	Goguryeo Kingdom. Goryeo (also Koryŏ), official name in the fifth century. Origin of the English name Korea.
918–1392	Goryeo, the Korean state known for unifying the peninsula.
1392–1910	Joseon Dynasty.
c. 1760–1815	Painters Kim Hong-do and Sin Yun-bok draw cartoon-like works, including Kim's *Ssirum* and a number of others by both that featured common peoples' daily activities and erotica.
1905	Japan wins Russo-Japanese War. Korea becomes Japanese protectorate.
1909	First recognized political cartoon by Lee Do-yeong.
1920	Korea's first female cartoonist, Na Hye-seok, with "What Is That?" in the magazine *Sin Yeoja*.
1920s	Origins of four-panel cartoon by Kim Dong-seong in the newspaper *Dong-A Ilbo*.
1945	Japanese occupation ends with conclusion of World War II. Soviet troops occupy territory north of thirty-eighth parallel; US military, the south.
1948	Formation of Republic of Korea (South Korea), with Syngman Rhee as president, and Democratic People's Republic of Korea (North Korea), with Kim Il-sung as premier. Jeju Uprising. Inauguration of North Korea's illustrated satire magazine *Hwalsal*.
1950	Korean War begins. Propaganda leaflet warfare starts.
1950s	*Soonjung* (girls') manhwa and comics factory/rental shop system start in South Korea. Animation treated merely as a form of film that is experimental in nature in North Korea.
1953	Korean War ends. Estimated two million lives lost.
1955	Four-panel political cartoons strongly reintroduced and popularly received in South Korea with *Gobau* by Kim Song-hwan.

1956	First acknowledged animation production in South Korea—a toothpaste advertisement.
1957	Startup of April 26 Children's Animation Film Studio (rebranded SEK Studio in 1997) in North Korea.
1958	Experimental Institution of Animation and Film launched in North Korea.
1960	South Korea's Second Republic formed when student protests force Rhee to resign.
1961	Military coup puts General Park Chung-hee in South Korean leadership. Revival of precensorship.
1963	Proclamation of Third Republic in South Korea. Some political freedom restored. Beginning of industrial advancement.
1960s–1970s	South Korea's golden age of manhwa. Beginning of offshore animation production. Cheerful (*myung rang*) manhwa genre dominant.
1967	South Korea's first feature animation, *Hong Gil Dong*, by Shin Dong-hun.
1967	Launching of the ideology of the Communist Party (*yuil sasang*) and the struggle to advance socialism in North Korea.
1970	Creation of Korean Ethics Committee for Books and Magazines in South Korea.
1972	Martial law in South Korea. Escalation of Park's powers.
1976	Establishment of Daiwon, South Korea's first and largest animation studio.
1979	Assassination of President Park Chung-hee.
1980	General Chun Doo-hwan seizes power. Declaration of martial law following student demonstrations. Beginning of Fifth Republic. Gwangju Uprising in South Korea.
1980s	In South Korea, rejuvenation of girls' comics with female creators; advent of comics magazines; beginning of manhwa spinoffs, the first being *Dooly the Little Dinosaur*.
1980s	North Korea's golden age of *kurimchaek* (comic books), many with war and spy themes.
1981	End of South Korean martial law. Chun elected to seven-year term as president.
1987	General Roh Tae-woo succeeds ousted Chun as South Korean president. Political freedom increased.
1991	*On Fine Art* by Kim Jong-il published in North Korea.
1993	Kim Young-sam becomes first freely elected president of South Korea.
1994	Death of Great Leader Kim Il-sung of North Korea; succeeded by son, Kim Jong-il. Beginning of North Korean famine.
1994	Recognition, with much financial support, of animation and cartoons as major export by South Korean government.
1995	First Seoul International Cartoon and Animation Festival.
1997–1998	Second major financial thrust for animation and cartoons by South Korean government.
1998	Swearing in of Kim Dae-jung as South Korean president. Implementation of government's "sunshine policy," offering unconditional aid to North Korea.
Late 1990s	Establishment of quota system requiring 50 percent of South Korean televised animation time to be of local origin.
Late 1990s	First web comics in South Korea.
Early 2000s	Cooperation between North and South Korean animation studios on *Ding the Lazy Cat*, *Pororo the Little Penguin*, and *Empress Chung*.
2000s	Advancement of internet use, webcomics, and new genres in South Korea.
2002–2007	South Korean presidency of Roh Moo-hyun.
2007–2012	South Korean presidency of conservative Lee Myung-bak.
2010s	Surge of South Korean investigative

	graphic novels, highlighted by Gendry-Kim Keum suk's *Grass*.
2011	Death of Kim Jong-il. Kim Jong-un new supreme leader of North Korea.
2012–2017	South Korea's first female president, Park Geun-hye, daughter of Park Chung-hee.
2014	Sinking of *Sewol* ferry, killing hundreds of high school students.
2017	Moon Jae-in, South Korean president, after impeachment of Park Geun-hye.

Comics Art in Korea

Chapter 1

Genesis and Dimensions

Let me begin with a personal setting.

My first visit to South Korea was in the summer of 1965. It was a short stay to meet up with a few Korean journalists I had met at an Asian editors' conference in Manila.

It was just a dozen years after the end of the Korean War and twenty since the country was freed from Japan's exploitative rule and then partitioned into the Democratic People's Republic of Korea (North Korea) and the Republic of Korea (South Korea).

South Korea was among the poorest countries worldwide, its per capita income comparable to that of Haiti in 1960; in the words of Michael J. Seth (2017), it was a "time of stagnation, inflation, corruption, and dependence on foreign assistance." Seoul still bore the scars of the Korean War. The city was anything but cosmopolitan, actually insular; Western products were not to be seen, nor was there any signage in any language except Korean. I recall walking into a restaurant full of Koreans, who spoke only their native language, naturally enough, and the menu was on small sheets of paper naming individual items, hanging from the wall like banners at the outer edges of the room. And they were in Korean, again, naturally enough. A large family was enjoying a feast of many dishes at a nearby table with a large bowl in the center. Not knowing how to tell the waiter what I wanted, I pointed to one dish on the adjoining table occupied by the large family. About thirty minutes later, the waiter appeared with a large, overloaded tray that held one of each of the many items my neighboring family was eating, including the bowl of soup, from which I pulled out a squab. The waiter had misunderstood; he thought I wanted the entire feast—my fault for not knowing his language.

I tell this anecdote not to be critical of Korea and its people but rather for comparative purposes, to say some words about what has been dubbed the country's "economic miracle."

My next visit was in 1982. I traveled the length of South Korea with a group of media and academic professionals, from the DMZ to Gwangju. We were proudly shown the rich agrarian countryside "modernized" during the New Village (Saemaŭl) movement begun in 1971–1972, a thriving steel mill in Pohang (Korea now ranks sixth in the world in steel production), and the Silla-period burial mounds of Gwangju. The highways were teeming with automobiles, among them Korean-made Hyundais. Seoul had become a metropolis populated with what seemed to be a high-spirited and highly motivated population. Six succeeding research trips throughout the 1990s and later made it very evident that South Korea had leapfrogged stages of economic development to become a major exporter of entertainment (witness the Korean Wave), a world-renowned technological innovator, and home of one of the world's highest-educated and healthiest populations. In the interim, in 1996, South Korea became one of the thirty members of the Organization for Economic Cooperation and Development (OECD), graduating "from a developing country to the ranks of the wealthy developed nations" (Seth 2017) in about thirty years—indeed, an "economic miracle."

The Korean Wave (*Hallyu*) and Comics Art

This transformation has traversed the globe through Korea's cuisine, music, film, soap operas, automobiles, food markets, television dramas, *mukbang* (livestreamed eating shows), beauty products, and comics, which are plentiful nearly everywhere. And, with comics, which were faltering generally worldwide, South Korea jump-started the industry with its "invention" of the webtoon at the beginning of the twenty-first century.

The manhwa (comics) webtoon phenomenon rode the Korean Wave to success, benefiting from how pop bands, soap operas, dramas, and so forth edged into the East Asian region and spread like a firestorm worldwide. The Korean Wave may be unique, though there have been many massive cultural exchanges/invasions in various parts of the world for millennia. It is different in many regards, such as not being militarily sparked or the result of government conquest; not hailing from the Western world; not isolated to one medium or form of entertainment (e.g., Hollywood movies, Japanese anime, the Filipino and British comics invasions); not limited to an intraregional presence (e.g., Hong Kong film); much faster spreading because of the internet and other new information technology; and, so far at least, not targeted as a type of cultural/media imperialism. The Korean Wave originally did not come from a preconceived government plan, though, in the case of animation and manhwa, when the authorities realized that animation had become a number one export, they pumped much funding into building an infrastructure around comics art and encouraging the making of "killer content."

The Korean Wave may be considered out of the ordinary also for its longevity, its continuation offsetting a couple of decades of skepticism, doubt, and indifference. In a 2012 survey conducted by a Korean government organization, 60 percent of the respondents gave the Wave only four more years to survive (KOFICE 2012); yet, since then, the world has enjoyed Psy's "Gangnam Style," the Oscar-winning film *Parasite*, and webcomics, to name a few.

Korea can take pride in making a number of contributions to the comics art world, some that were original, others that were enhancements of already existing features. No doubt, the webtoon is the most important comics art product "invented" in Korea; another is the vertical, four-small-panel political and social commentary newspaper comic strip that prevailed for a few decades before fading away and never becoming a transnational product. Other innovations in which Korean comics art either was at the forefront or altered the field significantly are: being one of the world's first and largest animation offshore providers (along with Japan and Taiwan); developing and advancing "investigative cartooning" through graphic novels; highlighting and perfecting the comics production factory/rental shop system; and welcoming women into the field in relatively large numbers, to the extent that the country has one of the world's very few female comics associations.

The Genesis and Dimensions of *Comics Art in Korea*

This book, as with my *Asian Comics* (Lent 2015), had a long gestation period. It likely embryoed in the late 1990s after I had interviewed South Korean cartoonists in Seoul in 1992, 1994, and 1995, and while supervising doctoral students Yu Kie-un and Kwon Jae-woong, both completing dissertations on Korean animation. In fact, Yu's dissertation was to be the basis of a book, but this plan fell by the wayside after Yu received his PhD and then pursued a degree in theology and became a pastor. In Kwon's case, he wrote a very detailed chapter on Korean animation that was to be used in a planned book I was to write and edit. That proposed book did not materialize as I was diverted to finish other writing and editing projects that begged for completion, and, in the process, Kwon's chapter became outdated, which I regret.

As the new millennium began, I worked with other graduate students researching Korean comics art—Noh Sueen on *soonjung manhwa* (girl's comics) and Kim Chunhyo on animation. We collaborated on articles. Noh also translated parts of books and articles for me. These four individuals, in addition to other South Korean graduate student advisees Kim Hoon-soon, Kim Myung-jun, and Lee Sang-kil, who helped as interpreters during interviews in Seoul, and Suh HaeLim, who checked the final manuscript for accuracy and consistency, are the surrogate parents of this book. Nearly all the research was done by me; I also did all of the conceptualizing, organizing, writing, and editing of the book. Therefore, I am responsible for its content.

The thought of writing on South and North Korean comics art stayed in the back of my mind during the intervening twenty-five or so years. What I could not comprehend was why no one else, as far as I know, has written a book-length treatment of the subject in English.

This deficiency was unfathomable to me in light of South Korea having become a major cultural exporter in the first few decades of this century, its films, music, fashion, food, soap operas, and, of course, comics art finding worldwide audiences in the already discussed Korean Wave. Specifically, in the area of comics art, the country's comic books have steadily rivaled Japanese manga; its graphic novels, some of which are known for their excellent "investigative cartooning," have found markets outside of Asia, in the United States and Europe, been translated into many languages, been adapted into movies and television series, and been winners in many international competitions. Some have also brought to light many Korean historical travesties, especially during the four decades of dictatorial rule. From its beginnings, the webcomics industry has been dominated and advanced by South Korea webtoonists who, in fact, "invented" these online, vertical-scroll comics. Although in the background now, for decades, Seoul newspapers' unique, four-panel editorial cartoons were the dailies' most popular feature, known for holding the powers-that-be accountable. Animation has thrived as well; for years, the country was one of the earliest and top offshore producers of US, Canadian, and European animated films and still harbors the world's third-largest animation industry, behind the United States and Japan. All of these achievements, yet, not deserving a single book in English?

I began interviewing cartoonists and animators in Seoul in July 1992, on the first leg of a research trip to Taiwan, Hong Kong, the Philippines, Singapore, and Indonesia. Five of the Korean interviewees were prominent newspaper political cartoonists; others were the president of Daiwon Animation, a magazine cartoonist, and a comics art historian. The interviewees during a second trip in July 1994 came from an assortment of positions, most prominent being the director or editor in chief of manhwa companies and periodicals (Daiwon Publishing, Jigyungsa Ltd., *Weekly IQ Jump*). Others were a member of a government-operated ethics in comics organization, cartoon studies professors, the owner of a comics rental shop, a cartoon columnist, a cartoon critic, an animation studio head, and more.

In August 1995, I interviewed three of South Korea's pioneer animators—Shin Dong-hun, Jung Wook, and Nelson Shin, head of AKOM Productions—while I was in Seoul to judge at the first Seoul International Cartoon and Animation Festival (SICAF) and address its symposium. I also interviewed the heads of the Hahn Shin Corporation, the Seoul Movie Company, Hanho Heung-Up, and LUK Studio as well as a lecturer/reviewer on comics and the chief of the country's first college program in comics. SICAF invited me to be its featured speaker again in August 2003, and during this visit to both Seoul and Bucheon, I had the opportunity to participate in a two-day symposium of Northeast Asian animators seeking ways to collaborate with Nelson Shin and Shin Dong-hun, and I interviewed them again as well as the directors of SICAF, the Seoul Animation Center, the Korean Film Commission, the Bucheon Cartoon Information Center, and Universal Contents; manhwa researchers Kim Nak-ho, Park In-ha, and Seon Jeong-u; and other animators.

Other occasions when I picked up information and opinions about Korean comics art were when I was invited to give a lecture at the Korea Creative Content Agency (KOCCA) International Symposium on Cultural Content in Seoul in September 2001, was the guest of film industry personnel in Jeonju in 2002; chaired the jury for the Puchon International Student Animation Festival (PISAF) in Bucheon, November 2010; and traveled on a research trip in August 2018 specifically to interview seven successful graphic novelists in Seoul and Bucheon (see the full list of interviewees in appendix I).

By now, it is more than obvious that interviewing was the major research technique I used in this book. Actually, interviewing has dominated much of my academic work of the past six decades. Likely, this preference stems from my early education in a journalism program that taught reportorial skills, based primarily on interviewing and also on observation and the use of public documents.

The interviews in Korea were loosely structured around a few questions and points, the purpose of which was to allow respondents much leeway in how they answered questions and for how long. The location of an interview was usually set by the respondent, wherever he or she felt most comfortable—offices, homes, restaurants, tea and coffee houses, my hotel room, museums, and conference and festival venues.

The rationale for favoring interviewing stems from an urge to get to the original source of information rather than rely on retellings and symbolic interpretations by others. It is very important to get interviewees' views and recountings, while they are still alive and mentally acute. Too often, especially in literature studies, researchers spend much time digging out (of their own minds) intriguing symbols to explain what a writer meant—an interesting mental exercise but mostly meaningless. Novelist William Faulkner, who did write stream of consciousness in a way that lent itself to symbolic analysis, said that if he wrote as symbolically as attributed to him, he would not have been able to finish a single novel.

Although interviews by phone, email, Zoom, and other mechanical devices are increasingly used, and sometimes are necessary, for this book, all interviews were in person, which has been the case during my entire career. Live interviews allow the interviewer to observe a person's facial expressions and movements, and the ambience of the surroundings and the mood of the occasion.

However, I have long been very much attuned to the pitfalls of interviewing and try to avoid them (e.g., asking long, loaded questions; interrupting respondents), as well as other shortcomings (e.g., age or illness memory loss, prejudices and biases, "playing" to a microphone, fear of freely expressing opinions, or the "half life" of memory pertaining to interviewers' remembering unrecorded answers). Usually, I account for these limitations by critically appraising what I am told, matching an interviewee's responses with known evidence or others' opinions, easing respondents into more serious questions, and, when called for, putting aside any recording devices, including pencil or pen, and listening attentively. In the latter situation, as soon as I leave the interview, I find a quiet place and write down what I just heard. Usually, I take notes during interviews and do not use audio or video technology. To test the accuracy of my written notes, a few times, I machine-recorded interviews while simultaneously taking notes; they matched nearly perfectly.

Observation and reading of documents, whenever available, were my other research techniques in writing this book. In a number of instances, I was able to see where artists worked (studios, offices, homes), how and with whom they worked, and how their comics art was distributed. For example, I spent part of a day in a manhwa studio that operated on a master/apprentices system, and a few hours each in a comics rental shop and a commercial bookstore. I observed many cartoonists' and animators' art while attending exhibitions, visiting museums and centers in Seoul and Bucheon, and evaluating animated films while chairing and/or serving on international festival juries, also in Seoul and Bucheon. The documents I used were summaries and chronologies of Korean comics art history, books, academic and trade periodical articles, corporate promotional materials, and cartoons compiled in anthologies, clipped from newspapers, or given to me by their creators, most of which were in the Korean language and translated by the already named graduate students.

The all-encompassing term "comics art" used here includes "cartoons," which normally refer to political and social commentary drawings that comment on or take a stand (that of the cartoonist, media management or owner, the public, or government officials), and those that present a joke or gag in a visual form. As mentioned earlier, for a time in the latter part of the twentieth century, popular political/social commentary cartoons in South Korea consisted of four small panels. Other categories under comics art are "comic strips," multiple connected panels that appear in newspapers (and sometimes magazines) to tell a humorous episode or continue a serialized (often cliff-hanging) story; and "comic books" (manhwa) (called *kurimchaek* in North Korea), rather hefty periodicals consisting of a number of stories that can be serialized or completed in one issue. A variation of comic books common in South Korea is the "graphic novel," usually hard-covered and limited to one extended story. "Animation" refers to filmed cartoons and occasionally docudramas that use movement and sound, and "caricature" means a likeness to an individual that captures a prominent physical or personality trait that is highly exaggerated. New to comics art are webcomics, online vertical-scrolling stories with characters conceived and drawn by both professional and amateur artists.

The major focus of this book is on South Korea, although one chapter is devoted to North Korea. I have not been to North Korea; thus, the contents of this chapter are not my firsthand accounts but those of a few who have spent time in the north and written about their comics-related experiences, notably Danish scholar Martin Petersen. The four chapters that deal predominantly with South Korea are organized by the comics art forms, namely political cartoons, comics and graphic novels, animation, and webcomics. The remaining two chapters that are inclusive of South and North Korea are this introduction and a conclusion. Each of the comics art forms/media has its own inherent history, but because some of the historical aspects are linked, there is a bit of repetition across chapters, though minimal. There are also five vignettes, shorter articles tucked within appropriate chapters and expanding on the careers of prominent comics artists: Park Jae-dong (political cartoonist, animator, and organizer of comics art events), Kim Song-hwan (prominent pioneer political cartoonist), Gendry-Kim Keum suk (award-winning investigative graphic novelist), and Nelson Shin (pioneer animator). A fifth vignette includes information on the precursors of Western-oriented or -influenced visual humor and satire during the Joseon Dynasty and before.

Individuals' names are given in the Revised Romanization system (2000) in most cases; however, in cases where the individual has a preferred spelling, that is the one used. The name order is Korean style: surname followed by given name. For the sake of consistency, given names are split, the second part lowercase (e.g., Kim Song-hwan). Birth and death dates are provided for individuals whenever they can be determined. Because the surnames Kim, Park, and Lee are so common in Korea, for clarity's sake, I have added the initials of their given names when citing them in the text.

The objectives of this project are no different from those of other Asian region or country comics art overviews I have completed. It is, paraphrasing from *Comics Art in China* (Lent and Xu 2017, xii), to present a comprehensive treatment of Korea's comics art; to point out important historical and contemporary happenings, individuals and groups, issues, problems, and trends; to place Korean comics art in the contexts of the country(ies)' politics, culture, society, and economics; to deal with the business/industrial and artistic/literary dimensions of cartoons, comics, and animation, with an emphasis on the former (e.g., organizational infrastructure, professionalism, financial stability, relationship with the government, the "freedom to cartoon"); and to encompass all forms and types of cartoons, comic books and strips, graphic novels, humor/cartoon periodicals, animation, and online cartoons and comics.

General questions I will address are: (1) Are there common threads that run through Korean comics art historically? If yes, what are they? Do they switch (add on) or tend to unravel? (2) Have outside factors played roles (nourishing or hindering) during the history of Korean comics art? (3) What has been the relationship between the Korean government and comics art? (4) What socio-economic-political factors may have altered the trajectory of Korean comics art? (5) Have Korean comics artists added useful dimensions to the industry and profession? If yes, what are they? (6) What is the professional standing of Korea comics art?

References

Korean Foundation for International Cultural Exchange (KOFICE). 2012. "The Annual Survey of Overseas Hallyu." Seoul: KOFICE.

Lent, John A. 2015. *Asian Comics*. Jackson: University Press of Mississippi.

Lent, John A., and Xu Ying. 2017. *Comics Art in China*. Jackson: University Press of Mississippi.

Seth, Michael J. 2017. "South Korea's Economic Development, 1948–1996." *Oxford Research Encyclopedias, Asian History*, December 19. https://doi.org/10.1093/acrcforc/9780190277727.013.271.

Vignette I

Semblances of the Comics in Ancient Art

Any attempt to trace comics elements (e.g., caricature; satire and parody; humor, wit, and playfulness; narrative and sequence) in ancient art must contend with two serious issues: the lack of an exact and universally accepted definition of comics/cartoons and the above elements of humor, and the difficulty in discerning the intention of the ancient artist.

Many researchers have grappled with the first problem (Will Eisner, Robert Harvey, Thierry Groensteen, Scott McCloud, and others), come up with definitions, and fallen short of placating the challenges that different cultures present. The second problem is equally difficult, because ancient artists drawing on cave walls and tombs did not leave a record of what they meant. (An aside: this is why there is a need for more interview-based research, while the artist is alive and fully cognitive.) Without that, the researcher must rely on intuition and general knowledge about the time under study.

With those disclaimers in mind, exemplars of some ancient Korean art that resemble cartoons survive, though much has been destroyed during wartime. Perhaps the oldest are frescoes recovered from Goguryeo-era royal tombs. The oldest known to exist are wall paintings in about eighty Goguryeo-era tombs. The Goguryeo Kingdom ruled northern Korea during the Three Kingdoms period (first century BCE to seventh century CE), a prosperous and artistic time. Historian Mark Cartwright (2016) describes the wall murals as being painted directly on the stone chambers or applied to lime plaster and as full of bright colors and flowing outlines. Several tombs have paintings of the occupant, one of the best preserved being Tomb no. 3 at Anak, 357 CE, portraying ruler Tong Shou receiving officials. Also famous are the fifth-century CE murals discovered at Muyongchong, the "Tomb of the Dancers," at Gungnae, in present-day Jilin Province, China. One mural shows rows of servants dancing with "arms raised as they bid farewell to their master who is leaving the family home on horseback," presumably into the next life. Cartwright (2016) reports that hunting scenes were most popular; other content includes warriors on horseback, mythical animals, animal trainers, acrobats, religious ceremonies,

Vig-I.1. Mural from a Goguryeo tomb. Public domain.

Vig-I.2. *Subakdo*. Fresco in a Goguryeo tomb from the fifth century showing two persons in comic book style practicing a traditional battle called *subak*. Public domain.

Vig-I.3. *Bomyeongshiudo*. A tenth-century comic strip–like drawing, narrating a tale about a farmer protecting his cow. Public domain.

Vig-I.4. *Ssirum* (Wrestling Match). This painting by court painter Kim Hong-do has been credited as being a predecessor of comics. Kim's works were out of the norm because of their focus on commoners' daily lives; their informality, harmony, and numerical balance. Public domain.

Vig-I.5. Kim Hong-do, *Who Will Be the Hero at the Brothel?* Hyewon Pongsokdo series. Eighteenth century.

political processions, and details about daily life. Goguryeo tombs show Chinese-influenced artwork.

Playfulness is evident in Goguryeo tomb paintings; in one, two people are shown engaging in a fight called *subak*. Researcher Park In-ha (2002, 14) thinks that the characters' movements suggest a manhwa style. Other engravings that merit consideration as predecessors of manhwa, according to Park, are *Byeonsangdo*, whose purpose was to diffuse the canons of Buddhism, and *Bomyeongshiudo* from the tenth century, detailing in ten successive panels a Buddhist fable about a farmer and his cow.

During the Joseon Dynasty (1392–1910), genre paintings with humorous portrayals of daily life were popular, particularly the works of court painter Kim Hong-do (1745–c. 1806). Kim sharply deviated from Korean traditional artists, the majority of whom used themes of nature and religion. He differed also because his painting had a style of directness and immediacy, and his subjects were commoners. But he also fit in with his predecessors over the centuries for the simplicity and spontaneity of his art. At least one researcher, Park Ki-jun, categorized him as a cartoonist, writing: "He surely had a talent for cartooning. He described the scene of a *Ssirum* [wrestling match] in a light and humorous manner. Two wrestlers' desperate looks straining to win, the looks full of excitement of the spectators around them, and its comic composition give us a hearty smile" (Park 1980, 4). *Ssirum* is Kim's best-known painting; others he did were *Threshing Rice* (1780), portraying a lazing, pipe-smoking farmer overseeing toiling peasants, and *Seodang* (Village School, late eighteenth century), showing a Confucian teacher and his students. Typical of this genre of painting, the focus is on the individuals and their expressions, all set on a blank background.

Both Kim and his contemporary, painter Sin Yun-bok (1758–1813), who also worked at Dohwaseo (the Bureau of Printing) for a while, drew *chunhwa* (erotic prints). These paintings were cartoonlike in composition and usually were humorous, a few examples being two monks hiding behind rocks as they enjoy watching a couple copulating, courtesans in let's-get-this-over-with poses, and a prostitute standing in front of a brothel, annoyingly waiting for a group of noblemen to decide whether to partake of her offerings.

Painted portraits done in a peaceful and humorous style were popular during the Joseon era, and at the beginning of the twentieth century, this pictorial tradition was found in illustrations of the covers of *ttakjibon* (romance novels) and on posters, tracts, and leaflets.

References

Cartwright, Mark. 2016. "The Tombs of Goguryeo." *World History Encyclopedia*, November 3. https://www.worldhistory.org/article/966/the-tombs-of-goguryeo/.

Park, In-ha. 2002. "Trajectoire de la bande dessinée coréenne." In *La dynamique de la BD coréenne: Catalogue d'exposition*, by Sung Wank-kyung, Park In-ha, Kim Nak-ho, Park Kwan-hyung, Mo Hae-gyu, Yamanaka Chie, and Jean-Pierre Mercier, 14–15. Seoul: Korea Creative Content Agency.

Park, Ki-jun. 1980. "Caricatures and Comic Strips: Essential to Korean Journalism." *Asian Culture* (January): 4–5.

Vignette II

Park Jae-dong

Die-Hard Advocate for the Koreanization of Comics Art

Vig-II.1. Park Jae-dong. Seoul, August 10, 2018. Photo by and courtesy of Kim Chunhyo.

It seems that each time I met up with Park Jae-dong between 1992 and 2018, he was in a different dimension of Korean comics art, but consistently advocating and working for the betterment of the profession.

When we met in 1992, Park was a prominent political cartoonist at *Hankyoreh Shinmun*, where he started his career in 1988, at the daily's founding. Previous to that, he had graduated from the University of Seoul, majoring in oriental painting, and taught art in a high school for six years. His cartoons were popular among intellectuals and young people for their no-holds-barred messages designed to raise social and historical consciousness.

Park did not hesitate in expressing his thinking about political cartooning in Korea nor in critiquing fellow cartoonists or the country's overall comics art scene. He said he switched from fine art because cartooning was much better suited to meet his desire to bring about social change; he viewed his work as "doing an exhibition every day." Park credited older political cartoonists with good technique, but he felt their "language of satire" was poor. He explained: "The government repressed them for years; they were raised by the government. Thus, they sometimes limit their criticism . . . and have become conservative."

Before describing his own political cartooning, Park provided some context by explaining what *Hankyoreh Shinmun* was all about:

> The founder of my paper believes that the government has repressed freedom of the press. He believes that the masses want their newspaper to be free to say what it wants, independent of government and established capital. We are autonomous. My work is characterized by these beliefs of the paper. Our stockholders are the sixty thousand people who bought into the paper. They are the people looking after democracy with progressive thoughts. This is very unique in Korea. I don't have criticism from government, no specific repression. The government says nothing to *Hankyoreh Shinmun*, because we don't listen to the government.

Park admitted that like other cartoonists, he followed the stance of his newspaper, the difference being that *Hankyoreh Shinmun* was liberal. He also thought that his young age (forty) benefited his political cartooning, because he had not cultivated debts to family and friends.

Park anticipated my final question, having written down some notes beforehand. What do you foresee for the future of Korean cartoons and comics? He rattled off six trends with some overlapping:

1. The big trend is the change of attitude about cartoons. Before, people did not think cartoons had a social function. Now, they think about cartoons as they do of a good novel, as a valuable work.
2. Cartoons have many uses now—for education, information, electioneering, advertising, television, and so forth.
3. Daily and sports newspapers now use better cartoon content, whereas previously, sports dailies carried a lot of pornographic comics for which they were criticized and resisted.
4. Many people are expecting to see healthier, wittier, and Koreanized cartoons and are striving to achieve this, but it is just the beginning.
5. There is a strong tendency to abandon the Japanese manga influence.
6. But, we are expecting to have many more manga coming into this country. Young cartoonists are trying to stop this, wanting Koreanized comics with Korean perspectives.

Shortly after this interview, a demonstration calling for the abandonment of manga was held in Seoul, at which Korean cartoonists imitating the manga style were publicly identified; the organizers made a call to not patronize them.

In fact, my second interview with Park Jae-dong in July 1994 occurred while he was cohosting an anti-manga exhibition at the Indeco Gallery in Seoul. The exhibit was pulled together by Park and other members of Uri Manhwa Hyeophoe (Our Cartoon Association), started in 1992 to promote Koreanized manhwa and play down manga.

Park compared the cartooning scene of 1994 with that of two years prior, saying that when he praised the government in one of his cartoons in 1992, he did so unwillingly, but in 1994, he drew favorable cartoons of the government because the

Vig-II.2. Political cartoon by Park Jae-dong. Permission of Park Jae-dong.

government had changed for the better. But he cautioned that good government can make cartoonists lazy and less sharp.

When we met in August 1995, Park had changed his career to animation. Early on, he faced obstacles that required innovative thinking. To obtain funding, he encouraged potential audience members to participate in the production of his film *Odolttogi* by purchasing cel drawings and paying for admission tickets in advance. Neither scheme worked for his financial benefit.

Park also struggled to tell the story of *Odolttogi* effectively, though true to his convictions, he used a Korean incident (a deadly post–World War II event on Jeju Island), Korean characters and settings, and what he called "realism animation" (a true story with real natural backgrounds).

He elaborated when we next met in August 2003, saying that he had more or less given up on producing an animation feature and admitting that *Odolttogi* was a project "too big" for him, "requiring a [financial] foundation and a system," neither of which he possessed. And, again, he said that the story of his feature was too difficult for him to write, and he lamented the lack of good stories for manhwa and animation, as discussed in chapter 4.

I found out at our August 2018 interview (jointly with his friend and fellow cartoonist Lee Hee-jae) that Park still harbored hopes of finishing *Odolttogi* but was diverted by the necessity of making a living by teaching at a university, doing consultative work for educational officials, and directing the Bucheon Fantastic Film Festival.

여자 하나는 다쳐서 앓다가 죽
여기 있다간 죽을 때까지 일만 할 거야.
맞아.
도망가다 잡히면 우린 모두 죽일 거
여기서 죽으나 도망가다 죽으나…….
어쩌려고?
어무이 아부지 한 번만이라도 죽으면 소원이 없

Determining South Korea's first political cartoon runs into a snag or two. In 1884, a German visitor to Seoul, Ernst von Hesse-Wartegg, reportedly saw some drawings that he called "political caricature," and going by his description of one of them, they seem to be political cartoons. He wrote:

> I saw a political caricature which was drawn by a Korean. It described Korea as an unusually shaped person. The person's head was small and bald. His arms and legs were skinny and thin. However, his body was fat. Look, said a Korean, this is the poor figure of my country. This head means king, arms and legs are squeezed and suppressed people. But, the fat body is noblemen and bureaucrats in this country. (Quoted in Lee H-c 1982, 9)

The markings of political cartoons are there; however, von Hesse-Wartegg failed to tell us where they appeared, only that they circulated among the intelligentsia. We are not certain that they were even published.

Questionable, too, is a drawing by Lee Do-yeong (1884–1933) published in *Daehan Minbo* on June 2, 1909, and usually accorded the status of Korea's first political cartoon. It depicts a man with a top hat and cane out of whose mouth four streams of words declare the paper's mission: to promote an understanding of the national situation, to unite people by restoring the Korean spirit, to represent real public opinion, and to report diverse facts on the basis of reality (Lee H-c 1982, 19–20). Maybe a political cartoon, but definitely more like a promotional plug for the newspaper.

Attention should be directed at *Daehan Minbo*, not for the drawing of the gentleman with top hat and cane but for other Lee Do-yeong works that strongly satirized the cruelty of the Japanese occupiers and the traitorous activities of some Japanophile Koreans. Lee's cartoons were often censored or removed; in the case of the latter, the editors covered the empty space with black ink, an early ruse later used worldwide to let readers know that a cartoon had been banned. The government closed *Daehan Minbo* on August 31, 1910 (Yoon 1986).

What appeared as political cartoons during much of the succeeding thirty years initially glorified Japanese culture and occupation policies and attacked Korean

Chapter 2

Political Cartoons

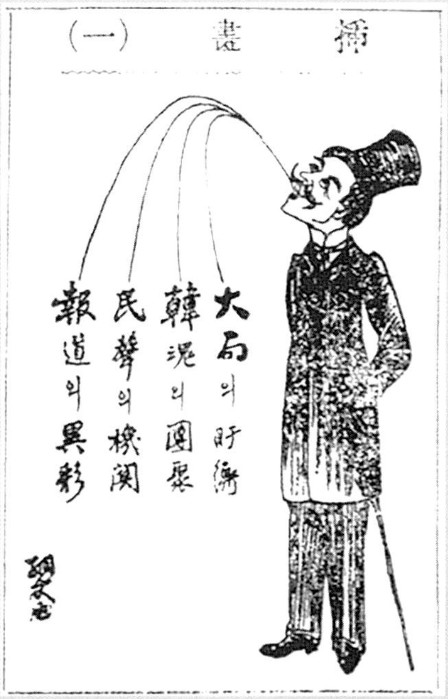

2.1. Recognized as Korea's first newspaper cartoon, this drawing of a top-hatted gentleman spewing out the purposes of his newspaper appeared in *Daehan Minbo*, June 2, 1909. Public domain.

2.2. *Daehan Minbo* carried cartoons on its front page daily, including those critical of Japanese groups and their newspapers. Some, as this December 27, 1909, drawing, show punishments meted out to pro-Japan individuals. Public domain.

2.3. When *Daehan Minbo* crossed the line by criticizing Japan in its June 26, 1910, issue, the colonial government ordered, for the first of a number of times, that the article be deleted. The editor let readers know that the newspaper was being censored by blackening the space. Public domain.

2.4. Just before the Japanese closed *Daehan Minbo* in August 1910, this cartoon of June 14, 1910, commented on the government's prohibition on Koreans congregating. The policeman asks: "Where are you going?" The Korean citizen replies: "I have nothing to do with . . ." Public domain.

2.5. This April 7, 1925, *Dong-A Ilbo* cartoon relates to the discrimination practiced at Korea's first modern university, now called Seoul National University (established May 2, 1924), the Japanese government giving entrance priority to their own students over Koreans. The right-side caption reads: "Korean students experience difficulty getting into Gyeongseong Jeguk Daehak." The rest of the caption requests readers' contributions, promises rewards, and lists Kim Ubeom as the cartoon's creator. Public domain.

2.6. A Kim Kyu-taek cartoon in a 1946 issue of *Chosun Ilbo* (reprinted in a 1975 anthology) portrays the thirty-eighth north latitude line dividing Korea as an immovable alligator. The name of the railroad is the Gyeongui Line, between Seoul and Sinuiju (North Korea); the writing on the alligator says "Military Demarcation Line [Hyujeonseon]." Public domain.

2.7. *Seoul Shinmun* carried this cartoon on October 8, 1945, showing a Chinese and a Korean shaking hands as a mark of good relations between the countries. Public domain.

underdevelopment, in the 1910s, and then, led by Japanese-owned *Kyungsong Ilbo*, emphasized cultural and educational themes after the bloody crackdown on the March 1, 1919, independence movement.

New outlets for political cartoons opened up with the launching of *Dong-A Ilbo* and *Chosun Ilbo*, both in 1920. *Dong-A Ilbo* used a cartoon in its very first issue, likely drawn by the daily's initial cartoonist, Kim Dong-seong (1890–1969). Kim wore many hats—comics artist, comics critic, translator, journalist, diplomat, and politician; his forte was drawing comic strips (Park H-s 2016). Also, in 1920, the first readers' cartoons appeared in special sections of daily newspapers—*Donga Manhwa* in *Dong-A Ilbo*, *Cheol Pil Sajin* in *Chosun Ilbo*, and *Jibang Manhwa* in *Sidae Ilbo*—allowing readers to voice their opinions through their own drawings. (Yoon 1986)[1]

By the mid-1920s, political cartooning took a turn for the worse. Critical newspapers were suspended or closed completely, readers' cartoons disappeared, and cartoons with political messages were replaced by children's and humor manhwa (Yoon 1992). During the following decade, the remaining newspapers, those favorable to the Japanese (e.g., *Maeil Sinbo* and *Kyungsong Ilbo*), used cartoons to legitimize Japan's buildup of militarism.

In the post–World War II era, political cartoons were slow in catching on until the Republic of Korea was established in 1948, when Kim Kyu-taek resumed his career at *Chosun Ilbo*. Others followed, usually with cartoons that featured ongoing characters. The issues political cartoons dealt with in this period were ideological battles between rightists and leftists, the thirty-eighth north latitude that split the peninsula, the cooperative China-Korea relationship, the housing crisis, the power shift from the American military to Korean civilian authorities, a comparison between US and Korean products, and the reestablishment of the nation (Lee W-b 1992).

During the Korean War (1950–1953), political cartoons continued but mainly to support the war, celebrate brave South Korean soldiers, and vilify the communists. Following the war, newspaper commentary and political cartoons experienced boon periods, particularly the four-panel political strips, officially reintroduced on February 1, 1955, by Kim Song-hwan (1932–2019) with his *Gobau*[2] (see vignette III on Kim's career).

2.8. A selection of very early Korean cartoons. Public domain.

The Four-Panel Political Cartoon Strip

The four-panel political cartoon strip is a unique feature of South Korean comics art. Though almost extinct now, it was a very important feature in nearly all dailies in the latter part of the twentieth century, so significant that the approximately one-column, one-inch space below the vertical panels was the most expensive and sought-after advertising slot in the entire newspaper.

The origins of the four-panel political cartoon strip go back to April 11, 1920, when Kim Dong-seong created one for *Dong-A Ilbo*, the daily of which he was a founder. The purpose of the strip was to promote the newspaper and increase its circulation (Park H-s 2016). Kim studied journalism in the United States (1908–1919), where he developed an interest in cartooning and published his first comic strips. Back in Korea, Kim created the first four-panel political strip, *Visual Storytelling*, in which he experimented with panel arrangements, initially starting from upper right to upper left, lower right, and lower left (Park H-s 2016). Kim and *Dong-A Ilbo* had much to do with the promotion of comics art in Korea, introducing foreign cartoons/comics, holding comics prize competitions, and publishing readers' cartoons. Kim himself translated American comics manuals and then wrote the first such comics guide for budding Korean cartoonists. In 1924, he founded the *Chosun Ilbo* newspaper and became its editor, and with other artists he created the first Korean manhwa, *A Dumb Man Who Digs a Wrong Well*. He ended his spectacular career as a politician, becoming the first minister of culture in independent South Korea (Park H-s 2016).

It was not long after *Gobau*'s birth that other four-panel commentary cartoons appeared: first, Ahn Ui-seop (1924–1998)'s *Dukkeobi* (Mr. Toad, a sign of good luck) and Chung Woon-kyung's (1936–) *Auntie Walsun* (A Tart-Tongued Housemaid), both in 1955, in *Kyunghyang Shinmun* and *JoongAng Ilbo*, respectively. Others subsequently were Yoon Yong-ok's *Kkaturi* (Mrs. Hen Pheasant, considered a "very bright, diligent, and intelligent bird" [Yoon 1992]) in *Seoul Shinmun*, and Kim Pan-kook's *Cheonggaeguri* (Blue Frog, representing resistance) in *Kyunghyang Shinmun* (Ahn 1992; Chung 1992; Yoon 1992; Kim P-k 1992). Kim (1992) said that his *Cheonggaeguri* integrated all perspectives, adding: "To draw a mouse, you must know the cat's

2.9. *Mijual* (Scrutiny) by Kim Eul-ho is considered the first four-panel political cartoon by a woman. *Hankyoreh Shinmun*, July 7, 1992. Public domain.

2.10. Yoon Yong-ok, *Seoul Shinmun* political cartoonist and creator of the four-panel political cartoon *Kkaturi*. Seoul, July 3, 1992. Photo by John A. Lent.

perspective." Only one woman drew a four-panel political cartoon, Kim Eul-ho, with her *Mijual* (Scrutiny), carried in *Hankyoreh Shinmun* in 1992.

The four-panel cartoons appeared on the next to the last page of dailies, usually reserved for cultural and social news and information. They were displayed vertically stacked, carried a regular title that denoted a symbolic meaning, featured the same character in every episode, and were numbered consecutively. For example, the last published episode of *Gobau* carried the number 14,139. Panel 1 of these cartoons was an introduction; panel 2, a reversion; panel 3, the emphasis; and panel 4, the punchline (Lee W-b 1992). This structure was derived from that of the classical essay on the Chinese civil service exam: introduction, development, twist, and punchline.

In their heyday, the four-panel cartoons were the main feature of newspapers for readers and advertisers alike. Advertisers vigorously vied for the tiny space directly under a four-panel commentary strip, usually priced at four to five times the normal fees. Kim Song-hwan said the revenue generated in one day by the one-column, one-inch advertisement under *Gobau* could pay ten reporters' salaries for a month (1992). Some advertisers secured that miniscule space by contracting it by the year (Yoon 1992).

The four-panel political cartoons hit their stride during the four-decade dictatorial era, which ended in 1988 with the Roh Tae-woo government (1988–1993). Yoon (1992) explained that the "former military governments closed people's ears and eyes. People wanted to know the truth, and articles could not give it. The cartoons, even though fictional, gave a different view, a hint at the truth. The people did not believe news stories but trusted a view if it was in a four-panel cartoon." He also said Koreans believed that without a four-panel political cartoon, a newspaper was not worth reading. Kim's *Gobau*, Ahn's *Dukkeobi*, and Chung's *Auntie Walsun* first appeared in 1955; within a year, all major dailies had their own four-panel cartoons.

Various four-panel cartoonists paid heavy prices for their subtle and even imagined criticism. Yoon (1992) gave some examples:

> It was a time that was very dangerous for cartoonists. *Gobau* once used a theme of a janitor cleaning the Blue House [Korea's presidential residence]. Kim Song-hwan was put on trial for

> this; authorities felt that it implied that even the Blue House janitor had political power. I remembered the period well as I lost my position in 1972 for five years. President Park [Chung-hee, 1962–1979] had a new community movement. I drew a cartoon about it, which the Blue House thought was critical of the movement. There were conscious and subconscious [*sic*] threats from the Blue House and the Korean CIA [KCIA]. All my colleagues received them. Kim was fined, I was fired, and Ahn of *Hankook Ilbo* had to stop work. The authorities pressured his paper to fire him rather than the government doing it. (Yoon 1986, 304–5)

Kim Song-hwan was a regular target of the Park Chung-hee government—imprisoned twice and tortured, fined, "set up" by the police as a communist, and made to explain in writing what certain of his cartoons meant. He was described as "walking on the edge of a razor blade." Kim described his ordeals:

> I was put in jail twice in 1974, the year the first lady was shot to death [Yuk Yong-su, Park's wife]. At various times, I was called up by the KCIA. In jail, the KCIA would interrogate me without sleep for days.
>
> After I gained popularity in the 1950s with *Gobau*, the police fined me twice in 1957–1958, when the KCIA did not exist. The police told me they were going to the authorities and say I was a red [communist]. The outside of this police headquarters was a gas station, but inside, the police were doing terrible things to us. They were in plain clothes and the gas station was a front. (1992)

Kim related a barrage of harassments, intimidations, and acts of censorship he had endured. He said that information about him was reported "spontaneously and regularly" to Park, and that the president knew everything about him. On one occasion, Park told a *Dong-A Ilbo* reporter to relate to Kim that the president hated a cartoon the artist had drawn of him. Out of fear of what might happen to him, Kim left work early for a week (Kim Song-hwan 1992).

The government attempted more than two hundred times to have Kim change his cartoons. "During martial law, I had to show my cartoons to the government four times a day before I was able to publish them," Kim (1992) recalled. Dreading the routine, Kim often dropped the political content and changed *Gobau* into a humorous strip, but that did not satisfy the censors, either; they suspected that hidden messages were in the humor and asked Kim to redraw the cartoon again. Kim further elaborated: "I would just put in a dog or something I thought was funny, and the censors would misread it to think I was calling them or the government 'dogs.' Seven censors regularly looked at my work. One time, all seven censors approved my cartoon, but just before it was on the press, they asked me to do it again" (1992).

Ridiculous as some of these shenanigans were, the authorities had ample reasons to keep close tabs on Kim. When asked what the government feared about *Gobau*, Kim described how the strip was different:

> (1) No one talked about the Blue House when I started, but I did; (2) I drew about democracy as it existed in some foreign countries [as a subtle contrast to the lack of democracy in South Korea]; (3) I touched on things with subtleness. For example, President Park wore black sunglasses. I had Gobau wear sunglasses. Park hated that, because I implied that because you can't see his eyes, you can't know if he is telling the truth; and (4) I used symbols in my cartoons. (1992)

Kim saved a large portion of his sarcasm for aspects of society, especially Korean pretentiousness. His "Blue House Janitor" of January 23, 1958, was an excellent example: a public toilet janitor walking on the street with Gobau encounters another janitor coming from the opposite direction and bows respectfully to him, after which he explains to Gobau: "He works at the Blue House." Kim's point was to mock the concept that for whom one works determines social status (Kang 2019).

At other times, Kim used a more direct approach. When a student was killed in 1987 under suspicious circumstances, Kim unveiled the suppressed story and accused the KCIA of the murder. After *Dong-A Ilbo*'s local edition appeared, the Blue House and the KCIA ordered that the cartoon be removed from the Seoul edition, because its publication there would lead to an unstable situation. Kim had it removed, but then other newspapers reported the death, prompting presidential candidate Roh Tae-woo to promise reforms if elected (Kim Song-hwan 1992; for more on Kim and *Gobau*, see Toler 2020; Salmon 2009).

Longtime *JoongAng Ilbo* cartoonist Chung Woon-kyung experienced "several" short stays (of three or four days) in police custody because of content in *Auntie Walsun*, the four-panel political cartoon he began while at *Youwon* (Woman's Garden), took to *Daehan Ilbo*, then moved to *Kyunghyang Shinmun* for seven years, before settling it at *JoongAng Ilbo*. Chung (1992) said that the authoritarianism of the governments beginning with Syngman Rhee (1948–1960), and continuing under Park and Chun Doo-hwan (1981–1988), changed cartoons from funny and witty to political with a resistant edge. Chung charged the KCIA and other spy networks with repressing cartoonists by maintaining files on them, questioning their motives, and warning them to desist from drawing critically in the future. The KCIA's rationale was that cartoons critical of the authorities would be used by North Korea in its propaganda campaigns, according to Chung. He took some delight in relating that he and other dissidents were called "instant noodles," meaning that they had been in jail, where the food served was solely instant noodles (Chung 1992).

With the advent of liberalization in 1988, political cartooning flourished. Four-panel political cartoonists I interviewed in 1992 had virtually no complaints about their living conditions or the degree of freedom they enjoyed. A few actually worried that liberalization had taken some of the spunk out of the profession. They followed, in part, the premise of *Far Eastern Economic Review* critic Shim Jae-hoon, that cartoonists' treatment of societal issues did not have the "punch" of the dictatorial era, when "a cartoonist was like a high-wire dancer: high above the mundane fray, the admiring crowd watching with bated breath, his direction clear-cut, his glory dependent wholly upon his daring" (Shim 1991, 54). Chung felt that some of the excitement had left cartooning, giving the example of President Roh allowing cartoonists to draw caricatures of him during his first two years in office. He said, "Cartoonists were confused. They came out of a terror period into a bright situation too soon" (Chung 1992). Yoon had a more analytical explanation:

2.11. Chung Woon-kyung, *JoongAng Ilbo* political cartoonist and creator of the four-panel cartoon *Auntie Walsun*. Seoul, July 7, 1992. Photo by John A. Lent.

> In times of difficulty, people want to know everything. If there is some kind of secrecy, people want to know something. If everything is known, no one cares as much, Before, even when I drew nonpolitical cartoons in bad times, the people thought there were hidden messages. Times are different now; the power of the political cartoon has lessened. When you are hungry, everything tastes good. When you are full, no food is that delicious. (1992)

In the early 1990s, four-panel political cartoonists accepted their newfound freedom with a sense of responsibility. At least Kim Song-hwan, Ahn Ui-seop, and Kim Pan-kook, no matter how critical they had been over the years, said they made concessions when they felt that the national interest or public welfare was at stake. For example, Ahn quit drawing beggars in his *Dukkeobi* when he was informed that North Korea used the strip to propagandize that the South was poverty stricken (Kim P-k 1992).

Political Cartoons in the Twenty-First Century

As the new millennium began, it was obvious that a significant number of changes were forthcoming. Topping the list, computer graphics and the internet had entered the profession, providing new ways of rendering drawings and adding venues. Initially, both artists and readers were leery about the new technology. Cartoonists such as Choi Min-sung of *Segye Ilbo* and Kim Sang-don of *Kyungin* continued to use pen and ink. Others, such as Hong Seung-woo of *Hankyoreh Shinmun*, combined pen and ink with computer software, while many others had no trouble completely going digital.

Early on, Korea's number one search engine and web portal, Naver, provided political cartoons from five national dailies—*Kookmin Ilbo*, *JoongAng Ilbo*, *Chosun Ilbo*, *Kyunghyang Shinmun*, and *Hankyoreh Shinmun*. Two internet newspapers were already in existence, *Up Korea* and *OhmyNews*, which irregularly posted cartoons, as did a cartoon magazine, *Newstoon*. A second web portal, Daum, had its own cartoonists by 2004, including Park Cheol-gwon with *Sisa Dwitbook* and Choi In-jong with *I Cut Sesang*, and provided political cartoons from *Chosun Ilbo*, *JoongAng Ilbo*, and *Kyunghyang Shinmun*. *Newstoon* was the first digital national political cartoon periodical in South Korea, started in 2003 by the National Editorial Cartoonists Association and made up of sixty-two members in the beginning. *Newstoon* provided cartoon pools, news of the cartoon community, and cartoonists' interviews.[3]

Some cartoonists thought the tone and feeling of political cartoons were changing to a style and content more appealing to the younger generation. Complicated, more obscure, and less direct approaches common during the authoritarian reigns, and still favored by some drawers such as Kim Sang-taek, were out (Kim N-h 2004), replaced by humor, gags, parodies of movies, and cuteness as the backbones of political cartoons. The epitome of cuteness was found in the works of Lee Jae-yong of *Munhwa Ilbo*, who proudly depicted all of his characters, even corrupt politicians, as cute, saying,

> I just want to get closer, friendly, with readers. Political cartoons are stereotyped as serious or authoritarian, and that results in some distance between them and the readers. My characters can reduce the distance to some degree. I want to draw things hilariously. Some people criticize my style, saying it is too light, but this is a new intention to approach readers. (Lee Jae-yong, quoted in Nam 2004)

A third trend at the beginning of this century was the hardening autonomy of political cartoonists. Perhaps it had to do with the formation of the National Editorial

2.12. *JoongAng Ilbo* cartoonist Kim Sang-taek's detailed, "nervous"-stroke political drawing. Caption: "Mr. Roh, who used to be seated at the end of the table, because he was the president. Cheer up! Placed at the end . . . again?" 2004. Courtesy of Kim Sang-taek.

Cartoonists Association, and before that, the labor strife between political cartoonists and their newspapers. The NECA was started in 2000, made up of members who had left their previous cartoon groups. Their aims were to contribute to the country's political cartoon nourishment (Choi M-s 2003) and to protect the rights of cartoonists (Lee S-k 2004). For much of their history, South Korean political cartoonists followed their newspapers' stances, which usually favored the government or large business concerns. In the latter part of the 1990s, a few political cartoonists no longer wished to abide by this unwritten policy. Son Mun-sang resigned from the conglomerate-owned *Dong-A Ilbo* because of ideological incompatibility (Lee O-s 2004) and accepted a cartoonist position at a Busan newspaper, from which he also resigned when the newspaper supported then-president Park Geun-hye (Park J-d 2018). Another artist, Choi Min-sung, led a strike against *Segye Ilbo* because of the company's frequent invasion of the editorial rights of reporters and political cartoonists. *Segye* fired Choi for instigating the strike but rehired him after a three-year legal battle. In 2004, the cartoonist was again suspended from *Segye* for two months, this time because of a cartoon he drew that was critical of a presidential impeachment bill. The NECA criticized the daily for its action, and Choi defiantly stated that a political cartoonist "is not an illustrator and need not follow the corporation's direction" (Kim J-h 2004).

Aligned with the "hardening autonomy" change of thought among younger cartoonists was a desire to reform

2.13. "Dead 16th National Assembly." Choi Min-sung. *Segye Ilbo*, March 13, 2004.

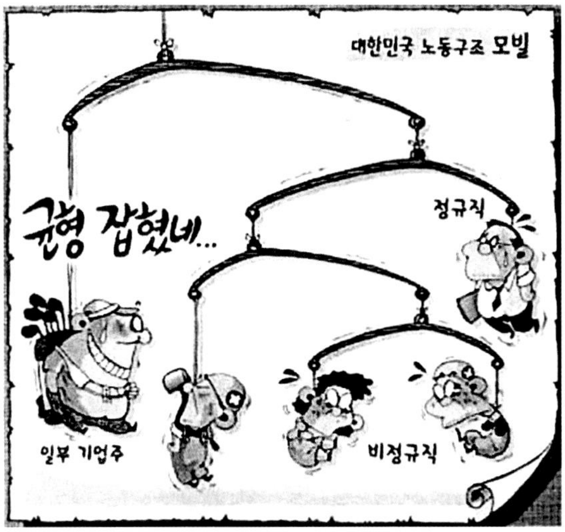

2.14. "Korean Labor Construction Mobile." Lee Jae-yong. *Munhwa Ilbo*, May 1, 2004. Caption: "What a balance: company president, employee, part-time employee."

the print media's usual practices, such as belonging to chaebols (family-owned conglomerates) and taking a conservative view on issues. These cartoonists often brought the conservative dailies *Chosun Ilbo*, *Dong-A Ilbo*, and *JoongAng Ilbo* into their drawings, lampooning them, such as showing them hanging around in groups with pens on their heads while holding sound magnifiers to blast out distorted opinions. Lee Jae-yong of *Munhwa Ilbo* satirized these newspapers as affected by "minor opinion addiction syndrome," listening only to trivial antigovernment opinions. These practices have been most apparent during periods of liberal government, beginning with Roh in 1988.

Lee Jae-yong described political cartoons in the chaebol-controlled conservative newspapers:

> Their works are emotional attacks rather than rational critiques. It is impossible not to be emotional when you criticize something, but the I-hate-you-like emotion went far beyond rational critique in their works. Nevertheless, it would be acceptable if the message contained verified reason, but you can not find any philosophy or logic in the cartoons. A political cartoon should be free of the newspaper's pressure. Even though it is published in the newspaper, it has to be independent and free like a floating boat. That is what readers want and expect from a political cartoon. However, they seem to follow their newspaper even when newspapers go the wrong way. That means the cartoonists do not work faithfully in my view, and it makes me feel sorry. Political cartoons should be independent but they are just swept away with the newspapers, and sometimes even go further than the newspaper. (Lee Jae-yong, quoted in Nam 2004)

Veteran political cartoonist Park Jae-dong answered my query about the most looming problems facing Korean political cartooning today, saying,

> A decrease in the number of newspapers, thus, fewer chances to publish cartoons. Now, only two papers carry political cartoons. Conservative daily newspapers ignore political cartoons, avoid punchy cartoons. Most political cartoons are webtoons and are in online newspapers.
>
> Newspaper owners in Korea are increasingly conservative and don't tolerate progressive cartoonists. In the current situation, it is not that political cartoonists ignore newspapers as venues, but there are fewer places to publish. (2018)

Conservative, chaebol-owned dailies have been accused of changing respected cartoonists such as Kim Sang-taek into their lapdogs. Cartoon researcher Kim Nak-ho said of Kim Sang-taek that he had lost his sharpness and satire and was left with conspiratorial and cynical views after joining *JoongAng Ilbo* (Kim N-h 2004).

Chaebols and Political Cartooning

For a country of its geographical size (38,600 square miles, equivalent to the state of Indiana in the United States) and population (51.3 million), South Korea has been well endowed with newspapers, the traditional havens for political cartoonists. Leading the thirty national general dailies are *Chosun Ilbo*, *JoongAng Ilbo*, and *Dong-A Ilbo*, pejoratively called Chojoongdong because of their conservatism, disproportionate power, collaboration with Japan during colonization and with domestic authoritarian administrations after the Korean War, and cozy alliances with the business world. About 58 percent of all newspaper subscribers in South Korea read one of the Chojoongdong dailies.

The largest South Korean daily newspapers are closely associated with the country's chaebols through informal ties of blood, marriage, school, and region. *Chosun Ilbo* is owned by the Bang family and their cultural foundation, *JoongAng Ilbo* by the Hong family, and *Dong-A Ilbo* by the Kim family and its cultural foundation (see Kim C-h 2016 for a comprehensive treatment of Korean media and chaebols).

Much of the interlinking, interlocking, and concentrated media ownership can be traced back to Samsung founder Lee Byung-chul, who, with Hong Jin-gi, cofounded *JoongAng Ilbo* in 1965. At a much more inclusive level than the Hearsts, Newhouses, and other world media moguls, Lee made sure a large proportion of his holdings were kept in the family, marrying his children to other chaebol heads and influential government officials. His third son, Lee Kun-hee, who headed the Samsung Group until 2014, married Hong Ra-hee, daughter of Hong Jin-gi, who chaired *JoongAng Ilbo*. One of their sons eventually headed *JoongAng*, and a daughter married the brother of *Dong-A Ilbo*'s chair. Researchers Kim Chunhyo (2016), and Kim Eun-mee and Lee Jae-woo (2021), managed to sort out the family and business entanglements, but it was a mean task.

In the late 1990s, Lee Kun-hee reorganized Samsung into six enterprises (actually, chaebols), which included Samsung, Cheil Jedang (CJ), and *JoongAng Ilbo*, all of which extensively expanded their media holdings, as well as Shinsaegae, Hansol, and Saehan (Kim C-h 2016, 83). Then, in 2005, *JoongAng Ilbo* divided into the *JoongAng Ilbo* and Bokwang Groups, which together with Samsung were closely linked by ties of blood and marriage. During *JoongAng Ilbo*'s vertical and horizontal diversification, its media properties increased from ten in 1998 to forty-eight in 2012 (Kim C-h 2016, 107, 109).

Over recent years, other chaebols came to own many newspapers to protect their interests, including Hyundai, Lotte, Daewoo, Duksan, Daenong, Hanhwa, and Line (Kim C-h 2016, 17). Although newspapers are the concern of this chapter, the chaebols have dominated in virtually all media: broadcasting, cable television, film production/distribution/exhibition, advertising, gaming, digital media, and recorded music.

By their own promotional material, the three largest Korean dailies can be labeled chaebols in their own right. The Dong-A Media Group consists of nine organizational networks: newspapers *Dong-A Ilbo*, *Sports Dong-A*, *Dong-A Children's Daily*, and *Weekly Dong-A*; books and magazines including *Shin Dong-A*, *Women's Dong-A*, *Dong-A Business Review*, *Science Dong-A*, and *Children's Science Dong-A*; website Dong-A.com; Dunet; Dong-A Science; Overseas Networks; Broadcasting; Sports and Cultural Activities; and Education. The group also has two museums and other centers, and hosts sporting and cultural events and festivals. The JoongAng Group maintains nineteen affiliates, including newspapers, the major ones being *JoongAng Ilbo* and *Korea JoongAng Daily*; magazines; a newspaper marketing and distribution firm; a news media company, which publishes the most Korean newspapers in eleven North American regions; a printing company; a design company; Joongang Tongyang Broadcasting Company (JTBC) and its many channels; a broadcasting advertising agency; multiplex cinemas with one hundred theater chains; a resort company that includes Phoenix Pyeongchang and Phoenix Jeju; cultural businesses; and new media and other production organizations. The third-largest media chaebol, Chosun Media, owns *Chosun Ilbo*, Digital Chosun, TV Chosun, the Chosun.com news website, the weekly *Jugan Chosun*, the monthly *Wolgan San*, other newspapers and magazines, Wolgan Chosun, Edu-Chosun, *Chosun Biz*, and more.

The impacts of chaebol control over newspapers and, by extension, over political cartooning are devastating. Kim Chunhyo reported on the uncovering of corporate censorship by the Lee family, stating that with their media holdings, "the Lee family published articles supporting its private interests, diluted the news regarding scandals of the Lee family and got involved in the presidential elections of Korea. The Lee family applied their economic and cultural power over Korean journalism to manufacture public opinion for their private interests" (2016, 133–34). She also stated that Chojoondong ignored media laws (124) and that media chaebols more generally bent the news to support their agendas through bribery, political support, and the denial of advertising revenues.[4] Both *Hankyoreh Shinmun* and *Kyunghyang Shinmun* lost chaebol contracts because of their critical reporting (Kim C-h 2016, 135–36). The chaebols overran the media advertising market, with the four largest (Samsung, Hyundai Automotive, SK, and LG) leading the way. The Korean Journalists Survey 2019 claimed that journalists felt pressure working in companies with different revenue and ownership structures, reporting that "advertisers (68.4%) were most frequently selected as one of the three biggest factors restricting freedom of the press" (Kim and Lee 2021, 403).

Kim and Lee warned about personal ties between media owners and nonmedia chaebols, stating that such relationships "are especially troubling because these affiliations are not readily noticed, yet can critically impair the independence of the press" (2021, 416).

These factors relating to chaebols definitely carried over to the political cartoonists, who had been some of the loudest and fiercest journalistic watchdogs of government and big business in South Korea. They thrived in the early years of the country's liberalization period of the late 1980s and early 1990s, as they were afforded public respect and high salaries, more venues with a significant increase in the number of magazines, and increased freedom to cartoon (Kim P-k 1992; Yoon 1992). However, at the same time, political cartoonists noticed that issues had become more complicated (Kim P-k 1992)—newly vested special interests protected the favorite targets of cartoonists, and the cartoonists were answerable to more constituencies. High on the list were the chaebols that owned the press (Shim 1991, 55). To protect their interests, chaebols such as Samsung, Hyundai, and Hanguk Hwayak (Korean Chemicals) purchased major dailies, whose cartoonists were intimidated by their new overseers and could not do their best work (Park J-d 1992).

By 2018, when I again interviewed political cartoonists, the profession was nearly nonexistent: both one- and four-panel cartoons had virtually disappeared, as stalwarts such as Kim Song-hwan and Jeong Un-kyeong had died; the number of newspapers had decreased; new venues such as webtoons took on political dimensions; and newspaper chaebols had become increasingly conservative, steering away from strong cartoons and no longer tolerating progressive cartoonists (Park J-d 2018). Two political cartoons survived—a four-panel in *Kyunghyang Shinmun* and a one-panel in *Hankyoreh Shinmun*. Other major dailies merely carried nondescript, small drawings that illustrated some articles.

Some political cartoonists scrambled to find ways to share their works—posting them at public events and creating caricaturized puppets of political figures accompanied by small patches of text for exhibitions and television (Park J-d 2018).

From its launching in 1988, *Hankyoreh Shinmun* set a course very different from the Chojoongdong press. The daily is owned by sixty thousand stockholders, none of whom has a more than 1 percent share; it was started by former journalists of *Dong-A Ilbo* and *Chosun Ilbo* who were disgruntled by government censorship and large capital interference, and it has maintained an independent, left-leaning, nationalist, and pro–human rights stance. For years, *Hankyoreh Shinmun* has been named the most trusted news organization by Korean journalists, and at the same time, the least influential.

The daily's major cartoonist from its beginning, Park Jae-dong (born 1952), said that other cartoonists envied him, calling him the "very happiest cartoonist" because he could do what he wanted to do (Park J-d 1992). Like other Korean political cartoonists, Park drew according to his newspaper's policy, the difference being that *Hankyoreh Shinmun* is uniquely liberal and "does not listen to government" (1992). The newspaper, in its initial years, sported

Park's daily, one-panel political cartoon, *Hankyoreh Picture*, and his weekly *Cartoon Story*.

Park has been a leading figure in the manhwa world since the 1980s. Besides his political cartooning years at *Hankyoreh* (1988–1996), he has devoted much energy to promoting manhwa generally, including the protection of Korean comic books from the manga onslaught in the early 1990s, by helping organize a group called Our Cartoon Association (Uri Manhwa Hyeophoe, started in 1992 and consisting of eighty members), which led a public demonstration in July 1992 at which manga were denounced and Korean cartoonists considered unduly influenced by them were identified and ridiculed; by pulling together an exhibition in July 1994 featuring Korean cartoonists who were attempting not to imitate manga; by lobbying for government action; and by participating in other anti-manga, as well as humanitarian, demonstrations and events (Park J-d 1994).

By the time of my second of four interviews with Park, he had turned to animation. For nine months, he created a weekly, two-and-a-half-minute animation related to the news for the Munhwa Broadcasting Company (MBC). At other times, he did animated shorts on voting and other issues. His goal has been to make a feature-length animation on the April 1948 Jeju massacre, but, as he said in 1993, he lacked a "foundation" (support), and after seven years he still had not written a "good scenario" (Park J-d 1993).

Park described the time he did the animated newsclips for MBC as being in "cartoon prison"; he said that he "did the storyboard, the idea for the story, everything but the technical part. All of this had to be done with speed, with a time limit in a creative war. Thursday night, I fixed the theme and had to do everything else in one and one-half days by Saturday morning. I did this for nine months. I was going crazy [trying to keep up]" (Park J-d 2018).

More recently, Park taught at a university, consulted for educational officials, and was in charge of a film festival.

Investigative Cartooning

In recent years, some of the most profound printed political commentary and criticism in South Korea have not

2.15. One of the displays at the 1994 anti-manga/pro-manhwa exhibition organized by Our Cartoon Association. Permission of Park Jae-dong.

been political cartoons in the traditional sense; they are not solely one or four panel, do not always comment on the most current events, sometimes are jointly produced, and do not appear in newspapers or magazines. Perhaps better termed as sociopolitical, historical-realism graphic novels, they are in book form, made up of multiple panels per page, and uncover news happenings that were silenced during decades of authoritarian rule and played down or ignored by contemporary chaebol-controlled dailies.

In the twenty-first century, a few factors gelled that brought about the emergence of investigative graphic novels: (1) most importantly, a series of liberal governments, (2) a strong manhwa presence and audience, (3) the diminishing role of newspapers and their political cartoons, (4) a publisher, the Bori Publishing Company, with its Footprints of Peace series, willing to bring out these controversial titles, and (5) the economic downturn of 1997 with its depleted job market that forced young aspiring artists to find other ways to make a living.

To be sure, Korea's most prominent investigative graphic novelists came to cartooning by accident and necessity. Born in the 1970s or after, they sought employment about

2.16. Kim Sung-hee. Permission of Kim Sung-hee.

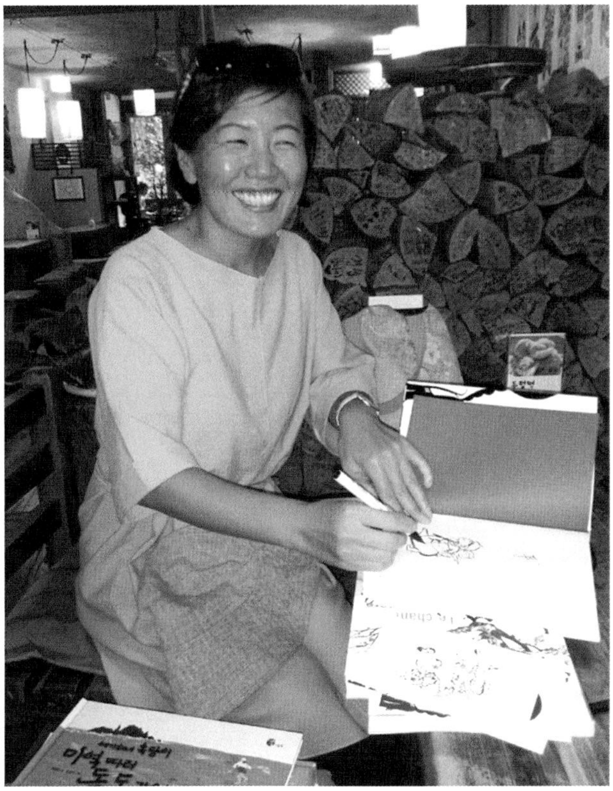

2.17. Gendry-Kim Keum suk. Seoul, August 8, 2018. Photo by and courtesy of Kim Chunhyo. Permission of Gendry-Kim Keum suk.

the time of the economic recession, when positions in their fields of training were scarce or nonexistent. For a time, they managed to make ends meet working at construction sites and on factory assembly lines, babysitting, cashiering, telemarketing, and holding similar jobs. For example, Kim Sung-hee (born 1975) and Gendry-Kim Keum suk (born 1971) separately came to cartooning in roundabout ways. Kim Sung-hee, who majored in international trade, despaired of finding a position in her field and decided to try cartooning. She devised a plan over nine years of working alternately three months at part-time menial jobs, followed by three months of only drawing cartoons (Kim Sung-hee 2018). Gendry-Kim studied Western painting, became "bored standing in one place to paint," moved to France, studied sculpture, worked in odd jobs to eke out an existence, and then drew cartoons for a Parisian Korean-language newspaper. She also translated Korean-language manhwa into French, at which time she figured that she, too, could tell people's stories. After seventeen years abroad, she returned to Korea and began writing and drawing graphic novels at breakneck speed (Gendry-Kim 2018; see also Melikian 2017). Kim and Gendry-Kim said they also wanted to escape from the discrimination of Korea's family-centered, patriarchal society. Others, such as Kim Soo-bak (born 1974) and Choi Kyu-seok (born 1977), also entered cartooning by side doors.

The exhumed stories the graphic novelists dug up and told span a period as far back as the "comfort women" (sex slaves to the Japanese military in World War II) to as recent as the *Sewol* ferry disaster of April 16, 2016, when 304 passengers died because of inept management and neglect of duty. Gendry-Kim told of one comfort woman's experiences in *Grass* (2019), which received numerous awards and was translated into fourteen languages, while Kim Soo-bak related the *Sewol* ferry tragedy in *Tale of a Sad and Funny Country*.

The range of subjects can be gleaned from this compilation I wrote elsewhere:

> Samsung's ongoing corporate denial and refusal to accept responsibility for the deaths and illnesses of 138 of its semiconductor employees exposed to toxic materials (e.g., Kim Sung-hee's *Dust Room* [2012] and Kim Soo-bak's *The One Thing Missing at Samsung: the Feel of Humanity*; [the already

2.18. Kim Soo-bak. Seoul, August 6, 2018. Permission of Kim Soo-bak.

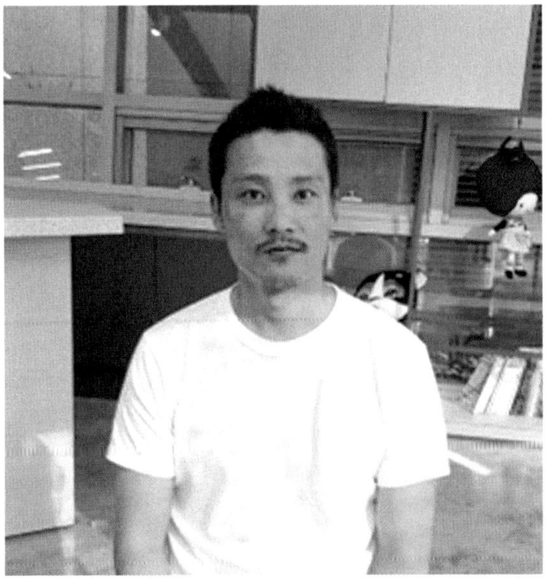

2.19. Choi Kyu-seok. Bucheon, August 11, 2018. Photo by and courtesy of Kwon Jae-woong. Permission of Choi Kyu-seok.

> mentioned *Grass* by Gendry-Kim Keum suk]; the 4-3 uprising (of April 3, 1948) during which 70 percent of Jeju Island's villages were destroyed and anywhere from fifteen thousand to sixty thousand people (most civilians) died in conflicts between Republic of Korea military and police (with the compliance of the US military), and communist insurgents (e.g., Park Kun-woong's *Story of Hong*) . . . ; the sad plight of Korean civilians working in Hiroshima and Nagasaki at the time of the US atomic bombings (e.g., Gendry-Kim's *A Day with Grandfather* [2017]); treasonous accusations wrongly brought against South Koreans during the Park Chung-hee regime (e.g., Park Kun-woong's *Spring of the Dead Year* [2021]); the torturing of civilians during the dictatorships; the killings of South Korean civilians by the South Korean military during the Korean War; the 1987 June Democracy Movement (e.g., Choi Kyu-seok's *Songgot* [2015]); the massacre of hundreds of South Korean citizens by the US military at the Bridge of No Gun Ri during the Korean War [e.g., *The Nogunri Bridge* by Park Kun-woong]; and the plight of dissidents Hur Young-chul and Kim Geun-tae (e.g., Park Kun-woong's *Time of the Beasts* [2014]). (Lent 2023, 68–69)

There have been others, such as *Yongsan, Where I Once Lived*, a team effort by six artists and writers to determine the truth behind a deadly 2009 fire in the Yongsan district of Seoul where the police and evicted housing residents clashed, and Gendry-Kim's *The Waiting* (2021), dealing with the separation of families after the Korean War (see Kwak 2021; Woodend 2021).

Much effort went into these investigations, finding and interviewing victims and knowledgeable individuals, both in Korea and abroad, and scouring public and historical documents, the latter often difficult to access since they are of government and chaebol origins. Some of the graphic novelists had to deal with their own emotions while gathering stories with such overbearing trauma (Park K-w 2018; Kim Sung-hee 2018; Kim S-b 2018).

Their hard work paid off, as some of the investigative graphic novels sold tens of thousands of copies, were made into movies, television shows, and webtoons, were translated into multiple languages, and were awarded a number of prizes. On the other hand, there was also a price to pay because of various repercussions emanating from conservative groups, the government, and chaebols, including the removal from libraries of Park Kun-woong's *Time of the Beasts* (also translated as *Animal Time*) by President Park Geun-hye supporters (Melikian 2016), the denial of advertising space for graphic novels in some print and online periodicals because of the latter's fear of losing chaebol (e.g., Samsung) advertising contracts, and the placement of cartoonists Kim Soo-bak and Park Kun-woong (born 1972) on Korea's artist blacklist under Presidents Lee Myung-bak (2008–2013) and Park Geun-hye (2013–2017), respectively. Kim and Park considered being on the blacklist an honor (Kim S-b 2018; Park K-w 2018).

2.20. A unique page from *Grass*. Gendry-Kim Keum suk. Permission of Gendry-Kim Keum suk.

2.21. *The Waiting*. Gendry-Kim Keum suk. Permission of Gendry-Kim Keum suk.

2.22. Investigative graphic novelist Park Kun-woong. Permission of Park Kun-woong.

2.23. The main method of dispersal of propaganda leaflets during the Korean War was by airdrops. This is an example of aerial distribution from a US warplane during the Korean War. Public domain.

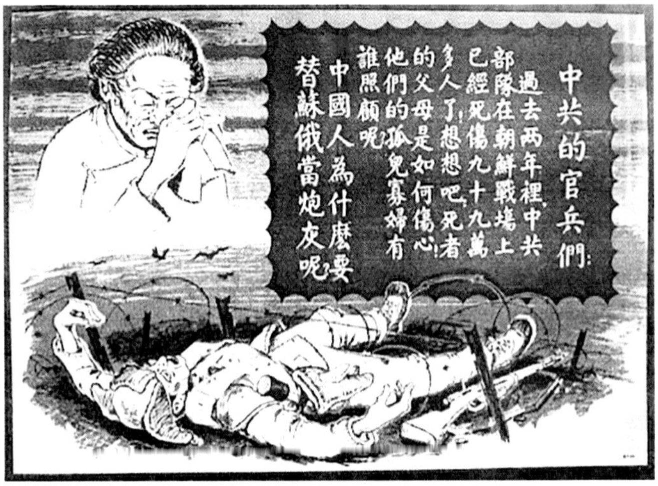

2.24. This US leaflet shows a mother grieving over a dead Chinese soldier with the message: "Over the past two years, 990,000 people have died. Who will take care of your old mother in your hometown, and why die for someone else?" Public domain.

Propaganda Leaflet Warfare

On and off since around 1950, both the South Korean and North Korean governments have bombarded each other's soldiers and citizens with propaganda (often political) leaflets, many of which use cartoons and other drawings. Cartoon leaflet warfare was employed during World War II by the Japanese to demoralize American and Australian troops and to encourage Asian people to rebel against the colonizers and be part of Japan's East Asian Co-Prosperity Sphere; by the Chinese to persuade private citizens to identify traitors and support China's military; and by the Americans to weaken the morale of the enemy. These leaflets were released over the landscape by airplanes (see Lent 2014, 258–301).

The Korean Peninsula experienced the Korea balloon propaganda campaign during the Korean War, when United Nations forces fired 2.5 billion leaflets into North Korea and China, while North Korea released 300 million into the South (Jung J-h 2014, 16). Only seventy-two hours after the first battle, the Psychological Warfare Section of the Far East Command in Tokyo began dropping leaflets on Communist forces at the rate of twenty million a week. United Nations forces disseminated them by leaflet bombs released from B-29 aircraft; 105-mm mortar shells, each packed with 738 leaflets, fired from heavy artillery on the ground; and patrols who handed them out (Kim J. K. 1993, 5). The leaflets, varying from three-by-five inches to newspaper size, were delivered in special bombs, each with 22,500 leaflets, whose hinged side blew off at a predetermined time, releasing their cargo (Hoh 2017). Initially, most of the North Korean leaflets were delivered by hand.

In his thorough account of Korean War leaflets, Kim Jin K. (1993) divides them both functionally and thematically. The functional types were strategic ("breaking the enemy's will to fight" to bring about victory and peace) (5), tactical ("assisting specific, imminent [or ongoing] military operations by creating a desired psychological impact") (5), and consolidating (restoring and sustaining civil order when hostilities cease) (6). Kim found that of UN leaflets, 49 percent were strategic and 42 percent tactical, while 84 percent of Communist leaflets were strategic and 14 percent tactical (6). The themes of Korean War leaflets in Kim's breakdown are: political ideology and leadership, nationalistic sentiment/foreign forces, military technology and tactical/strategic predicaments of war, history/culture/tradition, freedom/discrimination/censorship/deception, hardships on the battleground and in civilian life, health issues and the treatment of defectors and POWs, nostalgia for family, life and death, and information/bombing alerts/utility (6–15). Kim concludes: "U.N. leaflets, to a great extent, exploited nationalistic sentiments, political leadership/ideology, and hardships in military and civilian lives most frequently while the Communist Forces focused on hardships in military and civilian lives, nationalistic sentiments, and tactical/strategic predicaments of war" (14–15). Both sides were referred to derogatorily, for instance as warmongers, traitors, or Chinese barbarians, "(Chinky or Yankee troops) violating your wives and sisters" (18),

2.25. "Why die for Russia?" Propaganda leaflet showing Stalin pushing a Chinese military officer, who in turn is pushing a Korean soldier toward a Korea-labeled battlefield. Public domain.

2.26. North Korean leaflet equating the treatment by UN soldiers during the Korean War with the harsh treatment inflicted by the Japanese military during World War II. Public domain.

"this bum," internal security pigs, blood suckers, or clumsy fighters. Kim found that "Communist leaflets characterized (more frequently than the U.N. leaflets) their enemy as war criminals, servers of foreign interests (or loathsome foreigners) and perpetrators of abominable behaviors. The U.N. leaflets, on the other hand, engaged in name calling by focusing on their enemy's moral character, incompetence—especially their vulnerability to bombing—and class exploitation" (19).

Leaflets usually carried illustrative matter (often cartoons) on the front and text on the reverse side. A UN leaflet designed to damage North Korean soldiers' morale shows a beaten-up soldier sitting atop a pile of skulls on the front with text on the back questioning why the Communist soldier wanted to continue fighting when so many fellow soldiers were dying. The text goes on to offer a "warm hand" if the soldier surrendered. One meant to induce homesickness and at the same time invoke anger against North Korean soldiers portrays a sad South Korean soldier sitting with his gun resting against a tree, an older woman longingly staring at him. The reverse side, in the form of a letter from mother to son, details how the Communists had made life miserable for the mother and her family back home.

After the battles ended in 1953, the leaflet war continued into contemporary times with a succession of bombardments of both countries, agreements to cease the dropping of the leaflets, threats from North Korean authorities when agreements were broken, and placating actions by the South Korean government. When, in 2020, nongovernmental organizations (mostly Christian and evangelical groups) flew propaganda-laden balloons into North Korea, Kim Yo-jong (sister of North Korean leader Kim Jong-un) issued a lengthy document demanding that the South Korean government accept responsibility for the "scum" and "mongrel dogs" who had dispatched the balloons (BBC News 2020). Not long after, on December 14, 2020, the South Korean National Assembly passed a law to formally punish the distribution of anti–North Korean leaflets across the border (Rogin 2020). This sort of back-and-forth saber rattling and saber sheathing has been ongoing. Sometimes, the threatening language has been a bit frightening, as when in October 2014 the North Korean state newspaper *Rodong Sinmun* equated the South Korean government's tolerance of the balloon dispatchers with acts of war (Park J-m 2014).

Most recently, in June 2020, a resurgence of threats and counterthreats plagued the peninsula. North Korea officials announced that twelve million leaflets would be sent to the South as "punishment" for breaking a 2018 agreement to stop border hostilities, including psychological warfare involving leafleting and propaganda broadcasting. A top South Korean official warned that "immediate, swift and corresponding steps" would be taken to any North Korean provocation (Roos 2020); however, the South Korean Ministry of Unification simultaneously issued a statement calling on anti–North Korea groups (this time, mainly defectors) to stop sending the leaflets (Jung D-m 2020).

Content of the leaflets vary between North and South Korea. BBC reporter Kevin Kim describes slogans on

2.27. A North Korean cartoon leaflet portraying former South Korean president Park Geun-hye in a sexual encounter. Public domain.

North Korean leaflets as "very direct . . . spontaneous and lacking subtlety . . . quintessentially North Korean . . . right down to details like the colours and quality of paper used" (BBC News 2016). They have called former South Korean president Park Geun-hye a prostitute, pictured US president Barack Obama as a monkey, and depicted an angry President Donald Trump sporting a Hitler-like mustache, calling him a "barefaced robber" (Persio 2017). Another leaflet dropped on the South had Park Geun-hye in a red bikini being thrown in the rubbish can as "human filth." Others mocking Park were "exceptionally explicit" in depicting her romantic (sexual) relationships in cartoon form and describing her as a "notorious woman of loose morals and [an] oversexed witch" (Ji 2017). One cartoon said that Park had a "hard-on" for her lover, another showed the president in bed with a man during the tragic *Sewol* ferry sinking (Ji 2017), and a third portrayed her as a "dung fly flying toward a pile of feces with the words 'US poop'" (Ji 2017). Leaflets from South Korea tend to be more subtle and relate negatively to the family history of Kim Jong-un (BBC News 2016). They show off the South's growing affluence and the "miracles of capitalism," displaying South Koreans "vacationing on beaches and trumpeting the number of cars produced in the South" (Choe 2008). On one occasion, the South Korean government even filled North-bound balloons with candy, lighters, tobacco, and pornographic publications. The North Korean government countered by issuing alarming, false statements that the supplies were poisoned, and later that they carried the coronavirus, to deter the public from recovering and using the products, but North Koreans did not heed the warning (*Guardian* 2021).

Conclusion

A major common thread that has carried through much of the more than a century's history of South Korean political cartooning is that of government control, first by Japanese occupation forces and then by dictatorships from Syngman Rhee in the 1940s through Roh Tae-woo ending in 1993. During that time, the country experienced a major war, which curtailed full and accurate cartoon reportage and commentary; martial law initiated under Park Chung-hee, who considered cartoons to be one of six evils of society; and tragedies such as the Jeju and Gwangju Uprisings, which were off limits for coverage until the 2010s. In addition to censorship, political cartoonists were subjected to arrest, jailing, torture, fines, and other harassment.

A different aspect of South Korean political cartooning is that it was not introduced through European or American satirical magazines such as *Punch* and *Puck*, as happened elsewhere on the continent. In his exhaustive study of *Punch* imitators globally, Australian historian Richard Scully did not find a Korean *Punch*, though they existed in surrounding countries and territories such as Japan, China, and Hong Kong (Scully 2013, 6–35).

South Korea's trajectory of political cartooning has also been affected by socioeconomic factors, particularly that the major dailies—*Choson Ilbo*, *JoongAng Ilbo*, and *Dong-A Ilbo*, lumped together as Chojoongdong—are owned by chaebols (conglomerates), and their publishers and editors are very much aware of what can be reported and guide cartoonists accordingly. In recent years, many buried stories of past events have been uncovered not by newspaper cartoonists but by a number of independent artists who used whatever resources they could gather and the assistance of a small publishing house, Bori, to bring their revelations to light in graphic novels.

Such investigative cartooning is a useful dimension that can be credited to South Korean cartoonists; another is the vertical four-panel political strips that were extremely popular in the latter half of the twentieth century. The strong appeal of these strips seems limited to South Korea, and they have disappeared even there. Professionally, cartoonists made some strides toward bettering their labor conditions by forming the National Editorial Cartoonists Association and achieving some autonomy.

Overall, South Korea political cartooning is going down the same road traveled by the profession in other parts of the world. That road worldwide is potholed by dwindling numbers of newspapers, many dismissed and unemployed political cartoonists (particularly in the United States), the concentration of mass media outlets into fewer and fewer conglomerates, the use of subtle control mechanisms such as "guided cartooning" and self-censorship by editors and the cartoonists themselves, and inroads made by new information technology. However, the internet and social media, by providing added venues, have helped save political cartooning.[5]

Notes

1. The most prosperous period for readers' cartoons was the 1950s and 1960s, when more experienced cartoonists commented upon and instructed the amateurs (Yoon 1986). Eventually, reader cartoonists organized, and when dailies needed a cartoon, they pulled from that group. *Kyunghyang Shinmun* political cartoonist Kim Pan-kook credited the group with producing "the major cartoonists of today [1992]" (Kim P-k 1992).

2. Kim Song-hwan (1992) traced the four-panel political cartoons to 1945; however, most of the early ones did not last longer than ten appearances.

3. The author is indebted to his former graduate student Chung Min-ju for providing much of the information relating to the beginning of the 2000s.

4. In the 2000s, top Lee executives were indicted: Lee Kun-hee in 2008 for tax evasion and breach of trust, and his successor son, Lee Jae-yong, later for bribery. Lee Jae-yong reportedly paid US$17.5 million to Choi Soon-sil, a close confidant of then president and subsequently impeached Park Geun-hye, in return for government favors. Lee Kun-hee avoided a prison term by admitting to the wrongdoing and apologizing, and because of fears that his imprisonment would affect the functioning of a leading group. Other chaebol heads have kept the jailers at bay by donating large sums of money to charities, what one outspoken critic termed "bribing the society" (Choe 2011).

JoongAng Ilbo publisher Hong Seok-hyun was arrested on tax evasion charges in late 1999 after a probe of the Bokwang Group, of which he was the largest shareholder. He also did not see a prison cell, given a three-year suspended sentence and ordered to pay US$3.3 million in back taxes (CPJ 2000).

5. Suggesting that political cartooning as it has been known for centuries can be seen as "a relic of a bygone era," one researcher offered internet memes as its replacement. Memes, which dominate social media, are any aspect of popular culture that can be copied; they are easy to create (e.g., a photograph with a text overlay), quickly made, and democratic in nature (Grygiel 2019).

References

Ahn, Hyun-dong. 1992. Interview with John A. Lent. Seoul, July 6.

BBC News. 2016. "North Korea Is Dropping Leaflets on the South—What Do They Say?" January 19. https://www.bbc.com/news/world-asia-35349686.

BBC News. 2020. "South Korean Balloons: Plans to Stop People Sending Cross-Border Messages." June 4. https://www.bbc.com/news/world-asia-52917029.

Choe, Sang-hun. 2008. "Koreans Recall an Era of Propaganda Battles." *New York Times*, May 2. https://www.nytimes.com/2008/05/02/world/asia/02leaflet.html.

Choe, Sang-hun. 2011. "South Korean Family Conglomerates Pressured." *New York Times*, September 13. https://www.nytimes.com/2011/09/14/business/global/south-korean-chaebol-under-increasing-pressure.html.

Choi, Kyu-seok. 2018. Interview with John A. Lent. Seoul, August 11.

Choi, Min-sung. 2003. "Introducing the National Editorial Cartoonists Association." *Newstoon*, December 18.

Chung, Woon-kyung. 1992. Interview with John A. Lent. Seoul, July 7.

Committee to Protect Journalists (CPJ). 2000. "Attacks on the Press 1999: South Korea." March 22. https://cpj.org/2000/03/attacks-on-the-press-1999-south-korea/.

Gendry-Kim, Keum suk. 2018. Interview with John A. Lent. Seoul, August 8.

Grygiel, Jennifer. 2019. "Political Cartoonists Are Out of Touch—It's Time to Make Way for Memes." The Conversation, May 17. https://theconversation.com/political-cartoonists-are-out-of-touch-its-time-to-make-way-for-memes-116471.

Guardian. 2021. "North Korea Says Propaganda Leaflets Sent from South Could Carry Coronavirus." May 6. https://www.theguardian.com/world/2021/may/07/north-korea-says-propaganda-leaflets-sent-from-south-could-carry-coronavirus.

Hall, Emily Marie Anderson. 2019. "Kim Sŏnghwan's 'Mr. Kobau': Editorial Cartoons as Genre Weapons in South Korean Search for Democracy, 1945–1972." PhD diss., University of Washington.

Hoh, Anchi. 2017. "Korean War Propaganda Leaflet Collection at the Library of Congress." Library of Congress, September 26.

https://blogs.loc.gov/international-collections/2017/09/korean-war-propaganda-leaflet-collection-at-the-library-of-congress/.
Ji, Dagyum. 2017. "N. Korean Leaflets with Sexually Explicit Cartoons of Park Found in Seoul." NK News, February 27. https://nknews.org/2017/02/n-korean-leaflets-with-sexually-explicit-cartoons-of-park-found-in-seoul/.
Jung, Da-min. 2020. "Political Dynamics of Propaganda Leaflets and Inter-Korean Relations." *Korea Times*, June 11. https://www.koreatimes.co.kr/www/nation/2020/06/103_291046.html.
Jung, Jin-heon. 2014. "Ballooning Evangelism: Psychological Warfare and Christianity in the Divided Korea." MMG Working Paper 14-07, July. Max Planck Institute.
Kang, Hyun-kyung. 2019. "Satire Comic Strip Artist Dies at 87." *Korea Times*, September 9. https://www.koreatimes.co.kr/www/culture/2019/09/142_275335.html.
Kim, Chunhyo. 2016. *Samsung, Media Empire and Family: A Power Web*. Abingdon, Oxon., England: Routledge.
Kim, Eun-mee, and Lee Jae-woo. 2021. "South Korea: Relatively Healthy, Still Trying Hard to Adapt to Digitalisation." In *The Media for Democracy Monitor 2021: How Leading News Media Survive Digital Transformation*, edited by Josef Trappel and Tales Tomaz, 387–424. Gothenburg, Sweden: Nordicom, University of Gothenburg.
Kim, Jin K. 1993. "Themes in Korean War–Era Leaflets: Implications for Future North-South Korean and Korean-U.S. Dialogues." Unpublished paper. State University of New York at Plattsburgh. https://library.ndsu.edu/ndsuarchives/sites/default/files/Themes-in-Korean-War.pdf.
Kim, Jong-hwa. 2004. "*Segye Ilbo* Impeached the Political Cartoonist Who Drew an Impeachment Cartoon." *Mediatoday*.
Kim, Nak-ho. 2004. "The Limit of Kim Sang Taek's Cartoons: Superficial Sympathy of the Working Class and Over Date of Conspiracy." *People and Ideology*, June.
Kim, Pan-kook. 1992. Interview with John A. Lent. Seoul, July 2.
Kim, Song-hwan. 1992. Interview with John A. Lent. Seoul, July 4.
Kim, Soo-bak. 2018. Interview with John A. Lent. Seoul, August 6.
Kim, Sung-hee. 2018. Interview with John A. Lent. Seoul, August 6.
Kwak, Yeon-soo. 2021. "Harvey Award–Winning Graphic Novelist Highlights History in Cartoons." *Korea Times*, January 21. https://www.koreatimes.co.kr/www/culture/2021/01/135_302826.html.
Lee, Hae-chang. 1982. *History of Korean Political Cartoons*. Seoul: Iljeesa.
Lee, O.-s. 2004. "Send Me to Iraq as a War Political Cartoonist." *Newstoon*, February 20.
Lee, S.-k. 2004. "Controversy about the Layoff of Political Cartoonists of *Segye Ilbo*." *Hankyoreh Shinmun*, June 3.
Lee, Won-bok. 1992. Interview with John A. Lent. Seoul, July 2.
Lent, John A. 1995. "Korean Cartooning: Historical and Contemporary Perspectives." *Korean Culture* (Spring): 9–19.
Lent, John A. 2014. "Allied, Japanese, and Chinese Propaganda: Cartoon Leaflets during World War II." *International Journal of Comic Art* 16, no. 1 (Spring): 258–301.
Lent, John A. 2023. *Asian Political Cartoons*. Jackson: University Press of Mississippi.
Melikian, Laurent. 2016. "Park Kun-woong ('Je suis Communiste'): 'Nous ne sommes pas libérés de la guerre des idéologies'" [Park Kun-woong ("I Am a Communist"): "We Are Not Free from the War of Ideologies"]. *Actua BD*, March 16. https://www.actuabd.com/Park-Kun-woong-Je-suis-Communiste.
Melikian, Laurent. 2017. "Keum Suk Gendry-Kim: 'J'arrive chargée d'espoir'" [Keum Suk Gendry-Kim: "I'm Coming Full of Hope"]. *Actua BD*, May 23. https://www.actuabd.com/Keum-Suk-Gendry-Kim-J-arrive-chargee-d-espoir.
Nam, S.-h. 2004. "The Role of the Political Cartoon: To Lead the People to Have Interest; Interview with Lee Jae-yong." *OhmyNews*, January 10.
Park, Hye-su. 2016. "Dong-Sung Kim." Planetary Republic of Comics. https://professorlatinx.osu.edu/comics/dong-sung-kim.
Park, Jae-dong. 1992. Interview with John A. Lent. Seoul, July 7.
Park, Jae-dong. 1993. Interview with John A. Lent. Seoul, August 15.
Park, Jae-dong. 1994. Interview with John A. Lent. Seoul, July 3.
Park, Jae-dong. 2018. Interview with John A. Lent. Seoul, August 10.
Park, Ju-min. 2014. "South Korea Group Launches Anti-North Leaflets amid Threats from Pyongyang." Reuters, October 25. https://www.reuters.com/article/idUSKCN0IE041/.
Park, Kun-woong. 2018. Interview with John A. Lent. Seoul, August 9.
Persio, Sofia Lotto. 2017. "North Korea Mocks Trump in Propaganda Leaflets." Yahoo News, October 6. https://news.yahoo.com/north-korea-mocks-trump-propaganda-163757654.html?fr=yhssrp_catchall.
Rogin, Josh. 2020. "South Korea's New Anti-Leaflet Law Sparks Backlash in Washington." *Washington Post*, December 17. https://www.washingtonpost.com/opinions/2020/12/17/south-koreas-new-anti-leaflet-law-sparks-backlash-washington/.
Roos, Meghan. 2020. "North Korea to Drop 12 Million Propaganda Leaflets as 'Punishment' on South." *Newsweek*, June 22. https://www.newsweek.com/north-korea-drop-12-million-propaganda-leaflets-punishment-south-1512586.
Salmon, Andrew. 2009. "A Cartoonist at War: 'Gobau's' Korea, 1950." *Asia-Pacific Journal* 28, no. 3 (July 13). https://apjjf.org/Andrew-Salmon/3186.
Scully, Richard. 2013. "A Comic Empire: The Global Expansion of *Punch* as a Model Publication, 1841–1936." *International Journal of Comic Art* 15, no. 2 (Fall): 6–35.
Shim, Jae-hoon. 1991. "A Hard Act to Follow." *Far Eastern Economic Review*, June 13, 54–55.
Toler, Pamela D. 2020. "Sketching a War's Toll." *MHQ: The Quarterly Journal of Military History* 33, no. 1 (Autumn). https://www.historynet.com/sketching-a-wars-toll/.

Woodend, Dorothy. 2021. "'The Waiting' Is a Piercing Story of Family Separation in Korea." *The Tyee*, November 16. https://thetyee.ca/Culture/2021/11/16/The-Waiting-Piercing-Story-Family-Separation-Korea/.
Yoon, Yong-ok. 1986. *The History of Korean Newspaper Cartoons*. Seoul: Yorhwadang.
Yoon, Yong-ok. 1992. Interview with John A. Lent. Seoul, July 3.

Vig-III.2. Fleeing Koreans at the start of the Korean War sketched by teenager Kim Song-hwan. June 27, 1950. Public domain.

Vignette III

Kim Song-hwan

Korea's Dean of Political Cartooning

Kim Song-hwan is well known in Korea for his long-running four-panel political cartoon strip *Gobau* (strong rock), and he is often dubbed the "dean" of such cartoons.

Forgotten or never widely recognized is the valuable service Kim rendered by daringly using his pencils and watercolors to capture the everyday life of South Korea in late 1949, and the wartime destruction during the opening months of the Korean War (June to September 1950). Seventeen years old, Kim ventured into the streets of Kaesong and then Seoul to visually capture the refugees and soldiers fleeing from the North Korean military. To avoid capture by the North Koreans, he hid in his aunt's attic or under her kitchen floorboards while in Kaesong, and at other times he used clever ruses. When he learned that North Korea was conscripting young men into their army, Kim carried a cane and faked a limp to make himself look physically unfit to serve in the military.

Already in 1949, Kim set his sights on doing cartoons, serving as the "exclusive" artist for the *Yonhap Daily*, where he contributed one- and four-panel political cartoons. He told me in 1992 that, "in the long term, it is accurate that I started the four-panel cartoon," his reasoning being that among a few published in 1945, none lasted more than ten or so issues.

Vig-III.1. Kim Song-hwan (1932–2019). Seoul, July 1, 1992. Photo by John A. Lent.

When the US Army recaptured Seoul on September 28, 1950, the South Korean Ministry of Defense hired the still seventeen-year-old Kim as a war artist stationed near the front. However, for most of the rest of the war, Kim drew informational pamphlets for the public.

On February 1, 1955, Kim realized what he had imagined while hiding in his aunt's house nearly five years before and launched *Gobau* in the daily *Dong-A Ilbo*. The cartoon

Vig-III.3. Kim Song-hwan. 1999. A 1947 street scene. Gobau can be seen in the upstairs center window adjacent to the sign. Courtesy of Kim Song-hwan.

Vig-III.4. Two men watch artillery explosions on the first day of the Korean War. Eighteen year old Kim Song hwan sketched many wartime scenes during the summer of 1950. Courtesy of Kim Song-hwan.

series was made up of social and political criticism, wit, and a touch of humor and was meant for adults as well as children. The character Old Man Gobau was drawn simply without any facial expression, his mood or psychological state expressed by the positioning of a single hair on his head. *Gobau* remained at *Dong-A Ilbo* for twenty-six years before moving to *Chosun Ilbo*, where Kim became a member of the editorial council, as he had been at *Dong-A Ilbo*.

Gobau was an icon during its long run, made into two movies (*Gobau* in 1959 and *Master Upside-Down, Master Long Legs* in 1997); lauded in the poems "Mid-Stream" by acclaimed poetess Lee Young-do (1916–1975) and "Gobau Kim Song-whan" [*sic*] by Ko Eun (born 1933); merited a permanent exhibition room in the National Library of Korea; commemorated on a Korean postage stamp; and made the subject of about sixty books, exhibitions, and doctoral dissertations. Kim has also won individual awards, including the Order of Cultural Merit, Bogwan.

In our 1992 interview, Kim Song-hwan spent considerable time discussing political cartooning during the restrictive dictatorships, much of which is recounted in chapter 2 of this volume. Kim said that during Chun Doo-hwan's regime, the president wanted to meet him; Chun said there were calls for reform because of *Gobau* and suggested that Kim emigrate to the United States. One of the times he was imprisoned was in 1958, during President Syngman Rhee's regime, when Kim drew people hauling buckets of manure out of the Blue House (the presidential residence).

Kim summarized the status of Korean political cartooning in 1992, shortly after the demise of the dictatorships. He thought that his colleagues were drawing cartoons

> in a mellower way since liberalization. This is done on purpose. When liberalization was announced, extreme leftism started. Cartoonists moved to a softer side, because they thought too leftist was not good. They wanted to balance the situation.
>
> There are newspapers that severely criticize the government, but their circulations are going down. These papers are like students who throw firebombs at the police. This is not good. You must do it in a smoother, more democratic way.
>
> Personally, when the political situation is more stable, my cartoons will have more punch. It is unstable now, so I will move to the softer side.

Making Gobau an older man was done purposely, Kim said, mainly to gain readers, because college students had moved from political cartoon fare to drama cartoons in sports newspapers. Kim outlined his daily work routine as revolving primarily around choosing a theme or topic; his day began at 5:00 or 6:00 a.m., when he thoroughly scoured three daily newspapers, from which he found four or five topics. Kim said that during his bus trip to the office, he planned how he would develop the themes into a cartoon. At work, he read another ten newspapers, found four or five more themes, and then drew three or four sample cartoons to show to whomever was nearby, whether it was the editor or a rookie cartoonist. Then, he chose "the one I like and that is most popular with my colleague," Kim said. This he did for about half a century.

In his later life, Kim continued painting exquisite works about everyday life in a shantytown and collecting and publishing war-zone sketches he had done in 1950; he helped establish the Gobau Cartoon Award and served as an adviser to groups such as the Korea Cartoonists Association.

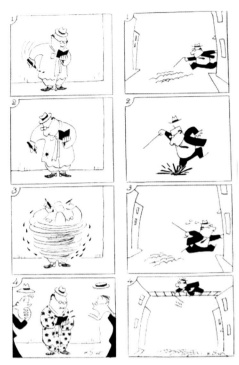

Vig-III.5. The birth of *Gobau*. 1950. Courtesy of Kim Song-hwan.

Vig-III.6. *Gobau* movie poster. 1958. Courtesy of Kim Song-hwan.

Vig-III.7. Fiftieth anniversary of Kim Song-hwan's popular strip character Gobau, seen pulling a cart of his belongings, surrounded by his well-wishing colleagues. Courtesy of Kim Song-hwan.

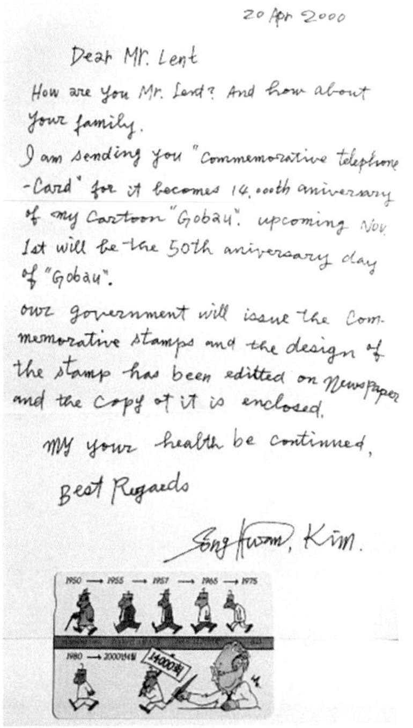

20 Apr 2000

Dear Mr. Lent

How are you Mr. Lent? And how about your family.

I am sending you "Commemorative telephone-Card" for it becomes 14,000th anniversary of my Cartoon "Gobau". upcoming Nov. 1st will be the 50th aniversary day of "Gobau".

Our government will issue the Commemorative stamps and the design of the stamp has been editted on Newspaper and the copy of it is enclosed.

My your health be continued,

Best Regards

Song Hwan, Kim.

Vig-III.8. A telephone card depicting Kim Song-hwan drawing the evolution of Gobau from 1950 to the fourteen-thousandth episode and fiftieth anniversary of the character, November 1, 2000, and Kim's letter to author. Courtesy of Kim Song-hwan.

Vignette IV

Gendry-Kim Keum suk

Graphic Novelist Extraordinaire

Vig-IV.1. A page from Gendry-Kim Keum suk's first graphic novel, *Le chant de mon père*. 2012. Permission of Gendry-Kim Keum suk.

The impression one gets while talking with Gendry-Kim Keum suk is that she loves to work and does a lot of it, "eight days a week," in her words. From the time that she wrote her first graphic novel, *Le chant de mon père*, in 2012, until our interview on August 8, 2018, Gendry-Kim wrote fifteen other books (yes, a total of sixteen in about six years). She had no difficulty convincing me that she works "all the time doing the books" and has a "lot of energy."

Gendry-Kim takes pride in being a one-woman show, pointing out, "I do everything—find and conceptualize the story, interview, write, draw, letter, and color my books." Some titles are about "who I am, my family history," such as *Le chant de mon père*, which tells about her father, a famous regional *pansori* (traditional music) singer; and she wrote three children's books about her life in the countryside. One of the latter was *Ggo ggang yi* (her father's nickname for her, meaning "an indispensable farmer's tool, the hoe").

The road to cartooning for Gendry-Kim was full of twists and turns. She was born in 1971 in the southern part of South Korea and moved to Seoul with her parents when she was seven. At university, she majored in Western painting, but, as she recalled,

> It made me frozen in place; standing in one place to paint was boring. So, I decided to go to France and change to sculpture. It was impossible to be successful in Korea as a woman, a lower-class one. Paris was a strange world, but also a new world. I knew no one, had no money, but had ambition.
>
> I went to art school in Strasbourg, near Germany. It had almost no tuition, so I could go. After graduating in fine arts, I went to Paris. Paris was very expensive, so I worked, worked, worked, as a babysitter, clothes saleswoman, museum keeper, cashier. I was physically exhausted; it was difficult to sculpt.

About that time, 2002–2003, Korean manhwa made their entry into France. Gendry-Kim saw an ad in a Parisian Korean-language newspaper seeking a translator, applied, and began translating Korean manhwa into French. Cognitive of the criticism heaped on comics because of their sexual and violent content, she also recognized their importance—"the 1 percent that were different." While translating and being impressed with Lee Hee-jae's graphic novel about the danger of briquet gases, the thought came to her: "I can do this; I can tell people's stories." And she did after returning to Korea in 2012, though her first cartoon was published in a French periodical in 2002.

Gendry-Kim went into some detail about how she finds stories and tells them, emphasizing her dislike of "market-only-oriented books" and her adherence to an artistic perspective that expresses her viewpoints, using "metaphors and symbols to show empathy, emotion; to share these feelings with other people." She said that ideas for stories come to her by meeting

> people of interest by accident. This is before I decide on a theme. I lived in France for seventeen years; that opened my eyes to other views. Also, my class is lower class; that is why I am attracted to these types of themes. I am interested in ordinary people's lives—their pain, emotions, sufferings, the power that oppresses them, their voice, life, color. Humans understand experiences before they experience them.
>
> I think of life, of death. My sister died when I was young; I took care of my sick sister. I always try to express humans' inner minds. My heartwarming memories of my sister influence my work and my thinking.

평화 발자국 19
풀
살아 있는 역사.
일본군 '위안부' 피해 할머니의 증언
김금숙 만화
보리

Vig-IV.2. *Grass*, the multi-awarded graphic novel about "comfort women" of World War II, by Gendry-Kim Keum suk. Permission of Gendry-Kim Keum suk.

The book that Gendry-Kim is most noted for is *Grass*, nominated for and awarded a number of prestigious prizes and already translated into French, Italian, English, and German by 2019. The story concerns Korean "comfort women" (young girls sold or seduced into sex slavery for the pleasure of Japanese soldiers during World War II). Gendry-Kim explained how she arrived at the book's title: "I call the book *Grass* because flowers are associated with women, but comfort women were like grass; though systematically exploited, they endured wind, cold, etc., but did not give up; they still sprouted."

Although considerable attention has been paid to comfort women in recent years, Gendry-Kim wanted to deal with "specific aspects, with different parts of the story, those of social class and gender issues." To accomplish this, she interviewed ten comfort women survivors and heard their stories, from which she "generalized for a world audience how authoritarian systems oppress women, especially poor women." In her quest for firsthand information on these enslaved girls, Gendry-Kim also went to China to interview Lee Oksun, a surviving comfort woman, who related her sad tale as well as others' woes, and she read many books on the Japanese occupation and talked with historians.

Gendry-Kim explained the class and gender implications of this sexual slavery:

> Rich girls did not need to make money. Poor girls did because they had to support their families. Also, if the girl went away, the family had one less mouth to feed. Before the occupation, poor girls were exploited by both the state and the upper class. Poor girls wanted an education but had no money to get one. Under the Japanese period, they were adopted by Korean families. You know the comfort woman history? From 70 to 80 percent of the Korean comfort women were cheated by other Koreans, who promised them jobs or an education but did not honor their pledges. [Instead, they sold them to the Japanese military.]

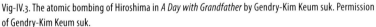

Vig-IV.3. The atomic bombing of Hiroshima in *A Day with Grandfather* by Gendry-Kim Keum suk. Permission of Gendry-Kim Keum suk.

Vig-IV.4. Cover of Gendry-Kim Keum suk's account of a group of women divers who, during hard times after the Korean War, camped out on an island where they collected seaweed that they sold to support their families. Permission of Gendry-Kim Keum suk.

> At the time of the Nanjing Massacre [1937–1938], many women were raped by Japanese soldiers, and the Japanese military authorities wanted this to change and started the comfort woman system.

Other graphic novels by Gendry-Kim either expose or add information to injustices that had been covered up for long periods, among them *The Waiting* and *A Day with Grandfather*. *The Waiting* deals with the splitting of families when the peninsula was divided into North and South Korea, inspired by the story of Gendry-Kim's mother, who was separated from her sister, while *A Day with Grandfather*, published in 2017 as a "picture book," provides a Korean view of the atomic bombings of Hiroshima and Nagasaki. Gendry-Kim said that many Koreans worked in these cities in 1945, including the real-life grandfather in her story. She explained:

> In telling of the atomic bombings, views of the minorities were ignored; everything was from the Japanese view. There was discrimination against the Korean workers, and when Japanese authorities provided some relief for Japanese victims of the bombings, the Korean workers were passed over. This was all covered up. How did I explain this horrible situation? Through *haru*, which has the double meaning of "spring" and "memorial day," through this grandfather's story of being in Japan working at the time. I interviewed him in Japan.

Gendry-Kim pointed out the diversity of themes she has used, mentioning *Jun*, the coming-of-age story of an autistic pianist–*pansori* singer she met during the eight years she herself studied *pansori*, and how through music he learned to live with his disability; and *Okrang-yi; or, The Young Women Divers Go to Dokdo Island to Pick Seaweed*, about a small group of women divers who during hard times after the Korean War left their Jeju Island homes to camp out on Dokdo Island for a few months, collecting seaweed to sell in order to support their families and provide education for children.

코주부三國志
金龍煥

Chapter 3

Manhwa

The Beginnings

We have already discussed in the previous chapter the strong possibility that the political cartoon was the first authentic form of comics art in Korea. Other pieces of art have tentatively been associated with comics art—such as illustrated picture books from the fifteenth and sixteen centuries used to teach children (Lee W-b 1992), even older murals, the drawing *Ssirum* (Korean Wrestling) done by Kim Hong-do (1745–1806), and the already mentioned sketch seen by Ernst von Hesse-Wartegg in 1884. The verdict is still out if these works are the first, or even they are comics art, because it is very likely that much more is to be found in archives and elsewhere, and it has not been (and possibly cannot be) substantiated that these drawings originally had the meanings ascribed to them by today's researchers, or that they existed at all, as in the case of von Hesse-Wartegg's report.

There is also the dilemma concerning the definition of "cartoon" and who is defining it. This is an old issue. Some, such as David Kunzle, have traced the origins of the comic strip to as early as medieval Europe (Kunzle 1973), others to Rodolphe Töpffer in the mid-nineteenth century, and still others, such as Maurice Horn, to *The Yellow Kid* in New York in 1895 (Horn 1976). Often, there is much hedging on the issue. When half-heartedly suggesting that *Ssirum* was Korea's first cartoon, Park Ki-jun (1980, 4) said of its creator and the drawing, "[I]n idea and plot, [it] had some feeling of the cartoon about it. But, we cannot call him a cartoonist." Park's hesitance to commit fully to calling the work a cartoon is derailed by this description: "He surely had a talent for cartooning. He described the scene of a *Ssirum* match much in a light and humorous manner. Two wrestlers' desperate looks straining to win, the looks full of excitement of the spectators around them, and its comic composition give us a hearty smile" (Park 1980, 4). Yoon Yong-ok, in his history of Korean newspaper cartoons

Some parts of the history section of this chapter are rewrites of the Korean chapter in my earlier volume *Asian Comics* (2015). This is justified because the repeated information emanated from interviews I conducted and is important to round out the history.

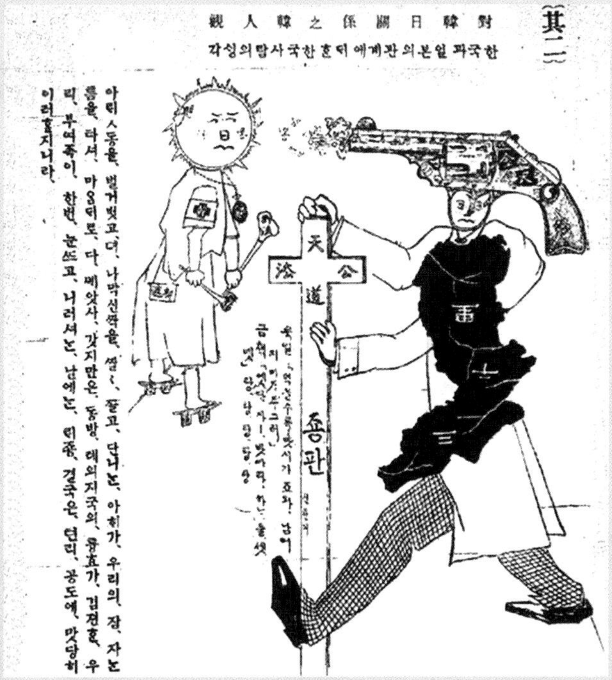

3.1. One of the very earliest Korean cartoons, "Haehwa," criticized the Japanese occupation of the peninsula. Published in 1909 in *Sinhan Minbo*. Public domain.

3.2. Cartoon depicting Korean people as lazy, idle, and idiotic in the "Japanified" Korean periodical *Chōsen Manga*, at the very beginning of the Japanese colonization. The caption reads: "Is he thick-skulled? Or just retarded? This is truly a work of art only Koreans can produce." The man is napping under his cow, not thinking that the cow might urinate upon him. Courtesy of Helen J. S. Lee.

3.3. Founder of *Sin Yeoja* Kim Won-ju (left), and *Sin Yeoja* artist Na Hye-seok. Public domain.

(1986), also found it difficult to term the illustrations in Korea's first newspaper, *Hanseong Sunbo* (started in October 1883), as comics art because of their usage—namely, to introduce Western science, advertise products, and spruce up the appearance of the newspaper. After *Hanseong Sunbo*, along with *Hanseong Jubo* (started in January 1885), were closed in 1894, satirical poetry, but not cartoons, was used in the Japanese newspapers that remained. Lee Hae-chang, in a 1982 history of political cartoons, expressed the belief that satirical drawings probably circulated informally in a limited manner.

I already stated in chapter 2 my reservations about calling Lee Do-yeong's 1909 drawing in *Daehan Minbo* the country's first political cartoon. Equally disputable is the claim that the illustration on Yu Gil-jun's book *Textbook for Workers' Night School* (*No Dong Ya Hak Dok Bon*) is a cartoon. Pictured is a man in a tailcoat addressing a nervous worker: "Please, work for the country. And people should learn." The worker replies, "Yes, I will, sir. Thank you" (Lee H-c 1982, 19–22).

Seldom mentioned as the country's first cartoon but certainly a contender is "Haehwa," which was published in *Sinhan Minbo* (the New Korea) in 1909. It was critical of Japanese interference in Korean affairs.

Such indecisiveness aside, and fully aware that cartoon-like drawings have existed in Korea at least for millennia, this brief history acknowledges the assertion of cartoonist Yoon Yong-ok, who has written a definitive history of Korean comics art, that domestic cartoons were not produced during the Joseon Dynasty (1392–1910), though newspapers knew of foreign cartoons and may have used some of them. Yoon (1992) said that at the end of the dynasty, publishers hired painters and showed them Western cartooning techniques.

Also, as noted in chapter 2, prominent among the first Korean-created cartoons in the late 1910s were satirical drawings that tended to favorably raise up Japanese culture and values while denigrating those of Korea. Such stigmatization of Korea was not new, occurring in Japan itself as early as 1876 through the cartoons of Charles Wirgman (1835–1891) in *Japan Punch* and an 1887 illustration by Georges Bigot (1860–1927) in *Tōbaé*. This mockery continued into the twentieth century as Helen Lee (2011, 42) described: "[T]he *manga* depiction of Korea in comic magazines mostly alluded to the changing political climate on the Korean peninsula, through the symbolic trope of a feminized and subservient body, an aimless yet malleable child, simply a 'backward' culture, or a subjugated political entity." Cartoonists Usuda Zan'un and Okamoto Ippei (1886–1948) both satirized Korean manners and customs in books of cartoons in 1909 and 1927, respectively (H. Lee 2011, 46). The 1909 *Chōsen Manga* (Cartoons of Korea) consistently depicted Koreans as "idiotic, vacant-minded, lazy, filthy subhumans whose facial features are likened to those of rats" (49). Just a few decades before, the same "barbaric" features were used by Europeans to describe the Japanese. By the time of Okamoto's book, *Chōsen Mangakō* (Cartoon Accounts of Travel in Korea), in 1927, a few decades into Japan's colonization of Korea, the colonized are changed into a people who are "almost the same [as the colonizer], but not quite" (58). Lee took some facetious pleasure in summing up: "Thus, in Okamoto's *manga*, Koreans behave in an orderly fashion and blend

3.4. An ignored contender for one of Korea's first cartoons, Na Hye-seok's "What Is That?" was published in the second issue of *Sin Yeoja*, 1920. Public domain.

in with Japanese (*almost the same*); but when acting on their own, apart from their colonial hosts, Koreans display distinctive habits such as napping on the steps of a bank (*but not quite*)" (58).

Though not credited among the earliest entertainment cartoons, a drawing that appeared in *Sin Yeoja* (New Woman) merits more attention. *Sin Yeoja* was the first feminist magazine published in Korea after the March 1919 independence movement.[1] It was the brainchild of Kim Won-ju (1896–1971) (pen name Il-yeop) and other young graduates of Ewha Hakdang (Ewha Women's School), a close-knit group of participants in anti-Japanese activities leading up to 1919. Three of the founders of *Sin Yeoja*, Park In-deok (1897–1980), Sin Chul-yeo (1898–1980), and Na Hye-seok (1896–1948), were arrested and imprisoned for months because of their protests, while Kim Hwa-lan (1899–1970) was whisked away and put into hiding; Kim Won-ju kept a low profile (Kim Y-h 2013, 48). The women benefited from the progressive tenets of Ewha as well as from study abroad. Their purpose for the group and the magazine was to promote women's liberation and women's rights.

In *Sin Yeoja*'s second issue of April 1920, Na Hye-seok, the first Korean female to paint in Western style, drew "What Is That?" (also called "New Woman with a Violin"). The one-panel drawing features four individuals and the following interaction:

> Two men in traditional dress on the right point to a "new woman" who is dressed in Western style and holding a violin case. A young man on the left, also dressed in a Western-style coat, is looking after her longingly. MAN A IN KOREAN DRESS: What's that? MAN B IN KOREAN DRESS: That's supposed to be a contemporary version of *yanggeum* [a traditional Korean stringed instrument]. MAN A: Gosh, she looks awfully arrogant. Who would marry such a woman? YOUNG MAN: Oh my, she is so pretty. If I weren't already married . . . [I would have liked to date her]. She is so fashionable. I would like to talk to her, but she doesn't even notice me.[2]

Na drew a second four-panel illustration (called a "cartoon" by Kim Yung-hee [2013, 51]) in the fourth and final issue of *Sin Yeoja*, admiringly depicting how Kim Won-ju managed her daily routine as housewife and career woman. Na boldly expressed her views against the traditional socialization of women also in poems, one such being "Nora," in which she stated, "I am a human being / before I am my husband's wife / before I am my children's mother" (Smith 2020, 224).

I contend that the *Sin Yeoja* drawing "What Is That?" is a cartoon and may have been the first (at least one of the first) of its kind, because: (1) It is more than an illustration decorating an article, standing alone as it does; (2) It contains dialogue between three individuals; (3) It has a story, brief as it is; and (4) It does not fit into another category—it is not political, because it does not take a stand, criticize, or otherwise politicize; it is not satirical, because it does not seem to mock the new woman; and it is not a comic strip, obviously, because it is one panel only.

Taking into consideration more acknowledged research, the first "plotted" (gag or humor) cartoon was *Pong-ui-i-wa Kim Pyolchangi*, created by Kim Kyu-son and published in the monthly magazine *Yadam* (Hidden Stories), and the initial comic strip was No Su-hyeon's *Meongteonguri*

3.5. Na Hye-seok's four-panel strip admiringly depicting the rigorous daily life of *Sin Yeoja's* founder, Kim Won-ju, maintaining a household and finding time to write. This drawing appeared in the fourth and final issue of *Sin Yeoja*. Public domain.

3.6. *Meongteonguri Heotmulkyeogi*. Korea's first newspaper strip. *Chosun Ilbo*, October 17–December 21, 1924. Public domain.

Heotmulkyeogi (The Vain Efforts of an Idiot), published in *Chosun Ilbo* in 1924. The latter was the first Korean comic to use speech balloons (actually more like rectangular boxes). Usually, the artwork and story of these cartoons were done by different individuals.

Cartoons took various forms and purposes throughout the 1920s. Ahn Seok-ju (1901–1950) introduced *manmun manhwa* in 1928, a form consisting of a cartoonish sketch united with a short essay to describe a societal trend or fashion. One of his cartoons showed a long row of female transit passengers, each holding onto a strap, drawn to emphasize their outstretched arms adorned with wristwatches, a mark of a "new woman." As mentioned previously, another new form, readers' cartoons, emerged in 1920, appearing in special sections.

Throughout the 1920s, magazines grew in number, and with them cartoons, caricatures, and illustrations. In 1920, the company Gaebyeoksa pioneered an assortment of magazines, starting with the monthly *Gaebyeok*, followed by *Byeolgeongon*, *Children*, *Shinsonyeon*, and *Student*. The most captivating and controversial was *Shinyeoseong* (Modern Women), started on September 1, 1923, and published monthly for a decade (with a nearly four-year suspension between 1926 and 1930). In about forty issues, *Shinyeoseong* shaped the image of the modern woman with a different front-cover caricature/illustration with each issue and inside visuals (Ann 2020). The early 1920s covers featured an "intelligent and sophisticated young woman dressed in a high school uniform. The appearance stayed similar. But by adding unique facial expressions," *Shinyeoseong* created new images of the modern woman (Ann 2020). After the mid-1920s, the magazine's cover women had a new image—not distinguished by nationality and shown in a more simplified manner, transformed, as Ann Da-young (2020) explained, "from the serious female student in the early 1920s to a more Westernized look with a freer spirit. Such a transformation was made by mutually exchanging influences with not only various social and cultural phenomena of the day, but also with the actual female readers of the time."

These and other magazines of the 1920s and early 1930s introduced the works of cartoonists who later led the field such as Kim Kyu-taek, who in 1933 debuted his cartoon *Byuk Chang Ho* on the pages of *Chosun Ilbo*. Others included Lee Sang-beom, Choi Yong-se, and Lee Ju-hong (Park I-h 2006).

3.7. Ahn Seok-ju's introduction of *manmun manhwa* with this 1928 drawing of wristwatch-adorned ladies showing off that they were among the "new women." Public domain.

3.8. *Kojubu Three Kingdoms* by Kim Yong-hwan. 1953. Permission of the Korea Society. From the exhibition catalog *Korean Comics: A Society through Small Frames*, page 10.

In the immediate post–World War II period, newspaper cartoons of any type were slow to reappear. No cause has been given for this slow startup, but it must have had something to do with the war's effects on the country's economic situation, for example lack of newsprint, smaller newspapers, or no space for cartoons. Cartoons were not prominent again until the Republic of Korea was established in 1948. Kim Kyu-taek resumed his career drawing commentary cartoons and the strip *Jung Su Dong*, and Kim Yong-hwan (1912–1998) returned from Japan, where he had started doing cartoons under the pen name Gita Koji, and drew the first widely recognized Korean character, Kojubu Samgukchi (Mr. Nosey), in the *Korea Times* and a strip, *Kkang tong Yosa*. Other pre–Korean War newspaper strips were *Meongteonguri Heotmulkyeogi*, whose authorship then changed from No Su-hyeon to Kim Chung-hyon; *Sam-par-i* (Thirty-Eight Degrees Latitude, the boundary between North and South Korea), drawn by Paek Mun-yong; and *So Cham Pan* by Lim Dong-eun (Oh 1981, 15).

Some artists also drew for magazines and comic books—Lim Dong-eun, Kim Kyu-taek, and Kim Ui-hwan (first work in 1940) published in children's magazines such as *Sohaksaeng*, *Sonyo*, *Chindallae*, and *Orini Nara*, and Kim Yong-hwan in the adult magazine *Sinin*. All of these artists as well as Kim Gi-chang and Choi Yong-soo also created irregularly published but popular comic books.

Between 1945 and 1950, at least three comics magazines designed for the public had brief runs. The first, *Manhwa Haengjin* (Comics March, est. 1948), started by Kim Yong-hwan and the poet Kim So-un, ran into trouble from its first issue, when, because of a political crisis, its street sales were prohibited. The sixteen-page tabloid was issued for street sales every ten days. *Manhwa Haengjin* lasted three issues before being shut down by the Ministry of Education. Featured cartoonists were Kim Yong-hwan, Kim Ui-hwan, and Lim Dong-eun (Oh 1981). Shortly after *Manhwa Haengjin*'s demise, the weekly *Manhwa News* (est. 1948) enjoyed a brief (one-year) but prosperous existence, attaining a circulation of forty-six thousand. Its cartoonists included Kim Yong-hwan, Kim Ui-hwan, Kim Song-hwan, Shin Dong-hun (1927–2017), and Yi Yong-jun. In 1950, Kim Yong-hwan had difficulties with the publisher, quit, and started *Manhwa Segye* (Comics World, est. 1952), which lasted two issues before the Korean War started but was resuscitated later (Oh 1981).

Manhwa had a central role in the propaganda of both sides during the Korean War. Some of the South's cartoonists drew for the Defense Department's *Manhwa Seungri* (Cartoon Victory) and the army's *Sabyeong Manhwa* (Soldiers' Cartoons); others, such as Kim Kyu-taek and Kim Ui-hwan, created cartoon flyers (see the section on cartoon leaflets in chapter 2), and still others fashioned comics stories that exalted brave South Korean soldiers, most notably Kim Yong-hwan's four issues (beginning in 1952) of *Totori Yongsa* (Brave Soldier Totori). The first anticommunist manhwa also came out of this period; an example is Kim Jung-rae's *Bool Geun Tang* (Red Land) (Oh 1981). Other Korean War comic books were the sixteen-page *Kojubu Tamjeong* (Detective Kojubu) by Kim Yong-hwan and *Ongtori Moggongso* (Phony Carpenter) by Shin Dong-hun. The cartoon magazine *Manhwa Sinbo* published seven or eight issues during the war. It was the creation of cartoonist Kim Song-hwan, sculptor Yun Hyo-jeong, and journalist Park Song-hwan. To soothe a society hard hit by the war, especially the children, morning magazines published many adventure and fantasy comics stories. Called *ttakji manhwa* and published in Busan, these were low-cost magazines printed on very poor-quality paper; they helped launch the careers of young artists and authors (Lima n.d.).

3.9. *The Baby Soldier*. Kim Won-bin. 1965. Permission of the Korea Society. From the exhibition catalog *Korean Comics: A Society through Small Frames*, page 30.

The 1960s–1970s: A Golden Age and Its Besmirchment

The postwar period running into the mid-1960s was very prolific for the cartoon/comics profession in Korea. Responsible for this thrust of manhwa were the success of the first comic book rooms (*manhwabangs*), the structuring of the market, the creation of specialized publishers, the launching of many independent publishers, the establishment of cartoonists' associations and standards codes, and the emergence of new two-hundred-page magazines containing full stories that encouraged long, dramatic narratives (Lima n.d.). *Manhwa myung rang* (cheerful manhwa of three or four pages) was the leading genre, but as the narrative comics flourished, a group of different *manhwagas* (manhwa artists) took hold, including those who created science fiction and fantasy comics such as Shin Dong-u (1935–1994), Kim San-ho (also known as Kim Chul-soo, born 1939), and Park Ki-dang (1922–1979), historic manhwa such as Park Ki-jeong (born 1935), historical drama such as Kim Won-bin (1935–2012), and *soonjung manhwa* (female comics) such as Kwon Yeong-seop (born 1939), Choe Sang-rok, Jo Won-gi, and Jang Eun-ju.

Kim San-ho is credited with starting Korea's first heroic science fiction comic, *Raipai, the Herald of Justice* (*Chongui ui Saja Raipal*), modeled after US superheroes and published between 1959 and 1962, and introducing diagonally drawn block-letter onomatopoeia to Korean comics (Kim Kyu Hyun 2014, 39). Between 1961 and 1967, Kim San-ho produced a large number of comic books, in the process raising the ire of government officials. In 1967, he immigrated to the United States, where he drew for Warren, Skywald, Marvel, and Charlton (J. Cooke 2023, 185). Park Ki-dang, who entered cartooning during the Korean War, was known for his graphic narratives, which were said to be similar to the "popular colonial-period literature such

3.10. *Challenger* was a sports comic book by Park Ki-jeong from 1964. Permission of the Korea Society. From the exhibition catalog *Korean Comics: A Society through Small Frames*, page 25.

as *ttakjibon* (colorful Korean equivalent of dime-store novels)." (Kim Kyu Hyun 2014, 18) New comics aimed chiefly at children also appeared in the 1960s, such as Im Chang's *Taengi* and Kim Won-bin's *First Boss* (*Chumok Taejang*, 1958), a hero endowed with a disproportioned fist (Toutenbd 2004).

Two cartoonists who stood out in this pool of manhwa talent, for their innovativeness and ability to work in multiple forms and genres, were Kim Won-bin and Park Ki-jeong. Kim, born in 1935 in China to a Korean independence fighter, debuted in 1953 with *The Secret of Mount Taebaek*, followed by several science fiction and police manhwa, before creating the new genre of historical drama. His *The Black Ribbon* and *The Baby Soldier* were the first of their kind. *First Boss* was Kim's best-known work, reissued four times, the second appearance in *School Chums* magazine (*Ŏkkaedongmu*, 1967–1987) in 1975. The stories revolved around "famous Korean legends supplemented with mythical motifs," going back to one of the country's best-known legendary figures, Super Baby (Agi Janjsu) (Korea Society 2005, 27).

Park Ki-jeong's career spans more than sixty years, beginning in 1956, and encompasses at least three phases: as a prominent comic book creator, bringing out more than a hundred titles between 1956 and 1978, and even more later; as a full-time political cartoonist with *JoongAng Ilbo* from 1978 to 2011; and as a champion for the rights of cartoonists. The genres he worked in were far-ranging, including sports (*Challenger* [*Tojŏnja*], *Wrestler*), spy (*Poktanah*), romance, drama, and history. The magnitude of his output can be gauged by the number of volumes of some titles—for instance, *Challenger*, forty-five, and *Poktanah*, sixty. Park said that drawing political cartoons was like sprinting the one-hundred-meter dash, while doing a comic book was like running a marathon. In 1968, Park started what is now the Korea Cartoonists Association (over which he presided during two different periods) to protect cartoonists against plagiarism, price fixing, and other injustices (Baek 2016).

During the repressive Park Chung-hee years, Park Ki-jeong dedicated himself to ensuring that his comics reached people clearly and independently. As he said:

> In order to point out wrongs in the government, it is necessary to have courage and keep a sharp eye. This is vital for news analysis as well. Editorials should not exist just to appease or curry favors from the government. Out of all the various newspaper articles, [those with an editorial perspective] must remain on the cutting edge by providing sharp and dispassionate criticism of wrongs committed by the government. [Comics with an editorial message] gain vital energy by keeping an eye on the government. However, they must deliver their message metaphorically rather than frankly if they're to be forceful. Straight talk actually diminishes the punch of some opinions, although of course, at times, it is necessary. Metaphor and satire are the essence of news criticism. (Korea Society 2005, 23)

Just a few years later, the boon period for comics lost some of its luster. As the prices of manhwa per copy dropped, so did the quality of the paper and the books' contents. As I wrote elsewhere: "To increase their profits, cartoonists churned out large numbers of poorly done cartoons which became the targets of press and lay critics" (Lent 1995, 12).

To capture readership, the industry switched from marketing in bookstores to rental shops, at the same time setting up professional organizations and standards codes to restore quality to comics art. In this regard, there was considerable action. There were separate groups for cartoonists who drew children's cartoons (the conservative Taehan Association of Cartoonists, later the Hanguk Association of Children's Cartoonists) and those who created adult cartoons (the Hyondae Association of Cartoonists). They cooperated with each other until both were dissolved after the 1961 coup. To put some muscle into the profession, and anticipating strengthened government regulation resulting from the military coup, children's cartoonists and publishers instituted the Korean Self-Regulation Body for Children's Cartoons, whose task was to get cartoonists to register and submit their works for evaluation by veteran cartoonists. The larger, well-established publishers agreed with the body's evaluations; the smaller, newly formed publishers ignored them. On August 31, 1968, the Ministry of Culture and Public Affairs replaced the self-censoring group with its own ethics committee, prompting the cartoonists to form the Hanguk Association of Children's Cartoonists (Oh 1981).

The golden age of manhwa was severely tarnished by a series of political and business changes in the 1960s and 1970s. A coup d'état in May 1961, the declaration of martial law in 1972, and another coup d'état in 1979 definitely curbed the "freedom to cartoon," and with it, the creativity of cartoonists. Pre-censorship reappeared with the 1961 coup. The Park Chung-hee government targeted manhwa in its "social cleansing" campaign,[3] resulting in the establishment of the Korean Ethics Committee for Books and Magazines (Hanguk Toso Chapchi Yulli Wiwonhoe) in 1970 (newspapers were added in 1976), and the impoundment and destruction of thousands of "degenerate comics." The procedure meant to curb manga made no sense at all. All Japanese popular culture, including manga, had been banned from entering Korea since the 1940s, yet this government ethics committee pre-censored manga that were not allowed in the country in the first place. The pre-censorship ended in 1992.

The ethics committee seriously scrutinized all publishing and sales of comic books, reporting that most were Japanese in origin, full of sex and violence and illegally produced by

3.11. *Myung rang* genre cartoonist Park Su-dong with John A. Lent. Seoul, July 7, 1992. Photo by Lee Sang-kil. Courtesy of Park Su-dong.

"money-grubbing" publishers. The only full-time member of the committee, Cha Ae-ock, told of what they targeted:

> What we are looking for are cases of obscenity and violent content. Some kisses are all right, but deep kisses are not. Generally, however, kissing is okay. But, there can be no nudity, profanity, stabbing, blood, shootings, amputations, etc. In children's cartoons, showing a weapon is allowed, but not its use. In rental comics, use of weapons can be depicted because these are not just for children. In Korea, communism is a big, big problem so artists cannot write about it in the comics. (Cha 1994)

A number of situations transpired throughout the 1960s that did not bode well for manhwa or *manhwabangs*. By 1964, about 10 percent of Seoul's *manhwabangs* had added television viewing as an extra attraction, bringing in more children. The collapse of one such viewing room, which injured twenty-one children in 1964, and a stabbing in another resulting from a quarrel over seating in 1966 raised the ire of the police and parents. In 1968, the National Council of Korean Women declared that manhwa were children's "methadone," that about one-quarter of them featured gunmen and violence, and that, generally, they were "poorly edited," "of low quality," "and lacking creativity."

3.12. *Young Dolmen* by Park Su-dong, the tale of a boy living in prehistoric times. Courtesy of Park Su-dong. Permission of the Korea Society. From the exhibition catalog *Korean Comics: A Society through Small Frames*, page 41.

The following year, police proposed that the ethics committee require prepublication censorship of all manhwa, the licensing of all comics rental stores, the removal of all "unhealthy" books by a deadline, and the content of 30 percent of titles to be cultural (VanVolkenburg 2019).

Because of the Park government's smothering of freedom of expression, contemporary events gave way to safer "long historical, emblematic" manhwa discreetly "critical of the current power," in which readers could recognize themselves among characters who struggled against feudalism in the late Joseon Dynasty (Lima n.d.). Readers relied on these hidden meanings, even finding them where they were not intended (Kim S-h 1992).

Famous manhwa artist Heo Young-man (born 1947) remembered that time:

> [I]n the late 1960s until the mid-1970s, on National Children's Day on May 5 police officers would collect comics and adult films and burn them in public. . . . We comics authors were in a constant struggle with the government to let us work in peace. [Heo's first hit, the masked hero Gaksital in 1974] was such a big success, it encouraged others to produce similar comics with masked heroes. And these led the state censors asking me to stop my series. . . . I was told that if I stopped, the others would do the same. . . . Since the 1960s, there has been a lot of censorship in Korea. For example, you couldn't show a brother and a sister in the same bed due to moral issues related to Confucianism.[4] Comics about sport were very successful, but it was difficult to propose a series on boxing because it was considered too violent. (quoted in Gravett 2017)

Added to these censorship woes, the distribution system was monopolized in 1967 when a cartel of comics publishers, United Publishers (Haptong Chulpansa), was established, "monopolizing the distribution routes of comic books (the majority of which by then relied on rental outlets), distributing projects to the comics artists in the manner of sweatshop factories, and blackballing any artist who resisted this oppression" (Kim Kyu Hyun 2014, 41).

Genres in which readers could find some comfort during these oppressive times were *myung rang* (cheerful) comics published in children's magazines and historical dramas meant for adults. The genre was published in children's magazines such as *School Chums* (*Ŏkkaedongmu*) and *Central Juvenile* (*Sonyeon Chungang*, 1968–1994), and was considered a tool of patriotic education in line with the Park Chung-hee regime.

A very successful and prolific cartoonist who started his career using the *myung rang* genre was Park Su-dong (born 1941); his best-known strip features a prehistoric kid and his two friends who regularly defy adult rules. *Young Dolmen* (*Sonyeon Koindol*) was two to four pages and serialized in *School Chums* from 1974 to 1982; it soon became the most popular strip in Korea, its appeal resulting from the brevity of the stories, its attraction to mature, adult audiences as well as to children, and its "simplicity, hilarious originality and dazzling humor of his characters" (Korea Society 2005, 39). No doubt, *Young Dolmen* was liked because it carried a sex-related theme with a humorous tone, dealing with male-female relationships while at the same time "discreetly presenting the forbidden eroticism" (Lima n.d.). Park used experiences from his days as an elementary school teacher, depicting children at play on their own terms, not regimented by institutional and adult supervision or "high tech gadgetry" (Korea Society 2005, 39). Park also drew *Housewife March* for many years, following a newly married couple in real time; by 1992, he regularly drew

3.13. *Mischievous Boy*. Kil Chang-deok. Permission of the Korea Society. From the exhibition catalog *Korean Comics: A Society through Small Frames*, page 32.

3.14. *Samgukchi*. Ko Woo-young. Permission of the Korea Society. From the exhibition catalog *Korean Comics: A Society through Small Frames*, page 44.

cartoons for about thirty magazines. His career was very lucrative, he agreed, pointing out, for example, that a set of five collections of *Koindol* sold more than one hundred thousand copies (Park S-d 1992).

Other cartoonists who worked in the *myung rang* genre included Lim Chang, Bang Yun-jin, Kil Chang-deok (1929–2010), Yun Seun-hun (with *Dunshimi's Shipwreck* [*Dunshimi Pyeoryugi*]), Shin Mun-su (born 1939), and Lee Jung-moon. Kil Chang-deok stood out as a pioneer of these cheerful comics, using "heavy dialogue and simple yet lively pictures" (Young 2010). He began cartooning in 1955, drawing comics for adults, but he focused on young people's comics after 1966. Kil's work is filled with nostalgia for the lifestyle of the 1970s and 1980s, reflecting on President Park Chung-hee's "New Village" (Saemaŭl) movement, which modernized agriculture and raised the living standard of rural people, in the process demolishing entire villages and replacing them with high-density row houses (Korea Society 2005, 31). Kil's best-known work is *My Neighbor Dol* (*Kkŏbŏngi Lutjip Dolne*, also *Mischievous Boy*) (1970), featuring a neighbor boy who is a troublemaker. Other hits are *Madam Vicious* (*Sunakjil Yŏsa*) (1970), *Sondali* (1977), *Independent Girl* (*Tolle*) (1978), and *Stubborn Boy* (*Kojipse*) (1982). Shin Mun-su, along with his mentor, Kil Chang-deok, dominated the *myung rang* line of manhwa. Shin's most popular titles, *Goblin's Hat* (1972) and *Robot Tchippa* (1978), often involved a "mischievous character learning a moralistic lesson"; they were "embedded with anti-communist storylines, such as capturing a North Korean spy or visiting North Korea and mocking its leader" (Korea Society 2005, 34).

Historical dramas for adults garnered the market in the 1970s, beginning with the series *Im Kkŏk-Jŏng* by Ko Woo-young (1938–2005) and published in the *Daily Sports* (*Ilgan Supochu*) in 1972. Ko had been sketching for a children's magazine when his brother, also a cartoonist, died suddenly, after which Ko continued the strip to keep his brother's legacy alive. Ko had been barely surviving by doing pictures for other artists when the president of the Hankook Ilbo Media Group, despite staff objections, decided to use serialized narrative comics with adult content in his newspapers. Comics with more than four panels had not been used in newspapers before. Ko's *Im Kkŏk-Jŏng*, full of graphic violence and "detailed, anatomically realistic depictions of human bodies," was an instant success and elevated the *Daily Sports*' circulation from twenty thousand in 1972 to three hundred thousand in 1975 (Kim Kyu Hyun 2014, 42; see also Lee Eun-joo 2008, 7). Ko was known for his adaptations of Chinese and Korean literary classics; his

3.15. Heo Young-man, one of Korea's most prolific cartoonists, who used hundreds of different themes. Public domain.

3.16. Sports comic *Silk Spider* by Heo Young-man. Permission of the Korea Society. From the exhibition catalog *Korean Comics: A Society through Small Frames*, page 62.

most successful title was *Samgukchi*, taken from China's *Romance of the Three Kingdoms*. Kyu-won Oh (1981) wrote that Ko succeeded because of his style of dramatization in stories about "love and friendship, history and conspiracy, the past and the present of his cartoon characters. His cartoons are historical stories of old times. However, he shows the present as well as the past at the same time by such sentences from [US] president Kennedy's inauguration speech as 'Before asking what your country can do for you, think what you can do for your country.'" Ko and Heo Young-man produced nationalist narrative comics that were exemplary, but they were also known for producing "a stunning number of works that covered a wide range of genres and approaches, from martial arts, sports, romance and period pieces to contemporary 'business' comics, and at each phase of their careers they were able to renew their appeals to new demographic and new generations of readers" (Kim Kyu Hyun 2014, 38). Extremely popular among their works were Ko's *The Great Ambition* (*Tae-yamang*), a nationalist sports manhwa about a taekwondo master, and Heo's *The Bridal Mask* (*Kaksital*) in 1974 and *The Iron Flute* (*Soetunso*) in 1982. In a nearly fifty-year career, Heo has authored more than 150,000 pages for more than one hundred series on every imaginable (and unimaginable) topic, including the invention of cars (*Asphalt Man*), music (*The Lonely Guitarist*), coffee, science fiction, various sports, and gambling (*48+1*)—on 215 different themes, by his account. About twenty have been made into television shows, films, and games (Gravett 2017). Heo thoroughly researches each topic; he stated: "If it's a comic about swordfights, then you have to draw the sword as if it's going to slice you" (NPR 2015).

Other cartoonist contemporaries of Heo were Kim Dong-hwa (born 1950), Kim Kwang-sung (born 1954), and Lee Hee-jae (born 1952). Kim Dong-hwa was called a "master of change" by Park In-ha (2007, 40). Fearful of becoming bored drawing the same themes and wanting to satisfy different age and gender audiences, Kim started out doing romance manhwa, resulting in *Our Story* (*Urideu-rui Iyagi*) in 1979, followed by *My Name Is Candy* (*Naui Ireumeun Sindi*), *Acacia*, and *Sapphire*. He then added fantasy and comedy to his work with *Pink the Fairy* (*Yojeong Pink*) in 1984, adventures for boys with *Bug Boy* (*Gonchung Sonyeon*) and *Youth Police* (*Gyeongchaldae*), Korean-style beauty (past and present; in landscape, music, tradition, etc.) with *Ugly* (*Monnani*), *A Yellow Story* (*Hwangtobit Iyagi*), and *A Story of Kisaeng* (*Gisaeng Iyagi*) (about the colorful lives of courtesans), and older people with *The Red*

3.17. Lee Hee-jae. Seoul, August 10, 2018. Photo by Kim Chunhyo. Permission of Lee Hee-jae.

Bicycle (*Ppalgan Jajeongeo*), about a postman who delivers mail in an imaginary village. Later, Kim created the trilogy *The Color of Earth*, *The Color of Water*, and *The Color of Heaven*, described as a "beautifully illustrated, poetically written tale of a young girl's sexual awakening and her relationship with her mother" (Lorah 2009; see also Culkin 2009). His series have been republished in France, Japan, and Taiwan (Park I-h 2007, 40–45).

In contrast, Kim Kwang-sung did not stray much afar from recording Korean history through fictional and nonfictional manhwa, his goal being to "evoke memories from those reminiscing their past. Those who had experienced the Korean War accumulated an odd mixture of compassion and pathos in their bones. So did many enlightened scholars, artists, and other democratic movement fighters who witnessed and protected against Chun [Doo-hwan]'s regime" (Ko 2016). Although some of his manhwa were visual novels, Kim carried out research much like the later investigative graphic novelists discussed in chapter 2. For a volume on World War II comfort women, he interviewed survivors "to understand their pain," their "beaten psychological ego"; for *Seoul, the Old Days*, a collection of Seoul scenes from the 1930s through the 1970s, he relied on his memory of "memorable scenes," old movies, and encyclopedias (Ko 2016).

One of the most diligent researchers among Korean history cartoonists has been Park Si-baek. A former *Hankyoreh* political cartoonist, Park decided in about 2002 to take on a task that would keep him busy for the rest of his life—to re-create the thousands of volumes of *Annals of the Joseon Dynasty* as graphic novels. He read the primary sources, then drew the historical events and converted the stories into modern language for easy reading. Park read more than one hundred books and filled 121 notebooks with handwritten notes as part of his research, and after thirteen years, he had drawn 2,077 volumes of the *Annals* (Wi and Chang 2015).

Lee Hee-jae debuted as a professional cartoonist in 1970, working with Kim Jong-rae, who liked his stories and became his mentor. Throughout the 1980s, he drew short stories on everyday life for magazines. Lee (2018) said that his subjects were ordinary people, because "they were me—tears, pain, joy, emotions. For my story ideas, I use what I have seen from experience." Working in the 1970s and 1980s was difficult, Lee said, because of strong censorship and a "sensitivity to expressing ordinary people's lives. It was dull." Among his thirty-some books are hits such as *Ganpanstar*, about a little girl who leaves her town to live in Seoul, and *The Way of the Paddle*, the story of a couple who have lost their three children. Works such as *Vedette* (2006) and *Grief in the Sky* (2007) were issued in French editions.

The 1980s: Spinoffs, *Soonjung Manhwa*, the Factory System

The 1980s ushered in phenomena that considerably advanced comics art. First, manhwa spinoffs to other media started when *Dooly the Little Dinosaur* was adapted to animation and also made into a musical. Created by Kim Su-jung (born 1950) in 1983, the character was spun off to merchandise,

3.18. *Dooly the Little Dinosaur*. Kim Su-jung. 1983. Permission of the Korea Society. From the exhibition catalog *Korean Comics: A Society through Small Frames*, page 54.

another first for manhwa. Second, the *manhwabangs* became important reading centers as well as influencers of production, even fostering a rental shop form or genre. Cartoonists began to draw exclusively for the rental shops, where they gained fame, before working for magazines. What they drew were dramatic epics. Chief among the *manhwabang* cartoonists were Lee Hyeon-se (born 1956), Heo Young-man, Park Ki-jeong, and Kim Su-jung.

Lee's blockbuster was *Gong Po Eui Wae In Gu Dan* (The Terrifying Mercenary Baseball Team), published in 1982. The story is about a baseball team of losers who, through intensive training and by overcoming a slew of obstacles, become powerful enough to defeat Japanese teams. Lee's *Mythology of the Heavens*, which first appeared in 1997, was the impetus for one of Korea's most controversial manhwa legal cases in the waning years of the century. The story, set in the legendary past, revolved around a man wishing to become king and a goddess who promises to grant his wish if he takes a snake as his queen, but warns that his own son will cause his death. She then demands that he have sex with her, during which she turns into a snake who gives birth to many other snakes, all of which he kills, except for one that survives. Lee was prosecuted, his story ruled legally obscene, and he was fined for contravening the Youth Protection Act of 1997. Upon appeal, he was acquitted four years later (Gravett 2006).

One of Heo's major hits for the rental shops was *Mudanggŏmi* (about boxing) in 1987, which Park In-ha (2006) wrote "best describe[s] the sentiments shared among the people who lived through the 80s."

Soonjung manhwa (girl's cartoons) also experienced a rejuvenation in the 1980s. These stories had been around since the 1950s; in those years, *soonjung* (pure heart) *manhwa* dealt with pure-hearted girls who overcame many difficulties. They were drawn by men, such as Kim Jeong-pa, Choe Sang-rok, Jo Won-gi, and Kwon Yeong-seop, and featured girls as heroines or narrators. In the 1950s, three comic book narratives emerged—action, *myung rang*, and family. *Soonjung* came out of the family genre. When *shōjo manga* began to glut the Korean market in the 1970s, they were perceived as Korean *soonjung* rather than the Japanese girls' comics that they actually were. This disguise (whether purposeful or not) got around the government's banning of Japanese cultural materials.[5]

About the same time a group of female cartoonists known as the 49ers joined the Japanese manga forces during the 1970s, similarly in Korea, the first generation of women cartoonists came on the scene. Among them were Uhm Hee-ja, Song Soon-hee, Chang Eun-ju, and Min Ae-ni. Girls' comics researcher Noh Sueen (2004b, 281) writes that the *soonjung manhwa* they produced were "for women, by women, of women" and that they "created their own stories or dramatized Western novels; for form, they followed the drawing styles of Japanese girls' comics."

The works of these pioneering women cartoonists were extremely popular, to the extent that publishers limited the print runs of their *soonjung* to deter a sales imbalance in the market (Park I-h 2000, 53). As much as the *soonjung* cartoonists may have wished to create a "pure" Korean product, some of them admitted they were strongly influenced by manga, not only because of the large influx of Japanese comics but also because some of them

3.19. *We Saw a Pitiful Bird Who Lost Its Way*. Hwang Mi-na. 1986. Permission of the Korea Society. From the exhibition catalog *Korean Comics: A Society through Small Frames*, page 88.

had studied the drawing of comics in Japan (Choe 1995, 82–83). Kukhee Choo (2010) gives a third reason: "[T]he dichotomous narrative structure of 'good versus evil' in Japanese *shōjo manga* affected both Korean readers and artists," elaborating, "Within these narratives, Korean readers may have found solace from the menial state of postwar society. Korean *sunjeong manhwa* by Min Ae-ni and Eom [Uhm] Hee-ja often depicted class struggle between the rich and the poor and the contrast between urban and rural spaces; their female protagonists would typically find happiness after enduring hardship." Two other early women cartoonists, Hwang Mi-na (born 1961) and Shin Il-suk (born 1962), moved away from the mushy *soonjung* love stories of the 1970s into plots dealing with the underclass, feminine issues, and social barriers. A third popular female cartoonist, Kim Hye-rin (born 1962), mixed resistance, oppression, and affection for the lower class with love in her portrayal of characters. Among her most successful works were *Thermidor*, *The Dance in the Sky*, and *The Sword of Fire*. These types of storylines cut muster with the prevailing military government, which censored according to Confucian values; thus, "the depiction of virtuous, humble women became a generic formula for *sunjeong manhwa*" (Choo 2010).

However, as others such as Lim Jung-in (1996) and Matt Thorn (1995a, 1995b) have argued, comics represented the only place where women could communicate so freely with one another. Also, contrary to some common belief, *soonjung manhwa* were not only different from but also superior to *shōjo manga*, able to "capture the feelings of characters, the complexity of relationships, [and] the turmoil of human drama" (Thorn 1995b). These less tangible traits are usually given as the differences between Korean manhwa and Japanese manga. For example, Sajima Akiko, a Japanese professor devoted to manhwa, credited Korean comics with having "deep thoughts" not present in manga (Kwon 1998), while Noh (2004b, 291) reported that key *soonjung* comics authors she interviewed said that Japanese comics differed because they were "highly planned and specialized in various genres such as food, politics, industry, medicine, animals, and so on." Newspaper critic Lim Bum (1994) asserted that Korean cartoonists "have to draw with a sense of familiarity and originality and touch Korean feeling." The editor in chief of Seoul Cultural Publishers, Kim Mun-hwan, leaned in a different direction, claiming that the differences were in the drawing of human features, the format of presentation, and the contents, explaining, "The shapes of Korean eyes and faces are drawn more softly than Japanese; Korean comics have round lines while manga have sharper, straighter ones. Korean books are read front to back; Japanese from back to front, and Korean comics do not have the blatant violence and sex, bleeding scenes, amputations, and so on" (Kim M-h 1994).

Others have given their opinions about the differences between manga and manhwa overall. Vernieda Vergara (2021) writes that manhwa use color more often, tend to portray heroes in individual rather than team roles ("Ensemble casts drive manga, whereas charismatic protagonists drive manhwa"), "stick to the format's historical roots and make social commentary its central premise," and alter the *isekai* genre in which the protagonist is transported to another world. Morgan (2017) adds: "The main characters [MCs] of manhwa are memorable because of their distinguished personalities, in contrast to manga heroes, who are usually an amalgamation of clichés. The MCs of manhwa are complex. The line between good and evil is blurry, and characters cheerfully cross it to get what they want." Morgan labels manhwa characters as having "organic personalities with complex motives," "the tendency to do the wrong thing," "violent emotions rather than a sense of justice," a "quickness to disregard the greater good for their own reasons," and a knack to "fight dirty, assault with a deluge of cussing, and never swallow their pride."

Then there are those who would agree with researcher Kim Nak-ho (2003), who said, "Publishers who say Korean comics do not have a manga style are talking trash; you can't tell Japanese and Korean comics apart." He explained:

> Japanese and Korean comics both have an Asian traditional way of drawing—using black and white lines, and emptiness between lines and panels. All share the same basic principles. It is not clever to say Korean comics are different from Japanese as they share the same Asian graphic style. The difference is what lies beneath the comics' style. Mainstream Korean comics use more drama, narrative. Mainstream Japanese manga are more concerned with building up individual characters and personalities. It is a cultural difference. Korea, through its cultural background, emphasizes more the forces of society and history beyond the individual. In Japan, the focus is more on the individual.

Another comics researcher, Seon Jeong-u (2003), said the difference between Japanese and Korean comics is that "the Japanese went their own way after the initial influences from outside, but Korean comics just kept being influenced from outside." He said that Korean comics are open to impacts from Japan, Europe, and elsewhere. "The Japanese market does not import much; someone called manga the comics of the Galápagos Islands in that they isolate themselves," Seon said.

When the Chun Doo-hwan military government came to power in 1979, it tightened legislation that banned anything Japanese, including *shōjo manga*, the most prevalent comics genre in Korea. *Manhwabangs*, curtailed from receiving *shōjo manga* and from meeting female readers' demands, came up with alternatives, most of which were illegal, but not bothersome, because the whole system was illegal. "Ghost artists" traced or redrew Japanese comics, often using different pen names to give the appearance that there were more *soonjung* artists than what existed. Choo (2010) called these plagiarized books "fly copies" (produced on the fly); they had advantages over earlier pirated manga, being economical to produce and appearing to be within the regulations banning Japanese cultural products because they carried Korean credit lines, though these pen names were not real, either (Choo 2010).

Also resulting from the Korean government's crackdown on Japanese *shōjo manga* was what Choo (2010) labeled "patch working," a process unique to *soonjung manhwa* that involved a "hodgepodge production of narratives, characters, and backgrounds from various Japanese *shōjo manga*," carried out by a number of ghost artists, each independently in charge of a section that was patched to the whole. This scheme was also called the "factory system."

Until the mid-1980s, almost all of the comic book activity in South Korea was confined to the comics factory/comics rental shop system. Simply stated, the writing and drawing were done by a master cartoonist and his student apprentices, who sent the finished product to one of eighty-six publishers for printing and binding. Three distributors then delivered the books to thousands of rental shops across the country, where fans paid for take-home privileges for a day or two, a system called *daibonso*, which dated to the 1950s. Starting in the late 1980s, the manhwa could be read on the premises; this was called *chaek-dae-yojom*. The latter rented all types of books but, by the mid-1990s, concentrated more on comics.

Under this system, all comics emanating from a given studio were produced in the style of the master cartoonist and credited solely to him; in a typical year, he could be listed as the author of as many as 464 titles, as was the case with Park Bong-seong (born 1949) in 1994. That same year, five other master cartoonists were given authorship to between 235 and 360 titles. Studios often employed anywhere from five to two hundred apprentices; the top ones were well organized, with a chain of command that included the master cartoonist, an editor, and a head team

3.20. *A Man Called God*. Park Bong-seong. 1995–2000. Likely a product of his "factory." Permission of the Korea Society. From the exhibition catalog *Korean Comics: A Society through Small Frames*, page 66.

of ten to fifteen members at the top, and other teams at the next level, each made up of five to fifteen apprentices divided by their specialties.

In 1995, I observed the work at one of these "factories," JWH Publications, and interviewed its head and master cartoonist, Jo Woon-hak. JWH Publications was one of the thirteen dominant studios among scores of others. Jo (1995) said that JWH was a medium-sized studio he set up in 1990. Himself a four-year apprentice of Heo Young-man, Jo said that when he struck out on his own, his work was criticized for imitating that of Heo. At that time (1995), JWH was producing six or seven titles yearly, each with ten to thirteen serialized volumes, for a total of sixty or seventy books. Jo said he created and wrote half the stories; the rest were done by freelancers. Apprentices had a two- to five-year period when they drew only backgrounds and characters.

The pinnacle of this system's success was in the 1960s and 1970s; by 1965, sixty different manhwa were published daily, and two years later, two-thirds of all Korean publications were comic books. Even as late as 1990–1991, fifteen to thirty manhwa were issued daily for the rental shops.

This changed in the 1990s as rental shops decreased in number from a high of 15,000 in the mid-1980s to 4,260 about a decade later. Accounting for this nosedive were: (1) studios began doing comic books for bookstores, (2) the Korean economy improved, and young people now had money to purchase books, (3) parents despised rental shops, viewing them as dens of inequity, and (4) legislation was passed in 1996 banning any comics rental shops within two hundred meters of any educational institution. Rental shop owners went out of business or had to hold a second job to survive, as in the case of Kim Chong, then owner of a Seoul shop, Kachei. Kim (1994) said that factors causing the slump in business were: (1) the elevated cost of renting the premises, (2) the dwindling readership of rental comics, largely because of poorer quality stories, (3) increased bookstore sales, and (4) deep inroads made by television and video.

To provide perspectives on the operation of a Korean comics rental shop in the mid-1990s, I reiterate what Kim (1994) told me about his shop, as I published elsewhere:

> Kim, who started Kachei in 1982, keeps an inventory of 9,000 comic books, 1,000 novels, and seven comics magazines, all neatly shelved in a basement outfitted with five to seven leather couches, a fan, and a television set. There are no computers, not even a cash register. Kim records the names and phone numbers of patrons who rent books overnight in a notebook and makes change from his pocket. With help from his wife, he keeps the shop open from 10 AM until Midnight, seven days a week, and there are no holiday closings.
>
> Kachei is supplied by four distributors who bring the books to him daily on their motorcycles. Kim purchases one copy of about 20 new titles monthly, and displays them for rental as long as possible, acknowledging that "many, many" are stolen. Usually, about 100 high school students and adolescents read comics on the premises, and 30 check them out daily. Generally, a patron reads 10 comics, often in a series, during an hour or two sitting; those taking out books rent 20 to 30 at a time. The fees are ₩150 (US 19 cents) per book to read in the shop and ₩250 (US 31 cents) for a two- or three-day takeout. Comics magazines can be checked out at ₩500 (US 62 cents) each. (Lent 1998, 33)

3.21. Comic book rental store Kachei. Seoul, July 2, 1994. Owner Kim Chong (left) with a customer. Photo by John A. Lent. Courtesy of Kim Chong.

The immense power that the master cartoonist factories/rental shops combo had wielded—almost solely responsible for which titles were bought—faded as increasing criticism was heaped upon the system: that it had compromised the quality of work (Jung 1994); that the studios imitated their master cartoonists and manga to the exclusion of new talent and forms (Roh 1994; Park S-h 2003; Jo 1995); and that rental shop owners, by their purchasing decisions, stifled creativity, encouraged imitation, and looked only at the bottom line, not the quality of work (Lee W-b 1991, 177).

Such disenchantment led to a new form of comics and a different business model. Beginning in the 1980s, comics magazines came onto the scene, retail bookstores became their outlets, and comics categorization switched from target age groups to genres. Comics magazines were intended to prime an audience and provide the storylines for the comic books reprinted from them and sold in bookstores. The then head of Daiwon Publishing, Hwang Kyung-Tae, told the logic behind the scheme: "You can't make money from comics magazines; the money comes from reprinting. We make comics magazines because, without them, we can't do reprints. Comics magazines are like advertisements for the reprints, attracting as many readers as possible to the reprinted books" (1994).

Cartoonists benefited from this setup, being paid when their art appeared in the magazines and again when it was reprinted. The problem was that few cartoonists had this opportunity, and as rental shops folded, many employed by the studios had no work. One way master cartoonists' studios survived was by providing comics to the bookstores in the form of books condensed from many-volumed serializations.

By 1995, twenty comics magazines were on the market, fifteen of which were published by Daiwon Publishing and Seoul Cultural Publishers. Daiwon Publishing is the dominant division of the five-pronged Daiwon, founded in 1974. By the beginning of the twenty-first century, the firm was producing domestic and foreign animation, comic books, comics magazines, videos, DVDs, film, an animation satellite broadcasting channel, characters, toys, games, and online entertainment content. It was publishing one hundred manhwa titles a month in Korea (Avila 2004). President of the animation division Ahn Hyun-dong said that the divisions spun off from one another with comics magazines appearing first, then leading to comic books, animation, and later video and merchandise (Ahn 1994). New comics magazines were started as readers advanced in age: the monthly *Wolgan Sonyeon Champ* (Monthly Boy Champ, established 1992) was meant for grade school pupils; the weekly *Sonyeon Champ* (Boy Champ, 1991) for junior high boys; the monthly *White* for middle to high school girls; the biweekly *Young Champ* (1994) for high school and college students; the biweekly *Twenty-Seven* for adults; and the biweekly *Touch* and the monthly *Pang Pang* for girls (Hwang 1994; see appendix II for a list of manhwa magazines).

Although most of these magazines were gender specific, this mode of operation ran counter to Hwang's thinking when he led the publishing arm of Daiwon. Instead of categorizing, Hwang said, "I was interested in how a story unfolds, regardless of gender ties. I liked to experiment, to handle topics differently. Instead of telling an artist what to draw, I want to see what the artist can do best; I want to develop each artist's abilities" (1994).

Daiwon picked up artists through two annual competitions it held. Hwang (1994) said that he maintained a pool of about a thousand artists from whom he chose about one hundred fifty on a freelance basis. At the time, cartoonists were attracted not only by wages received but by the prospect of receiving book royalties if their stories were popular enough to have long serializations and then be condensed into books.

To make stories last longer, Hwang implored artists and writers to "stage a story" and fashion interesting characters. He also sought readers' advice and tried out scriptwriters, playwrights, and novelists as developers of stories; the latter failed, he said (1994). The next plan was to conceptualize stories, using a staff of eighteen Daiwon editors who collaborated with the artists, each editor assigned a specific title according to his or her ability and preference.[6] To obtain readers' reactions, Daiwon inserted a postcard questionnaire in each magazine. Hwang said that about ten thousand were returned monthly, and they helped in determining which stories to develop.

The number of pages and prices of Daiwon comics magazines varied. Most magazines averaged 350 to 375 pages, containing about twenty-two stories in each issue. Monthlies such as *Wolgan Sonyeon* topped 550 pages. Prices per copy depended on number of pages, quality of paper, and circulation but generally fell within the range of US$1.90 to $3.80. Distributors took 10 percent of the cover price, and bookstores, 20 percent. Newsstands were seldom used because they demanded 60 percent (Hwang 1994).

Running parallel to Daiwon with similar operational procedures in the mid-1990s was Seoul Cultural Publishers (SCP), which had started in 1988 as the publisher of *Woman Sense*, followed by *Weekly IQ Jump*, its first comics magazine, in the same year. As with Daiwon later, SCP grew comics magazines to fit children's to adults' age groups: *Weekly IQ Jump*, fourth grade through middle school pupils; *Monthly IQ Jump* (est. 1992), pre-fourth grade; *Comic Young Jump* (est. 1994), eighteen- to twenty-three-year-old adolescents; and *Wink* (est. 1993), for women. *Weekly IQ Jump* and *Comic Young Jump*, each with two hundred thousand circulation, rather quickly became Korea's largest comics magazines (Kim M-h 1994).

Seoul Cultural Publishers turned comics magazines into stories and then books, some of which sold one hundred thousand copies per volume. In 1994, the company published 102 books from twenty-eight series, totaling three to four million circulation, or about thirty thousand per book.

Both the stories and the drawings in SCP's magazines and books were completely controlled by the editor in chief, who was Kim Mun-hwan in the 1990s. The company employed sixteen full-time and eleven part-time cartoonists, all of whom were paid higher-than-average rates. Beginning cartoonists, expected to turn out sixteen pages a week, could earn US$2,400 monthly, a star up to

3.22. Started as *Boy Champ* in December 1991, *Comic Champ* (*Komik Chaempeu*) was published by Daewon as a competitor of Seoul Cultural Publisher's *IQ Jump*. July 15, 2008, issue. Public domain.

$8,000; however, the catch was that they had to pay two or three assistants out of these earnings (Kim M-h 1994).

The 1990s: Manhwa Magazines, Infrastructure Buildup, and *Donginji*

There is no question that manhwa became a vital part of South Korean culture in the 1990s, chiefly because of strong government funding; the already mentioned buildup of a supportive infrastructure of ministry divisions, centers, museums, festivals, and competitions (see chapter 4); and the letting up of government control. A comparison of industry figures over a decade's time makes that clear. In 1990, 4,130 comic book titles were published in Korea, making up 9 percent of the country's total periodicals output, and selling 6,833,691 copies, or 2.7 percent of total periodicals sales. In 2001, the figures had skyrocketed to 9,177 titles, or 21.5 percent of total periodicals, and 421,151,591 copies sold, or 36 percent of total sales (Kim N-h 2003). Simplified, this means that in 2001, more than one of every five periodicals was comics

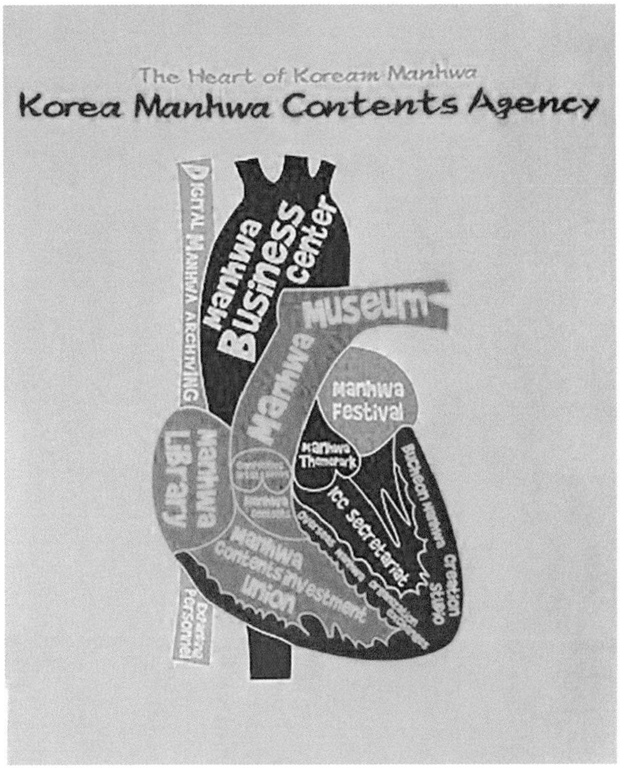

3.23. A heart design illustration displaying the divisions of the Korea Manhwa Contents Agency. Public domain.

3.24. Mural of Korean comics and cartoon characters. Bucheon Cartoon Information Center, August 2003. Photo by John A. Lent.

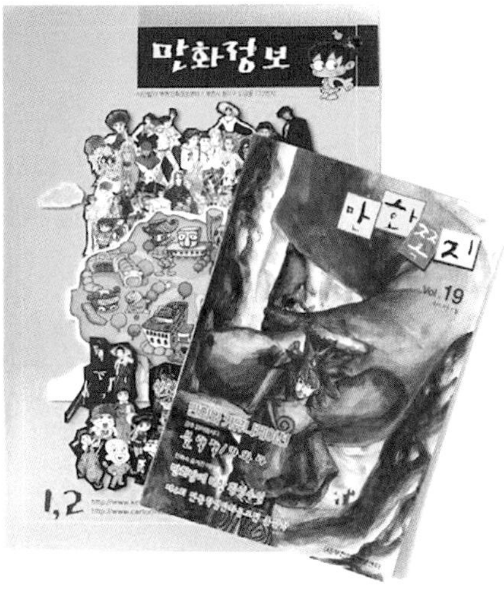

3.25. *Manhwa Jookji* (Comics Paper) (left), produced for children, and *Manhwa Jungbo* (Cartoon Information) (right), published for Korean cartoonists, both in 2003, by the Bucheon Cartoon Information Center.

related, and more than one-third of all periodicals sold were comic books.

As in the case of animation, discussed in chapter 4, comics were represented by their own professional associations, such as the Korean Alliance of Cartoonists, the Korea Cartoonists Association, the Association of Comic Books, the Korean Women's Comics Association, and the Korean Society of Cartoon and Animation Studies. They, along with the previously discussed Seoul Animation Center and the Bucheon Cartoon Information Center (BCIC, renamed the Korea Manhwa Contents Agency [KOMACON] in 2009), did much to meet professionalization goals. The BCIC was established on December 4, 1998, and consisted of the Korea Comics Museum, Comics Library, Cartoon and Animation Academy, and Kyujangkak Center.[7] Director Cho Kwan-je said that the center's purposes were to raise the public image of comics and to preserve Korea's old comics (2003). Eighty percent of the center's budget comes from the Bucheon city government, the rest from the provincial government and cultural industries. Cho enunciated a number of functions performed and services provided by the BCIC, summarized as: (1) arrange Korea's manhwa history for use online and in books through the Kyujangkak Center, (2) rent office space at affordable rates to character-producing companies and publishers through a comic book business center, (3) teach children "to open up their imaginations" and provide learning resources, and (4) publish two informational newsletters—*Manhwa Jungbo* (Cartoon Information), news of the manhwa industry for the cartoonists' community, issued every two months, and *Manhwa Jookji* (Comics Paper), produced by and for students (Cho 2003).

Under its new designation, KOMACON, the center's missions were:

1. Strengthening the capacity of the manhwa industry:
   a. Developing infrastructures for highly competitive artists and companies;
   b. Discovering and developing talented individuals;
   c. Creating superior manhwa and business projects;
   d. Organizing and operating professional investment unions for cultural contents.
2. Expanding manhwa cultural infrastructures:
   a. Operating the Korean manhwa archive;

3.26. Displays at the initial Seoul International Cartoon and Animation Festival (SICAF). August 12, 1995. Photo by John A. Lent.

   b. Developing the Korean manhwa digital archiving business;
   c. Constructing and operating the manhwa theme park;
   d. Expanding new artwork creations through contests.
3. Pioneering an overseas market and building a global network:
   a. Organizing the Bucheon International Comics Festival (BICOF);
   b. Exchanging ideas, resources, and talents with overseas comics organizations and pioneering the overseas market;
   c. Promoting excellent works in the International Comic Artist Conference (ICC). (Korea Manhwa Contents Agency n.d. [c. 2009], 11)

In 2003, Cho was especially proud of the annual Bucheon International Comics Festival (BICOF), held through the BCIC (and then KOMACON) since 1998, which he said was the first festival that dealt exclusively with manhwa. The Seoul International Cartoon and Animation Festival (SICAF) preceded it, started in 1995, but that focused on both cartoons and animation (Park S-h 2003). BICOF received help from the Bucheon Fantastic Film Festival to organize its first festival in 1998; in 2002, it became an international event, after which foreign artists were invited and exhibitions of French, Italian, Hong Kong, and Taiwanese comics were mounted. The four- to five-day event includes drawing workshops for children, familiarization sessions to instruct other businesses on how they can benefit from connections to comics, and various competitions.

Comics and animation education followed in the tracks of the professionalism surge. A single junior college, Kongju National Junior College, offered a program in comics and animation in 1994; by the decade's end, at least 156 university, college, and high school comics art departments existed.

Surprisingly, much of the growth of manhwa occurred during Korea's economic downtown of 1997 and 1998, which researcher Kim Nak-ho credited to the large number of newly unemployed starting rental shops, which they perceived as easy to operate ("someone gives you the comic books and you run the shop"), and to publishers increasing output of titles to give the unemployed something to while away their time (Kim N-h 2003). Cho (2003) estimated that there were about twenty thousand comics rental shops across Korea in 1998–1999. During that period, sales jumped from 23.6 million individual issues to 33 million (Russell 2008, 200).

This upward trend changed as the economy recovered, and the need for comics as a diversion ended and rental shops closed. Publishers were swamped with too many titles on hand. Especially affected were the four largest

3.27. Fans lining up to enter the first SICAF. August 15, 1995. Photo by John A. Lent.

companies, which each had been bringing out 1,400 titles yearly. The errant strategies of these major publishers ushered in a new lineup of small presses, long-standing publishers new to comics, and a so-called very independent press (Kim N-h 2003; Park I-h 2003). What had happened was that the majors published new titles "so quickly and often, they could not stick with one title and make it sell well," while the small presses, each with about twenty titles yearly, took the time to promote them (Kim N-h 2003). Many of the small-press comics were autobiographical, artist-oriented, reprinted classics, or products of independent artists. Older publishing firms such as Munji, Hyunmun, and Anibooks published comics for the first time in the late 1990s, and in a number of cases, they were very successful, having their own distribution and promotional systems and the savvy to turn out bestsellers. Park In-ha (2003) characterized their titles as essayistic, of short breadth, sensitive, and about everyday happenings.

The "very independent press" was similar to Japan's *dōjinshi* press—fan-produced books for self-expression, not profit. Actually, these amateur underground comics book clubs and magazines, called *donginji*, started in Korea in 1982, when *Korea Woman Amateur Comics* was published.[8] Six others opened in Seoul by the late 1980s, with a total membership of one hundred. These venues were dominated by women, although men participated "comfortably in *donginji* culture because it emphasized its underground rather than *sunjeong* (with connotations of a 'pure,' 'emotional,' feminine sensibility) aspects" (Choo 2010). Another characteristic of *donginji* was the mixture of styles from Japanese girls' comics and underground comics, both of which related women's desires at the time. Kukhee Choo writes: "Many *donginji* flaunted their affinity for the more contemporary and thus 'modern' Japanese shōjo manga narratives of the time, rather than the narratives popular among established artists, which had quasi-medieval settings. However, *donginji* artists were nevertheless influenced by the epic political sagas depicting human alienation and social injustice that established artists produced" (2010). Throughout the 1980s, these seven groups held annual exhibitions together, leading to the establishment of the Amateur Comics Association (ACA) in 1989, which, since, has been the representative organization of amateur comics in Korea (Kim H-j 2011).

Free of government censorship, *donginji* openly depicted heterosexual and homosexual relationships and contained nudity; they provided "female comic book artists a safe space in which they not only nurtured their artistic creativity, but also articulated their sexual desires and political consciousness" (Choo 2010).

Tying in with the success of girl's comics magazines after 1988, the ACA prospered in the 1990s, as a number of its members found fame drawing for these magazines. In the Korean *donginji* community, the original amateur comics and *yaoi* (boys' love) novels held strong positions. The Youth Protection Act in 1997 changed the scene drastically, defining manhwa as meant for children only, severely punishing those who included obscenity in their works, and forcing the boys' love novel groups to go underground, become exclusive, and separate themselves from the amateur comics community (Kim H-j 2011). The ACA lost favor in the 2000s after it showed preference for original works by semiprofessionals over fanart (art by amateurs who enjoyed fanart as a hobby). In 1999, a Japanese company, Comic World, began to sponsor "large scale all genre fanzine events" throughout Korea that treated original works and fanart equally. The result was that the ACA lost traction and closed in 2003 (Kim H-j 2011).

3.28. An early issue of *Renaissance* (est. 1988), Korea's first girls' comics magazine.

3.29. The best-selling manhwa *Unplugged Boy*, by Chun Kye-young.

The 2000s: The Internet and New Genres

Manhwa were on the cusp of another major transformation as they entered a new millennium. First and foremost among the change agents was the internet, advanced to the stage that it had become an important communicator among and between cartoonists, a purveyor of instantaneous information useful in the creative process, a technical aid to artists, and even a distributor of comics. Korean manhwa stood to benefit immensely from this new technology, because the country quickly became a leader in the adoption of high-speed broadband internet in the early 2000s.

Seen as both a blessing and a curse, the internet, on the one hand, led to a surge of online comics with new talent (including amateurs) and different forms, as well as offering the advantages mentioned directly above; on the other hand, games and other diversions had devastating effects on sales of printed manhwa—from 42.2 million copies in 2001 to 20.7 million copies in 2006. The internet rebirthed manhwa with webtoons (see chapter 5).

A second factor that changed the manhwa scene in the new century was the increasing and more open female roles as practitioners and readers. After 1988, women had their first comics magazine, *Renaissance*, followed by others,[9] and in the 2000s, *soonjung manhwa* gained a modicum of respect as they dealt with every type of human relationship (everyday life, history, horror, sports, and science fiction), not just romance and sexuality. Women's work was not confined to drawing *soonjung manhwa*; actually, women made up more than one half of young artists employed by boys' magazines (Noh 2004b) and 40 percent of Korea's total comics work pool. In the "very independent" genre, nine of every ten creators were females. Readership of manhwa by women also rose sharply; first of all, girls' comics magazines such as *Renaissance* were sold in retail bookstores, which girls were more apt to frequent than rental shops; second, with online manhwa, women could discreetly view comics that otherwise they would avoid (e.g., boys' love). Tied to the increased readership, of course, were augmented sales. Some statistics enforce the point. The girls' comics magazine *Daengi* (est. 1991) once sold 150,000 copies of each new issue, and famous girls' comics author Chun Kye-young earned US$250,000 in a year from sales of 300,000 copies of her *Unplugged Boy* and 100,000 copies of *Audition* (Kim C-j 2001). *Unplugged* characters were spun off into merchandise that brought in $6.7 million (Lee Eun-jung 1999, quoted in Noh 2004b, 289).

Study (*haksup*) and educational comics made a significant breakthrough after 2000, marketed mainly to parents as study tools in the highly competitive Korean educational environment. Manhwa researcher Kim Nak-ho (2003) thought that changes in the makeup of comics audiences helped germinate *haksup*, explaining that readership in the 1990s was high in the fourteen- to eighteen-year-old range, but as this group aged or turned their attention to other media, comics for small children gained strength. Some *haksup* had astronomical sales; an eighteen-volume mythology series (*Greek and Roman Mythology Read by*

3.30. An example of a *haksup* (study) manhwa on mythology.

Comics) sold more than ten million copies, following the trend in Japan at the time when manga on gourmet cooking and other topics sold in the millions. Noh Sueen (2004a) reported that by the 2000s, *haksup* made up half of the industry. Some of the *haksup* were of dubious pragmatic use, such as the best seller *How to Survive on a One-Man Island*, with sequels, according to Kim Nak-ho (2003), such as how to survive a theme park, a volcano, and so on.

Haksup differed from another popular genre in the early 2000s, *hakwon* (school) *manhwa*, which dealt with everyday life revolving around school activities and which could take a romantic turn, popular with girls, or portray organized crime in school, popular with boys (Kim N-h 2003). The crime genre had been around for years, depicting a nationalistic form of organized crime directed against the Japanese; however, influenced by Japanese manga, it switched to street fighting after the 1990s (Kim N-h 2003).

Other educational and instructional manhwa popped up from unlikely institutions, such as the Korean National Police Agency, which in 2009 published a comic book warning students about the dangers posed by North Korea (Rowland and Hwang 2009), and the national Chamber of Commerce with a series on the successes of real-life chaebol chief executive officers (*Dong-A Ilbo* 2009). The latter came about because domestic textbooks negatively described companies, turning teenagers' attention away from entrepreneurs (Park Y-k 2009). In 2010, commercial publisher Dasan Books, through its offshoot firm Joyful Stories Press in the United States, brought out fifty graphic novel biographies of famous Americans (Chung 2010). Lim Yeo-joo (2012), through a focus group study of seven- to eleven-year-old Korean children, found that the children read educational comics primarily for fun, not to learn from them.

Another new Korean genre, *yori manhwa* (food comics), appeared in the late 1990s. Food researcher Jeong Jae-hyeon describes *yori manhwa* as a subgenre of *jeomun manhwa* (professional comics), which "include food as an important factor in developing narratives; present cooking processes; [and] show a specialty in food" (2017, 301). The first Korean food comics, *Cooking of AB Studio* (*AB Hwasileui Yorijori*), was published in 1997. Jeong (302) maintains that significant socioeconomic changes in Korea in the late 1990s and early 2000s had impacts on the Korean comics industry overall and led to the emergence of *yori manhwa*. Using an argument by Theodor Adorno (1991) that all mass culture is identical and merely adaptation, Jeong (299, 303–12) textually analyzes fourteen named "food comics" and shows how they actually hybridized with *hapsup*, school violence, *myung rang*, *daebonso* (comics factory), martial arts, sports, other media, or *soonjung*. It seems only natural that a manhwa genre would be built around food, since Korean cuisine has become part of the Korean Wave. It also makes sense that some *yori* advocates would credit these comics with increased sales of certain products; when wine sales in Korea had an unprecedented boom in the mid-2000s, one of three reasons given for the jump was a Japanese manga on wine, *Drops of God* (*Kami no Shizuku*), translated into Korean and published by Haksan in nine volumes, which sold seven hundred thousand copies in about a year and half (Kamiya 2007).

A look at the promotional materials of two major comics publishers (Daiwon and Sigongsa Comics) at the advent of the new millennium provides clues as to the contents and popularity of various series. Daiwon Comics' best-selling series (setting a Korean record in sales) was *The Ruler of the Land* (*Yul-Hyul-Kang-Ho*), written by Jeon Keuk-jin and illustrated by Yang Jae-hyun. The twenty-eight volumes each sold more than one hundred thousand copies. The story revolves around two parties, Evil and Righteous, bent on ruling the country. The Evil leader "accidentally" receives help from a young man, Hanbikwang, after which he wants to make him his heir. But Hanbikwang does not want to be tied down. He falls in love with Damwharin, granddaughter of the Righteous Party leader, and risks his life to protect her from would-be murderers without telling her of his love for her. Another popular Daiwon series of twenty-nine graphic novel–size volumes, *The Unwritten Law*, tells the story of Korean street knights who help Korea gain independence from Japan, but who themselves are threatened into extinction when the United States takes control of Korea. *Sense and Sensibility* is a school setting love story series, featuring what the Daiwon catalog calls "cute, lovely characters, humorous and containing excellent descriptions of the characters' minds." Like many Daiwon school romance comics, it first appeared in the popular girls' comics magazine *Issue*. Other Daiwon titles were based on battle games or themselves were turned into online computer games. Sigongsa Comics featured 346 series titles in its 2003 catalog, broken into about fifteen divisions relating to adventure and detective, school romance, adult, and educational. An increasingly important venue of comics at the time was the internet, discussed in chapter 5.

The 2010s and Beyond: Sociocultural Factors, Adaptations, and Manhwa

Korean manhwa in contemporary times (arbitrarily set as the 2010s and beyond) faced some major sociocultural and economic changes that would affect the medium's actual form, its audience, and its marketing procedures. Once Korea became the world's most wired country, increasingly, manhwa converted to being online, employing the country's own invention, webtoons, to do this (see chapter 5). A second factor worthy of mention is the growth of a "solo economy." As birthrates fell, divorce rates increased, and the number of one-person households skyrocketed, the focus has turned to single customers, many of whom enjoy time alone. To accommodate these individuals, places of isolation have sprung up all over Seoul—coin-operated *noraebang* (pay-per-song karaoke booths) and reading cubbyholes in manhwa cafés, many open twenty-four

3.31. Examples of *yori* (food) comics, *I Love Kimchi* and *Jjang*. Courtesy of *International Journal of Comic Art*.

hours daily. Still to be determined is the effect of the solo economy on manhwa storytelling and genres—on family comics, for example, stories about isolation; or, to reverse it, those on gatherings, partygoing, and the like.

Tied to this is the so-called *sampo* generation. The term "sampo," broken down as *sam* and *po*, means "three" and "giving up"; it is applied to the young generation's willingness to give up relationships, marriage, and childbirth. It may not be too farfetched to say that the *sampo* generation has created interest in the already mentioned *yori* manhwa; if someone does not have or want someone to eat with, perhaps he or she may seek alternative pleasures through food comics or food television.

For a while, around 2002, Koreans indulged in other alternative pleasures through avatars, cartoonized cyber versions of themselves able to interact with other avatars controlled by their online users through chat rooms. Avatars allow people to be someone they could never be in "buttoned-down" Korean society, and, unbelievable as it would seem to older generations, these people (80 percent of whom were teens and twenty-somethings) were willing to pay for "goods" to improve their appearance, even though the accessories only existed in cyberspace. In about the first fourteen months of their availability, avatar services were purchased by about 13.6 million Koreans (Kim J-m 2002), and more than two million bought virtual accessories.

Another societal phenomenon that had the potential to alter manhwa, and did, was *hallyu*, which led to the popularization of Korean popular culture globally. Manhwa figured in the Korean Wave in a number of ways: (1) in a lesser way through their readership and sales; (2) through their change

3.32. A special printing of Kim Hye-rin's *Thermidor* and the wooden humidor-like box in which the books were encased. Courtesy of *International Journal of Comic Art* (John A. Lent).

3.33. Promotional poster for the 2003 television series *Damo*, which ushered in a new subgenre of historical drama (*sageuk*) and sparked what was called the "*Damo* syndrome," a form of hybridity. It was adopted from the manhwa *Damo Nam-soon* by Bang Hak-gi.

of origin and format with the creation of webtoons, which became extremely popular; (3) through being the story and character sources of other parts of *hallyu*, such as K-drama; and (4) through attempts to stem decreasing domestic sales with innovative approaches such as the reprinting of quality comics from the 1960s to the early 1990s. The reprints contained higher-grade paper, with clearer impressions and thicker bindings; occasionally they were produced in hard cover (even encased in attractive wooden boxes, as with Kim Hye-rin's *Thermidor*). Besides generating easy profits, the reprints fulfilled adults' nostalgia for stories they'd read as children, offered works serialized in magazines but never published in book form, and completed unfinished stories and those that had been censored during the dictatorships. Noh Sueen (2003) said that the reprinting of classic comics was done by both large and small comics publishers. She said that large publishers, of which there were eleven in 2001 publishing more than a hundred titles yearly, produced reprints on a massive scale for profit, even reprinting unfinished works in a different version, while the 388 small comics publishers, which produced fewer than ten titles each, reprinted them to satisfy diehard fans and the publishers themselves, some of whom considered the classics as works of art, not commodities (Noh 2003).

There were also unique twists in genres and story forms. One example is *Fairy's Landing* (*Sun-Yor-Kang-Rim*), written and illustrated by Yoo Hyun and published by Daiwon, a fantasy/romance/comedy story about 108 evil destinies designed as a computer game in which, conundrum-like, one solution leads to another problem leads to a solution, and so on.

Manhwa have been nurtured in recent years by their adaptability to other forms besides mass media, such as television and cinema;[10] to other entertainment, such as gaming and merchandising; or to an entirely new product through fusion or hybridity,[11] as explained by Kim and Choi: "Now the best ability of the cultural producer is not creativity any longer. The skill to collect the diverse elements favored by the audience, mix them, and create an entirely new-looking product is regarded as the best expertise. . . . In a hybrid age, the distinction between genres is meaningless. Fun is more important than genre. . . . Sticking to the orthodox is foolish" (2004). The authors were applying this notion to a popular television drama, *Chosun Female Police Damo* (shortened to *Damo*), which had a huge fan base in the early 2000s. Noh (2004a), terming this multiple-media strategy as the "*Damo* syndrome," traced its trajectory: first, it was a comic strip by Bang Hak-gi serialized in a sports daily, then it was compiled into paperbacks for the manhwa rental market, followed by its re-creation as a television historical drama mixed with *muhyup* (an action genre based on Asian martial arts) with the original soundtrack released as a compact disk, then it was reedited for DVD sales, rebroadcast through cable and satellite television, republished in its original form for the manhwa sales market, and finally made into a movie, *Dualist*.

Much of the expansion of *Damo* resulted from fan demands, and some of the economic gains were unexpected. The director of the televised *Damo*, Lee Jae-kyu, told Noh that there were no plans to package the drama as a DVD until fans demanded it (Lee J-k 2004), a business process

Noh (2004a) called "maniac marketing." Concerning profit turning, although the manhwa *Damo* itself was not successful, the televised version made a profit, as did the show's sponsor, LG, which saw an unexpected 10 to 15 percent increase in sales of its high-definition television sets after the telecasting of *Damo*, as well as the network that aired the drama, through advertising, DVD sales, and exportation.

Many countries have complemented comics with cinema, some much earlier than others. The Philippines was an early adapter, spinning movies from *komiks*, starting stories in *komiks* and ending them in movies, and employing various other ruses to capture both audiences. At one point in the 1980s, about 40 percent of all Filipino films were *komiks*-based (Lent 2009, 96–97).

Over the years, Korean manhwa inspired many films, television serials, and even musicals; however, the major thrusts of this phenomenon seem to have been during the contemporary period, when one manhwa was made into a Hollywood film, another into an extremely successful game, and many others into Korean films and television programs, some rather successful at the box office. The manhwa *Priest* by Hyung Min-woo boosted the presence of Korean comics in the United States when Hollywood released a 3-D film of the horror story in 2011 (Nakagawa 2011). Similarly, Lee Myung-jin's (born 1974) epic fantasy *Ragnarök*, first published in *Comic Champ*, besides becoming a successful online game also was the first manhwa to inspire a Japanese anime series. Another popular manhwa-based game was *Lineage*, created by Shin Il-suk, an animator and cartoonist known for her fantasy, epic, and romance titles, such as *Four Daughters of Armian* and *Pharaoh's Lover*. *Lineage* attracted a million players in the first fifteen months after its 1999 release.

In recent years, filmic and televised adaptations often were more profitably successful than their source manhwa. The manhwa industry began feeling a squeeze about 2005, blamed on increased illegal downloads, continuing competition from foreign titles, and market shrinkage because of an entertainment overload. As early as 2006, a report by the Manhwa Contents Agency showed that comics sales were down by 9.5 percent from the previous year (Sung 2010). A number of cases verify that the success of adaptations did not guarantee increased sales of the manhwa on which they were based. When Heo Young-man's *Tazza* was made into the film *The War of Flowers* in 2006, it brought in about seven million moviegoers and was made into a television series the following year, while the manhwa sales were not impressive. Other exceptional movie hits from Heo's strips were *Beat* in 1997 and *Le Grand Chef* in 2007.

3.34. A panel from the horror manhwa turned into a film, *Priest*, by Hyung Min-woo.

Scores of additional manhwa-sourced K-dramas with extended runs have filled television guides and theater marquees, the majority of which in recent years started out as webtoons, to be discussed in chapter 5. A small sampling of non-webtoon spin-offs includes *Pained* and *Late Blossom*, both drama/romances, in 2011; *26 Years* and *The Neighbors*, both drama/thrillers, in 2012; *Fists of Legend* (action), *Mr. Go* (comedy/drama/sport), *Recently Greatly* (action/comedy/drama), and *Deo pa-i-beu* (action/drama/thriller), all 2013; *Tazza: The Hidden Card* (crime/drama), 2014; *Cat Funeral* (drama/romance) and *Inside Man* (action/crime/drama), both 2015; and *I Married an Anti-Fan* (comedy/romance), 2016.

One of the most popular television serials that emanated from a manhwa was *Goodbye Mr. Black* (*Gutbai Miseuteo Beullaeb*), released by the Munhwa Broadcasting Company as a live-action series of twenty episodes that aired in 2016. Written by Hwang Mi-na (born 1961) and published in 1983, it is likely the oldest Korean comic book story to be resurrected for another medium (Albert 2020).

Others rated the best manhwa-based television dramas of the 2010s by MyAnimeList were: *Cheese in the Trap* (2010–2017), about the goings-on among a group of hardworking college students; *Orange Marmalade* (2011–2013), featuring vampires that hide their traits and live among humans; *Noblesse* (2007–2019), written by Son Je-ho and

3.35. A page from *Misaeng: An Incomplete Life*, written by Yoon Tae-ho, describing office workers' struggles.

illustrated by Lee Gwang-su; *What's Wrong with Secretary Kim?* (2016–2018), a combination of comedy, drama, and romance that has become "one of the highest-rated Korean dramas in cable television history" (Albert 2020); and *Misaeng: An Incomplete Life* (2012–2018), written and illustrated by Yoon Tae-ho, about the daily struggles of a group of workers in an office and labeled by Brianna Albert (2020) as "probably the rawest depiction of work-life in South Korea."

The 2010s and Beyond: Foreign Markets and Professional Prestige

A second major trend in contemporary manhwa, which has been on the industry's agenda for a time, has been the expansion of international markets.[12] Once again, the government provided motivation to address the issue, granting a third major stimulus package in 2008 to create "killer content" for a global manhwa market. To meet that challenge by 2013, the renamed Ministry of Culture, Sports, and Tourism allocated US$33.3 million, in addition to another $67 million for animation, $40 million for the development of character-driven content, and $134 million for human resources (Han 2008).

To open international markets, the comics art industries had to expose and bring awareness to their products, which they did by holding international festivals and exhibitions in Korea and abroad, establishing manhwa publishing companies in the United States, and providing more and better translations of stories. Between 2003 and

2008 alone, major manhwa exhibitions were held at some of the world's most prestigious book, culture, and comics festivals and fairs in Germany, France, Japan, China, Korea, and the United States.

In that time span, manhwa publishers set up affiliates in the United States and Canada such as Ice Kunion, jointly created by Sigongsa, Seoul Cultural Publishers, and Haksan; Netcomics as a branch of Korea's leading online manhwa publisher, Ecomix Media; and Dasan Books. By 2007, US publishers including Dark Horse, First Second Books, Central Park Media, and Tokyopop started stocking manhwa. That year, about a hundred manhwa titles were distributed in the United States (Lee Sunyoung 2007). In those early days, Tokyopop did not bother with distinguishing between manga and manhwa, according to founder and CEO Stu Levy (Alverson 2022b; for profiles of the heads of Yen Press and Ablaze, see Alverson 2022a and 2022c, respectively). However, Tokyopop must have changed its mode of identification in 2008 when it featured four of Park Hee-jung's books—*Fever, Hotel Africa, Martin and John,* and *Too Long,* as manhwa with pages in color and in trim-size (Alverson 2008).

Yen Press, founded in 2006, absorbed Ice Kunion's manhwa series in 2007 when the latter firm folded. Many companies such as Yen published manga and manhwa and benefited from the manga boom of the early 2000s, but the economic recession of 2008 and other factors dampened manga sales, and some companies folded, leaving series unfinished; for a while, new manhwa titles were rare. Yen took over some of these titles and continued books such as *Goong* by Park So-hee, *Angel Diary* by Lee Yoon-hee, and others.

Two other North American publishers launched manhwa lines in 2007, Nantier Beall Minoustchine (NBM) and Udon Entertainment. NBM published *Buja's Diary* by O Seyeong in 2006 and *Run, Bong Gu, Run!* by Byun Byung-jun in 2007. The latter tells a moving story of a woman and son who go to the city in search of their husband/father and the coldness and pressures they face (Alverson 2007). Udon, a Canadian-based art collective started in 2000, moved into manhwa in 2007 with three titles and the following year joined up with Seoul Visual Works to publish the English edition of *APPLE* (A Place for People Who Love Entertainment), a Korean illustration and comics anthology.

Other North American publishers brought out manhwa in the succeeding decade. Drawn and Quarterly published several titles after 2017, including Gendry-Kim Keum suk's multi-awarded *Grass* (2019) and *The Waiting*; Hong Yeon-sik's *Uncomfortably Happily* (2017), a tale of an urban couple who move to the countryside, and his *Umma's Table*, relating how cooking brings a family together; as well as three titles about Korean women, *Nineteen* and *Bad Friends* by Ancco, and *Moms* by Ma Yeong-shin. The senior editor of Drawn and Quarterly credited the company's strong entry into manhwa to superb translation and the ability to find new titles (Alverson 2021). Drawn and Quarterly treated manhwa as Korean; unlike other US publishers, it did not pass them off as manga.

At the outset of the 2010s, manhwa began climbing to a peak in popularity overseas while losing ground in Korea. Simultaneously, manga and US comics experienced major sales slumps. One writer believed that as fans aged, they were moving away from the "gritty post-apocalyptic manga for teenagers," preferring the "realistic dramas of manhwa" (Cain 2010).

Other appeals of manhwa over manga for foreign readers included: they were more personal and less explicit in content; they featured a "diverse range of genres, from raucous comedies and tense science fiction and fantasy to high-octane adventure, period dramas and slice-of-life romances" (Welsh 2007); they possessed universal traits that made them easier for different countries' readers to accept, for instance their fictional worlds and their characters' undistinguishable nationalities; they featured stronger, more modern female lead characters (Lee Sunyoung 2007); and their creators/producers were more globally inclined, lenient with licensing rights, and flexible and experimental. Japanese artists have been said to be almost bonded to the publishers and editors, shying away from doing anything different (Lee Sunyoung 2007). Some manhwa, in addition to webtoons, are in color.

The expanded marketing strategy, appealing features of manhwa, and later, government largesse paid large dividends for the internationalization of the industry. As domestic sales dropped dramatically, those in foreign markets grew—from US$240,000 worth of manhwa exported in 1999, to $1.9 million in 2004 and $4.2 million in 2009, almost a sixteenfold jump. Some popular titles were translated into multiple languages, such as Seoul Cultural Publishers' romantic comedy series *Goong* (Palace Story) by Park So-hee, seventeen languages and with huge sales in at least seven countries; and *Priest*, fifteen languages and sales of a million-plus copies in thirty-three countries (Jobst 2022).

Until more recent times, Europe had the largest readership of printed manhwa outside of Korea, accounting for 38.5 percent of total exports, followed by North America with 21.5 percent; Japan, 16 percent; Southeast Asia, 12.5 percent; and Latin America, Oceania, and Africa, the remaining 11.5 percent. More up-to-date figures deal with webtoons only and indicate changes. Japan leads with 31.8 percent of total webtoon exports from Korea, followed by China and Hong Kong, 23.4 percent; North America, 15.7 percent; Thailand, 13.5 percent; Europe, 5.9 percent; Indonesia and Malaysia, 4.8 percent; Taiwan, 3.4 percent; Vietnam, 1.6 percent; and others, 0.6 percent (Jobst 2022).

Manhwa began to move into European markets in 2002, when Daiwon, Korea's largest comics company, started exporting, followed by Haksan. In 2009, Daiwon exported Cho Jung-man's *Witch Hunter* to Algeria, the first African country to receive manhwa (Sung 2009). Manhwa also moved into South America when Conrad Editora of Brazil published *Chonchu, the Damned Warrior* by Kim Sung-jae in 2004. In a short time, about fifteen manhwa followed in Brazil.

Another indication that manhwa had become popular outside of Korea was the growing number of Japanese anime films that emanated from Korean comics or their offshoots. A sampling includes *True Beauty* (actually a webtoon), *Ragnarök, Timing, Freezing, When I Woke Up I Became a Bagel Girl, Blade of the Phantom Master, Noblesse, The God of High School,* and *Tower of God* (Mitra 2022).

Besides these achievements, manhwa in contemporary times have been able to attain what many Korean cartoonists regularly complained they had lacked—respect and prestige. This complaint has been difficult to fathom. For at least a quarter of a century, the South Korean government has singled out animation and comics as special, pouring huge sums of money into their continued development and professionalization. That the government made these gestures to reap economic rewards is besides the point; an end result has been that much respect and prestige have trickled down to the cartoonists in the form of many top-level centers and institutions that train and educate, monitor content, advance cartoonists' rights and labor, honor them with national awards, provide occasions to show off their work and intermingle with colleagues at international conferences in Seoul and Bucheon, and display their cartoons in local museums. South Korea has at least five top-of-the-line cartoon/comics/animation museums; the United States, a much larger country, has struggled for many decades to maintain even one. Since 2013, the Seoul city government has marked off a 450-meter section of a street as an open-air cartoon gallery. Named Zaemiro (the Street of Manhwa, or Cartoon Street), the street includes five manhwa culture stations (parks); a four-floor building with comics galleries, working spaces, and shops for comics; a Webtoon Workshop Center; and walls covered with cartoons and other art by seventy local cartoonists (Wikipedia n.d.).

Added prestige accrued to the profession in 2013 when the National Cultural Heritage Foundation conferred the honor of Registered Cultural Property on *Rabbit and Monkey, 30,000 Ri to Finding Mom,* and *Gobau Yeonggam* (Old Man). *Rabbit and Monkey* was made by Kim Yong-hwan (1912–1998) on May 1, 1946, and might be Korea's oldest surviving cartoon book. It was described to have used "animals and the tool of personification as well as metaphor and symbolism to criticize Japan's unjust colonization of Korea and expresses the wish for Korea's independence and sovereignty" (Kim H-e 2013). Created by Kim Jong-rae (1927–2001) and published in 1958, *30,000 Ri to Finding Mom* is set in the Joseon Dynasty but is an indirect way to portray the destitution of postwar Korea. The story revolves around a boy who embarks on a 30,000 *ri* search for his mother, who had been sold into slavery (5,847 miles, with one *ri* measuring 1,289 feet). Very popular, *30,000 Ri to Finding Mom* was Korea's first comic book best seller, going through ten printings in six years (Kim H-e 2013).

Manhwa that were honored as Registered Cultural Property by the National Cultural Heritage Foundation in 2013, left to right: *Gobau Yeonggam*, *Rabbit and Monkey*, and *30,000 Ri to Finding Mom*.

The third honored cartoon work, *Gobau*, has already been discussed in these pages.

2010s and Beyond: Regulations and Ethics

During these expansive years, and certainly in comparison with the repressive last two-fifths of the twentieth century, manhwa did not face much government/political interference nor many hassles. As explained earlier, the preponderance of government criticism and action was directed at political cartoons, especially the four-panel strips, when the dictators ruled, and in today's Korea, both of these forms are nearly extinct, and those that do appear are closely guided by editors or publishers, some of whom are beholden to chaebol owners.

Regulations exist in South Korea as they do in all countries, perhaps the most threatening being the National Security Act of 1948. The purpose of this law, which grants the government broad control over media, is to prevent the dissemination of information threatening to the country. Unlike similar laws in other Asian countries (Malaysia readily comes to mind), this law has not been applied to cartoonists in recent years.

Self-censorship is prevalent among manhwa and webtoon publishers. A recent example involved the internet portal site Naver, which in the summer of 2020 experienced a rash of objections about scenes of violence and sexual references in some of its webtoons. The scenes were removed or reedited, and Naver promised stricter guidelines. Naver only makes changes in collaboration with the authors but often finds itself in a no-win situation, being chastised because the offensive material is present in the first place and blasted by fans who believe that the censorship is too severe, disrupting the reader's experience. Some scenarios lose much of their meaning after being reedited. Fans gave examples of a knife being removed from an attacker's hand, leaving the empty hand suspended in midair, or an alcoholic beverage replaced by a soft drink, leaving the impression that the drunkard became inebriated by the latter. Punching scenes are blurred or removed, as are "provocative" scenes of female characters (Lim J-w 2020). The end result is that Naver editors, the authors, and the readers are left in a perplexed state.

Defamation laws are strict, prompting a United Nations official evaluating Korean freedom of expression to state that certain laws declaring defamation as a crime are "inherently harsh and [have a] disproportionate chilling effect." At least one cartoonist surnamed Choi felt the raft of these laws when in 2010 he was slapped with a three million won (US$2,600) fine for drawing a cartoon with abusive words against President Lee Myung-bak. The cartoon, published in a municipal public relations magazine, depicted family members paying respect at a soldier's monument, and it included an offensive comment against the president hidden in a pattern on the monument (Park S-s 2010).

Pornography regulations have not been imposed often in contemporary Korea; in 2019, the Ministry of Gender Equality and Family tried to implement guidelines to censor "unhealthy" content of K-pop stars, but faced strong opposition and withdrew the proposal. Distribution of pornographic material is a felony; however, legislation does not exist that punishes the watching, downloading, and storing of such material. The government has blocked pornographic websites, of which some were manhwa. Crackdowns that led to the arrest of manhwa dealers and

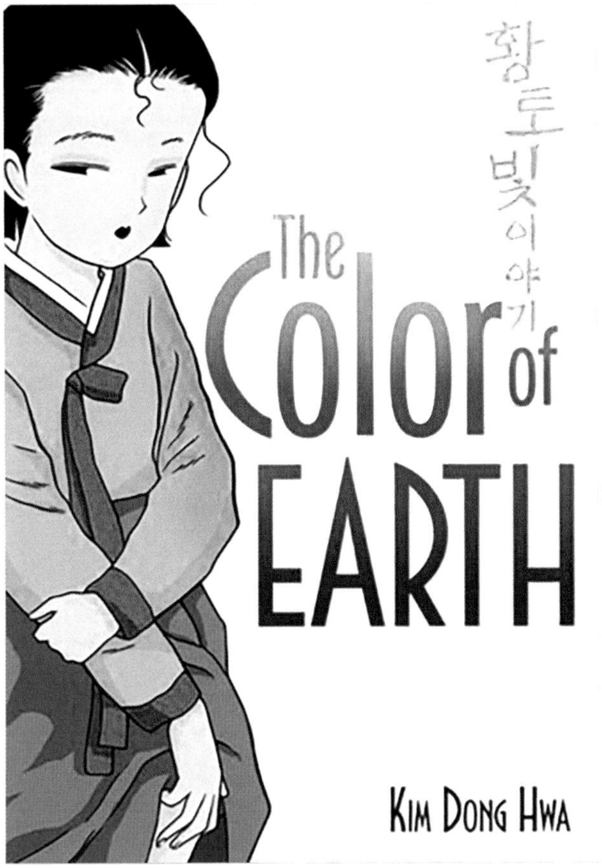

3.37. Kim Dong-hwa's *The Color of Earth*, reprinted in the United States, was the second most frequently challenged book in the United States in 2011.

the closing of their operations were common in the 1980s. The premises then were that most of the offensive comics were pirated Japanese books, illegal because they were pirated or illegally copied; they violated a Korean mandate that banned all Japanese cultural products, and most were considered pornographic.

A strong element that Korean manhwa writers and artists possess is their power to control their copyrights; in this regard, they have more power than artists in other media. This seems like an absolutely good thing, but journalist and researcher Mark Russell disagrees: "[H]aving all the rights in the world does not matter much when the rights are worthless. Strong companies, able to capitalize on those rights to expand their markets, are also good for the comics industry. . . . Comics creators may lose some freedom, but as working as part of the much larger corporate machine, they get the benefits of having their stories marketed in many forms" (Russell 2008, 199).

The Korean Ministry of Culture, Sports, and Tourism involved itself in copyright protection in early 2023 following the suicide of a manhwa creator involved in a long, drawn-out copyright suit with his publisher. The victim, Lee Yoo-young, with his brother, Woo-jin, were the creators of *Black Rubber Shoes*, a popular children's manhwa that ran for fifteen years and was spawned off into multiple films and television shows. The Lees complained that over the course of their contract with Hyungseol, they had earned a mere US$9,000. In 2019, the brothers were sued for $219,000 in damages by Hyungseol, which had taken over the contract and business rights for *Black Rubber Shoes*; the publisher alleged that the Lees used the characters without its consent. The ministry began an investigation to determine if Hyungseol had violated any provisions set down by the Protection of Artists' Rights Act of 2022; it also promised to set up a copyright legal aid center to help artists (Simons 2023).

As manhwa moved online in the 2000s, cartoonists' control over their copyrights with their publishers was challenged in another direction as illegal copyright violations by readers spiked, resulting in huge losses to the hardcopy comics industry. Cartoonists were faced with the dilemma of whether to bring legal action against their readers, which they hesitated to do.

Before ending this section, it is noteworthy to mention that when the American Library Association's Office for Intellectual Freedom released its 2011 list of "Ten Most Frequently Challenged Books" in US libraries and schools, Kim Dong-hwa's *The Color of Earth*, published in the United States by First Second Books, ranked second, but it seems not to have ruffled feathers in its home country of Korea.

Not unlike in other countries, the Korean manhwa industry has had a few cases of unethical behavior among publishers and cartoonists. One that stood out in 2007 involved a best-selling children's comic book accused of being anti-Semitic by a prominent watchdog organization. The manhwa was part of a series entitled Far Countries, Near Countries (Meon Nara, Yiwoot Nara), which sold more than ten million comics between its 1987 launch and 2007. One of the three books about the United States, published in 2004, devoted a chapter to the role of Jews, claiming they were the "driving force for the hatred that led to the September 11 attacks," that US media were Jewish controlled, and that Jews were responsible for Korean Americans not succeeding in the United States (Herman 2007).

The statements were revealed to the world in March 2008, when the US State Department submitted a report on global anti-Semitism to the US Congress. After considerable angry discourse, the author, Lee Won-bok, pledged to write more responsibly, and the publisher, Grimm-Young, pulled the controversial book from stores (Van Gelder 2007).

Another brouhaha erupted among Koreans and Americans in 2007 after a Korean cartoonist released a cartoon on the website of *Seoul Shinmun* that was considered distastefully unethical. The drawing, referring to the killing of thirty-three people at Virginia Tech by a lone gunman, depicted President George W. Bush as saying: "The life of 33 people killed at a time, our excellence of firearm technology was shown again." Intended as a satire of the US government for allowing the widespread possession of firearms, the cartoon was instead widely perceived as a mockery of death (Bae 2007).

The 2010s and Beyond: Graphic Novels

If we think of graphic novels as enlarged-by-number-of-pages comic books, and some researchers do, then manhwa and manga have merited the term for generations. For most of their existence, they have carried hundreds of pages. As an entry point, let us describe a graphic novel as a book-length visual narrative, though we are aware that anthologies and an assortment of short stories often are dumped into this category.

Graphic novels as investigative works are discussed elsewhere in these pages in the chapter on political cartoons; here, the emphasis is on their use as entertainment. Some titles are fictional, an example being Hyung Min-woo's bestseller *Priest*; there are also true-to-life stories, such as Kim Hyun-sook and Ryan Estrada's *Banned Book Club*, based on Kim's experiences as an activist in the 1980s; others are diarist stories, such as Ma Yeong-shin's *Moms* (2015); and still others are adaptations of successful books or films, such as Kim Young's rendition of the *Twilight* series by Stephenie Meyer or JR Comics' conversion of Chinese classics into graphic novels.

Graphic novels have had phenomenal sales in Korea, with the number that sold on the internet growing by 31.1 percent and sales increasing by 6.9 percent during 2019–2020. From 2010 to 2020, the number of Korean graphic novels published nearly quadrupled, from 37 to 140 (Park J-w 2021). These figures include investigative graphic novels. A survey by leading online bookstore Yes24 found that women in their forties were the major consumers of graphic novels (Park J-w 2021).

The surge in interest can be attributed to the quality of stories and how they are told, no doubt, but other factors might have been involved, including: graphic novels generally offer adult fare, elevating their prestige as something more than kids' reading material; they tend to be autobiographical, extracting sensitivities not often talked about but common among the public; and they have become fashionable—even sophisticated—in some high-profile countries, and as such they stimulate a "keep-up-with-the-Joneses" effect.

One graphic novel that exemplifies most of these traits is *Moms* by Ma Yeong-shin. Ma lived with his mother until he was in his thirties, and it was only after moving out that he realized "how difficult and frustrating household tasks are." Feeling upset for having treated her as an invisible middle-aged woman, he gave her a notebook and pen and asked her to keep a diary and "honestly" write about herself and her friends, about her love life and theirs (Menezes 2020). Ma polished and revised her story into the graphic novel *Moms*, published by Drawn and Quarterly. *Moms* broke some new ground in that older women very rarely appear as the main character in Korean pop culture (Cain 2020). One reviewer wrote that Ma's mother gave him a "great gift by helping him to understand that older women do not suddenly put aside longing and desire, jealousy and rage" (R. Cooke 2020). (See more on graphic novels in the section "Investigative Cartooning" in chapter 2.)

Conclusion

Common to the history of Korean manhwa for at least two-thirds of their existence has been the continual influx and influence of Japanese manga, even though they were banned for more than fifty of those years—at the same time that they were inexplicably censored. The Korean comics industry and the government expended considerable energy contending with the associated issues of piracy and censorship during the long run of dictatorships.

Manga as an outside factor can be seen as both a hindrance, making economic inroads into the limited local comics market, and as a nutrient, providing a model for Korean creators to imitate, though they can also be considered a deterrent blocking creativity. Mainly in the 2000s, another foreign phenomenon that affected manhwa positively was the opening up of international markets, as some US publishers started manhwa lines.

As mentioned above, for a long period, manhwa's relationship with the government was not cordial, steeped as it was in much restriction and regulation. However, beginning in 1994, and subsequently in 1997 and the early 2000s, the Korean government facilitated the advancement of comics and animation through large financial subsidies and the buildup of a strong and innovative infrastructure.

Sociocultural factors played heavily in the history of Korean manhwa. Perhaps most prominent was the role of women, who became more visible in the last third of the twentieth century, replacing most males as creators of *soonjung* comics, widening the scope of girls' comics, initiating the first women's comics magazine in 1988, and eventually making up about half of the country's comics labor pool. They also led the public outcry against manhwa's sexual and violent content in the 1960s. Manhwa were closely linked to the cultural phenomenon known as the Korean Wave, and loosely to the antisocial *sampo* generation.

Manhwa cartoonists and the community more generally added aspects to the field that they either innovated or improved, such as genres like study (*haksup*), school (*hakwon*), food (*yori*), boys' love (*yaoi*), girls' love (*yuri*), and cheerfulness (*myung rang*); the comics

3.38. *Moms.* Ma Yeong-shin. A graphic novel taken from a brutally frank notebook Ma asked his mother to write, detailing her life.

factory/comics rental shops system of production and distribution; widespread connections to the internet; and webcomics, a new way of making and reading comics. They also professionalized comics with the establishment of codes, associations, festivals, educational facilities, competitions, centers, and museums.

Overall, Korean comics have found their own identity separate from manga; endured and survived a long Japanese occupation, two wars, decades of dictatorships, and serious economic setbacks; secured a spot on the world map through their export to every continent and their exhibition and winning of awards internationally; and kept their stories alive through plentiful adaptations to every conceivable medium. Adding to all of that, manhwa have received long-sought public and government recognition as more than kids' stuff, occasionally boosted into the art world.

Notes

1. A second women's magazine, *Pu'in* (Madame), appeared three months later, in June 1920; it changed its name to *Sin Yosong* in October 1923. Written chiefly by men, the magazine brought awareness to the status of women and issues about the "new woman."

2. Kim Young-na (2003, 227) interpreted the drawing in the same manner, except for a more positive ending: "She is very stylish—I should go up and say hello."

3. An interesting sidebar is that while Park Chung-hee railed against manhwa as a social evil, his second wife, Yuk Yong-su, through her Yugyong Foundation, funded and published *Shoulder to Shoulder with Friends* (*Okkae Tongmu*, est. 1967), one of the three essential children's manhwa of the late 1960s and 1970s.

4. Another source claimed that girls and boys could not be "depicted together in a single comic strip" (Muirhead 2012). Bucheon Cartoon Information Center director Cho Kwan-je (2003) added that before 1988, drawing a mother and father sleeping together was forbidden, reminiscent of the restrictions of the Hayes Commission in the United States a half century before.

5. Although manga were the dominant comic books that entered South Korea, there was a presence of US superhero titles during and after the Korean War, left behind by departing Western soldiers. Roald Maliangkay (2015, 54) writes that several Western superhero comics were published in South Korea over the years, but given the quality of the drawings and inking, they were likely reproduced illegally. According to Maliangkay's research, Superman was introduced to Korea in 1953 in Yi Chong-hyon's *Superman of Transformation* (*Hwasŏng-ŭi Choin*) (54). Yi redesigned the character in his 1956 anticommunist comic book *The Three Brothers from the Homeland* (*Choguk-ŭi Samnanimae*), and still another rendering of Superman appeared in 1960 in Kim Su-yeong's Lucky Boy series. Maliangkay (2015, 55) writes that the US impact was marginal in Korea in the early years. Since 2014, Marvel Comics has recognized South Korea as an important market for their superhero comics because of the webtoon. In fact, a Korean female character created by Ko Yeong-hun was accepted in the company's *Avengers* comic book team in the United States.

6. Only two of the editors were women, because, according to Hwang's assessment, "the job requirements are very difficult, and males think of the job as permanent while females view it as premarriage" (Hwang 1994).

7. I was given guided tours of both the Bucheon Cartoon Information Center and the Seoul Animation Center in 2003, early in their existence. The Bucheon center impressed me with its various murals of Korean cartoon characters, exhibitions, and large library very well organized into reference and general reading sections. I was there on a Saturday afternoon and was overwhelmed by the large number of children and teenagers occupying all seats and sitting on the floor in the stacks.

The same afternoon, August 16, the director of the Korea Comics Museum, Song Dae-ho, drove me to the museum, which at that time was nestled under a professional soccer field; it has since moved into even more elaborate facilities. I quote from my notes taken that day:

> The first room provides a chronology going back to cave drawings found in Korea and a seventeenth-century, four-panel narrative about a farmer trying to protect his cow from a tiger. Then, the earliest political cartoons through each decade of the twentieth century to one of the present and future. On the walls there are examples and explanations of cartoons and comics of each period, and underneath, glass enclosed, are books and newspapers that contain cartoons and comics. All this was accompanied by visual and audio screens adding explanations.
>
> The second section was organized by genres (cartoons, comics, animation, etc.), followed by a space dealing with the process of making the drawings via materials and a TV monitor. The fourth space consists of rare comic books, the oldest being from 1950 and a few others from the 1950s. Song said that Kim Song-hwan has older books but does not want to part with them. A bigger room is for special exhibitions that change regularly. This one is on Korean comics magazines. Then, an artists' hall of fame, again with [each] artist's photograph, [career] information, and main character on the wall, and underneath, encased, either an original of the artist's work or paraphernalia (like personal or drawing implements). Only one woman was among the masters, Kim Sang-bo (born 1940, first science fiction comics). A children's section, a reading room with lots of 1970s and 1980s comics that have been reprinted. Again, the room is full of children and adults reading comics. There is a "Comics Café in Old Fashion" with a little stove and a mock-up of a man reading comics; [and] a Comics Information Search area with three or four computer stands where people can search for information, pictures of comic books, artists, stories, etc. One can actually see the inside pages of all of the old comics in the glass-encased places. There are platforms in front of each computer for little kids to stand on. There are a number of places in the museum where people can obtain information by computer or interact by computer. A "Derivative Room" has products and books for sale. In that room are a books for children section and a section of scholarly books about comics (Korean and elsewhere). Sold are things like thirty-two postcards of old Korean comic book covers for 6,000 won, stuffed animal characters, etc. Also, there are an audio-visual theater of 3-D animation where you have to wear 3-D glasses; [and] an Education Room, where little kids draw pictures with special pens and then have a woman attendant iron their drawings onto T-shirts for 5,000 won. Outside, there are statues of comics characters along with a walkway leading

> to an amusement park next door. Song said the previous day, National Day, the museum had 1,500 visitors. By the way, this museum has as much or more than the Tezuka Museum in Japan [or others I have visited in Canada, Poland, Cuba, Japan, Switzerland, England, Iran, China, Taiwan, and elsewhere].

Why such elaboration, the reader may ask? Indulge me for a few minutes . . . because the United States, with its rich history of humor magazines dating back to the nineteenth century, hard-hitting political cartoons that have set the standard for the rest of the world, animation that has included numerous characters known in every corner of the globe, and comic books that have sold hundreds and hundreds of millions of copies, has not been able to sustain even just one museum, although serious attempts have been made by individuals such as Mort Walker, Art Wood, and others. Something to think about.

8. In another publication, Choo Kukhee (2009) has the startup date of the first *donginji* as 1983, when Kang Kyung-ok set up PAC. What the abbreviation PAC stands for was not revealed.

9. Such magazines included *Mink*, *Wink*, and *Sugar* (Seoul Cultural Publishers), *Party* (Haksan Cultural Publishers), *Bijou* and *Owho* (Sigongsa), and *Issue* (Daiwon). As a contrast, the male comics magazines were *IQ Jump* (Seoul Cultural Publishers), *Chance* and *Booking* (Haksan Cultural Publishers), and *Comic Champ*, *Young Champ*, and *Pang Pang* (Daiwon). Seoul Cultural Publishers ceased publishing some boys' comics magazines and added a third girls' comics magazine, *Sugar*, because the latter was more profitable (Noh 2004b, 288).

10. Film adaptations of manhwa began with *Meongteonguri*, released in 1926.

11. Another term for this phenomenon is "glocalization," described by Jang Won-ho and Lee Byung-min as "[t]he specific socio-cultural characteristics of local society reshap[ing] and chang[ing] global cultural contents, and produc[ing] a new culture, which has both universal and particular cultural characteristics" (2016, 7). Hong Soo Jung (2014, 1), in an analysis of the manga *Boys over Flowers* and its adaptation in Japan, South Korea, and Taiwan, uses globalization and glocalization perspectives to show differences and similarities of all three versions (2014, 1). She concludes:

> The three storylines, although similar, have several modifications due to the differing audiences and goals of each series. Based on the idea of globalization: fidelity in the adaptation can be understood as emphasizing the shared values and community spirit between cultures while modifications can be interpreted as organizational gatekeeping. [Applying these principles to *Boys over Flowers*,] fidelity could be interpreted as presenting the glocalized cultural values or socio-cultural popular memory in the Asian context while modification could be considered as being reflective of a wide variety of different socio-cultural contexts where the series were created.

12. Korean manhwa was identified with transnationalism as early as 1969 (perhaps earlier, in January 1964, though that hasn't been verified), when Kim San-ho, working for Charlton, became the first Korean cartoonist to be published abroad in English (Gravett 2009).

References

Adorno, Theodor W. 1991. *The Culture Industry: Selected Essays on Mass Culture*. Abingdon, Oxon., England: Routledge.

Ahn, Hyun-dong. 1994. Interview with John A. Lent. Seoul, July 2.

Albert, Brianna. 2020. "10 Must-Read Manhwa and Manga Series for K-Drama Fans." CBR, March 20. https://www.cbr.com/must-read-manhwa-manga-k-drama.

Alverson, Brigid. 2007. "New Korean Manhwa from NBM." *Publishers Weekly*, June 5.

Alverson, Brigid. 2008. "Tokyopop Showcases Korea's Hee Jung Park." *Publishers Weekly*, May 27. https://www.publishersweekly.com/pw/by-topic/new-titles/adult-announcements/article/10889-tokyopop-showcases-korea-s-hee-jung-park.html.

Alverson, Brigid. 2021. "Korean Comics Gain Popularity in North America." *Publishers Weekly*, August 4. https://www.publishersweekly.com/pw/by-topic/industry-news/comics/article/87045-korean-comics-gain-popularity-in-north-america.html.

Alverson, Brigid. 2022a. "Manhwa in America, Part 1: Juyoun Lee of Yen Press." ICv2, March 3. https://icv2.com/articles/news/view/50589/manhwa-america-part-1-juyoun-lee-yen-press.

Alverson, Brigid. 2022b. "Manhwa in America, Part 2: Stu Levy of Tokyopop." ICv2, March 3. https://icv2.com/articles/news/view/50590/manhwa-america-part-2-stu-levy-tokyopop.

Alverson, Brigid. 2022c. "Manhwa in America, Part 3: Rich Young of Ablaze." ICv2, March 3. https://icv2.com/articles/news/view/50591/manhwa-america-part-3-rich-young-ablaze.

Ann, Da-young. 2020. "Following the Changing Faces of Modern Korean Women." *Korea JoongAng Daily*, September 1. https://koreajoongangdaily.joins.com/2020/09/01/culture/koreanHeritage/modern-women-magazine-korea/20200901184100420.html.

Avila, Kat. 2004. "Korean Comics in the U.S." *Jade Magazine*, September.

Bae, Ji-sook. 2007. "Cartoon Angers Americans." *Korea Times*, April 18. http://www.koreatimes.co.kr/www/news/nation/2007/04/1137_1216.html.

Baek, Byung-yeul. 2016. "Museum Archives 60s Star Cartoonist Park Ki-jeong." *Korea Times*, December 15. https://www.koreatimes.co.kr/www/news/culture/2016/12/203_220248.html.

Cain, Sian. 2020. "What Is It Like to Be a Middle-Aged Woman? A Son Asked His Mother—Then Wrote a Comic." *Guardian*, September 1. https://www.theguardian.com/books/2020/sep/01/what-is-it-like-to-be-a-middle-aged-woman-a-son-asked-his-mother-then-wrote-a-comic.

Cha, Ae-ock. 1994. Interview with John A. Lent. Seoul, July 2.

Cho, Kwan-jc. 2003. Interview with John A. Lent. Seoul, August 16.

Choi, Yeol. 1995. *Hanguk Manhwa-ui Yeoksa: Uri Manhwa-ui Baljachuri Ilcheonnyeon* [A History of Korea Comics: One Thousand Years of Our Comics]. Seoul: Yorhwadang.

Choo, Kukhee. 2009. "Usinawareta Koe wo Sagutte: Guniis-eikinki no Okeru Kankoku no Jyunjyo Manhwa Sakka Tachi no Teikō to Kenri Fuyo" [Searching for Lost Voices: The Resistance and Right Endowment of Korean Women's Comics Artists under the Military Regime]. In *Ekkyosuru Popyurā Karuchā: Li Cōran kara Takkï Made* [Popular Culture that Crosses Borders: From Li Cōran to Takkï], 47–79. Tokyo: Seikyūsha.

Choo, Kukhee. 2010. "Consuming Japan: Early Korean Girls Comic Book Artists' Resistance and Empowerment." In *Complicated Currents: Media Flows, Soft Power and East Asia*, edited by Daniel Black, Stephen Epstein, and Alison Tokita. Melbourne: Monash University Publishing.

Chung, Ah-young. 2010. "Comic Books Hailed as New Education Tools." *Korea Times*, March 19. https://www.koreatimes.co.kr/www/culture/2024/05/135_62659.html.

Cooke, Jon B. 2023. *The Charlton Companion*. Raleigh, NC: TwoMorrows Publishing.

Cooke, Rachel. 2020. "*Moms* by Yeong-Shin Ma Review: A Joyous Celebration." *Guardian*, November 10. https://www.theguardian.com/books/2020/nov/10/moms-by-yeong-shin-ma-review-a-joyous-celebration.

Culkin, Kate. 2009. "Colorful Kim Dong-Hwa Is a Big New Voice in American Comics." *Publishers Weekly*, April 7. https://www.publishersweekly.com/pw/by-topic/new-titles/adult-announcements/article/5077-colorful-kim-dong-hwa-is-a-big-new-voice-in-american-comics.html.

Dong-A Ilbo. 2009. "Comics on CEO Success Stories." August 25.

Gravett, Paul. 2006. "Hyun Se Lee: Manhwa's Modern Master." November 26. http://paulgravett.com/articles/article/hyun_se_lee.

Gravett, Paul. 2009. "Make Mine Manhwa! Exporting Korean Comics." September 27. http://www.paulgravett.com/articles/article/make_mine_manhwa/.

Gravett, Paul. 2017. "Hur Young-man: My Brilliant Korea." http://paulgravett.com/articles/article/hur_young_man.

Han, Sunhee. 2008. "South Korean Gov Invests in Content: Third Stimulus Package for Local Cultural Units." *Variety*, November 24. https://variety.com/2008/biz/news/south-korean-gov-invests-in-content-1117996414/.

Herman, Burt. 2007. "Controversial S. Korea Comic Book Pulled." *Guardian*, March 15.

Hong, Soo Jung. 2014. "Three Adaptations of the Japanese Comic Book *Boys over Flowers* in the Asian Cultural Community: Analyzing Fidelity and Modification from the Perspective of Globalization and Glocalization." *Qualitative Report* 19, no. 1: 1–18.

Horn, Maurice, ed. 1976. *The World Encyclopedia of Comics*. New York: Chelsea House.

Hwang, Kyung-tae. 1994. Interview with John A. Lent. Seoul, July 2.

Jang, Won-ho, and Byung-min Lee. 2016. "The Glocalizing Dynamics of the Korean Wave." *Korean Regional Sociology* 17, no. 2: 5–19.

Jeong, Jae-hyeon. 2017. "Genre Hybridity as the Scheme of the Comics Industry." *International Journal of Comic Art* 19, no. 1 (Spring–Summer): 296–315.

Jo, Woon-hak. 1995. Interview with John A. Lent. Seoul, August 14.

Jobst, Nina. 2022. "Leading Destination Countries of Webtoon Exports from South Korea in 2021." Statista, January 6. https://www.statista.com/statistics/1234132/south-korea-webtoon-export-leading-destination-countries/.

Jung, Joon-young. 1994. Interview with John A. Lent. Seoul, July 3.

Kamiya, Takeshi. 2007. "S. Koreans Get Taste for Wine from Manga." *Asahi Shimbun*, April 19. http://www.asahi.com/english/Herald-asahi/TKY200704190056.html.

Kim, Chong. 1994. Interview with John A. Lent. Seoul, July 2.

Kim, Chul-jin. 2001. "Yearning for an Unsatisfied 'Decadent Mood.'" *Sports Today*, November 4.

Kim, D., and J. Choi. 2004. "Reading the Culture 2004 (5): Hybrid." *Hankook Ilbo*, January 8.

Kim, Hyo-jin. 2011. "Crossing Double Borders: Korean Female Amateur Comics Artists in the Globalization of Japanese Dōjin Culture." *International Journal of Comic Art* 13, no. 2 (Fall): 116–33.

Kim, Hyung-eun. 2013. "3 Cartoons Deemed Registered Cultural Property." *Korea JoongAng Daily*, February 18. https://koreajoongangdaily.joins.com/2013/02/17/artsDesign/3-cartoons-deemed-registered-cultural-property/2967225.html.

Kim, Jung-min. 2002. "Altered Egos: Dressing Up Online Cartoon Characters Is a Booming Business in Buttoned-Down South Korea." *Far Eastern Economic Review*, January 24, 40.

Kim, Kyu Hyun. 2014. "Fisticuffs, High Kicks, and Colonial Histories: The Ambivalence of Modern Korean Identity in Postwar Narrative Comics." In *The Korean Popular Culture Reader*, edited by Kim Kyung Hyun and Choe Youngmin, 34–54. Durham, NC: Duke University Press.

Kim, Mun-hwan. 1994. Interview with John A. Lent. Seoul, July 7.

Kim, Nak-ho. 2003. Interview with John A. Lent. Seoul, August 17.

Kim, Song-hwan. 1992. Interview with John A. Lent. Seoul, July 4.

Kim, Young-na. 2003. "Being Modern: Representing the 'New Woman' and 'Modern Girl' in Korean Art." *German Culture Study* 12: 216–43.

Kim, Yung-hee. 2013. "In Quest of Modern Womanhood: *Sinyŏja*, a Feminist Journal in Colonial Korea." *Korean Studies* 37: 44–78.

Ko, Dong-hwan. 2016. "Unfolding History, Coloring Humanity." *Korea Times*, November 16. http://koreatimes.co.kr/www/culture/2016/11/135_218371.html.

Korea Manhwa Contents Agency. n.d. *The New Beginning of 100 Years of Korean Cartoons: The Korea Manhwa Contents Agency*. Bucheon: Korea Manhwa Contents Agency.

Korea Society. 2005 *Korean Comics: A Society through Small Frames*. Exhibition catalog. New York: Korea Society.

Kunzle, David. 1973. *The Early Comic Strip: Narrative Strips and Picture Stories in the European Broadsheet from c. 1450 to 1825*. Berkeley: University of California Press.

Kwon, Hyuk-jong. 1998. "An Evangelist of Korean Comics, Sajima Akiko." *Chosun Ilbo*, November 21.

Lee, Eun-joo. 2008. "Ko's Cartoons Still a Big Draw." *Korea JoongAng Daily*, July 10, 7.

Lee, Eun-jung. 1999. "The Most Famous Author among Teenagers, Chun Kye-young of *Audition*." *Kyunghyang Shinmun*, June 7.

Lee, Hae-chang. 1982. *History of Korean Political Cartoons*. Seoul: Iljeesa.

Lee, Hee-jae. 2018. Interview with John A. Lent. Seoul, August 10.

Lee, Helen J. S. 2011. "Out of *Sōdesuka-shi*, Creating *Yobo-san*: Cartooning the Korean Other in Japan's Colonial Discourse." *Japanese Language and Literature* 45, no. 1 (April): 31–66.

Lee, Jae-kyu. 2004. Email interview with Noh Sueen. April 19.

Lee, Sunyoung. 2007. "The Koreans Are Coming: Manhwa in America." *Publishers Weekly*, January 2. https://www.publishersweekly.com/pw/by-topic/industry-news/comics/article/11971-the-koreans-are-coming-manhwa-in-america.html.

Lee, Won-bok. 1991. *The World of Cartoons and the Cartoons of the World*. Seoul: Mijinsa.

Lee, Won-bok. 1992. Interview with John A. Lent. Seoul, July 2.

Lent, John A. 1994. "Cartoon Schools around the World: Kongju Nat'l Junior College, Seoul." *WittyWorld International Cartoon Magazine*, no. 18: 22.

Lent, John A. 1995. "Korean Cartooning: Historical and Contemporary Perspectives." *Korean Culture* (Spring): 8–20.

Lent, John A. 1998. "The Multi-Tiered Korean Comics." *Comics Journal*, no. 207 (September): 31–34.

Lent, John A. 2009. *The First One Hundred Years of Philippine Komiks and Cartoons*. Tagaytay, Philippines: Yonzon Associates.

Lent, John A. 2015. *Asian Comics*. Jackson: University Press of Mississippi.

Lim, Bum. 1994. Interview with John A. Lent. Seoul, July 8.

Lim, Cheong-san. 1994. Interview with John A. Lent. Seoul, July 5.

Lim, Jang-won. 2020. "Naver Accused of Excessive Censorship of Webtoons after String of Controversies." *Korea Herald*, October 21. https://www.koreaherald.com/view.php?ud=20201021000905.

Lim, Jung-in. 1996. "What Should Be Read?" In *Critical I*, 17–36. Unpublished manuscript.

Lim, Yeo-joo. 2012. "Seriously, What Are They Reading? An Analysis of Korean Children's Reading Behavior Regarding Educational Graphic Novels." PhD diss., University of Illinois.

Lima, Acervo. n.d. "Manhwa." https://wiki-acervolima.com/manhwa/.

Lorah, Michael C. 2009. "The Colors of Kim Dong-Hwa: The 'Color' Trilogy." Newsrama. April 16.

Maliangkay, Roald. 2015. "Embedding Nostalgia: The Political Appropriation of Foreign Comic Book Superheroes in Korea." *Situations* 8, no. 2: 49–65.

Menezes, Vivek. 2020. "Reading Yeong-Shin Ma's 'Moms' to Understand Why the Korean Wave Has Swept through Parts of India." Scroll, September 30. https://scroll.in/article/974451/reading-yeong-shin-mas-moms-to-understand-why-the-korean-wave-has-swept-through-parts-of-india.

Mitra, Ritwik. 2022. "10 Best Anime Based on Manhwa." Gamerant, January 12. https://gamerant.com/best-anime-based-on-manhwa/.

Morgan. 2017. "Beyond Manga: You Have to Check Out Korean Manhwa!" ComicsVerse, June 3. https://comicsverse.com/beyond-manga-manhwa/.

Muirhead, Justin. 2012. "History of Manhwa Comics." HubPages, December 8. https://discover.hubpages.com/literature/History-of-Manhwa-Comics.

Nakagawa, Ulara. 2011. "Priest to Promote Korean Comics?" *Diplomat*, February 1. https://thediplomat.com/2011/02/priest-to-promote-korean-comics/.

Noh, Sueen. 2003. Conversation with John A. Lent. Philadelphia, September 25.

Noh, Sueen. 2004a. "'*Damo* Syndrome': A Coup of a 'Fusion' Historical Drama in Korea." Graduate paper, Temple University.

Noh, Sueen. 2004b. "The Gendered Comics Market in Korea: An Overview of Korean Girls' Comics, *Soonjung Manhwa*." *International Journal of Comic Art* 6, no. 1 (Spring): 281–98.

NPR. 2015. "The Story of South Korea Told through One Cartoonist." *All Things Considered*, July 22. https://www.npr.org/2015/07/22/425377071/the-story-of-south-korea-told-through-one-cartoonist.

Oh, Kyu-won. 1981. *The Reality of Korean Cartoons*. Seoul: Yorhwadang.

Park, In-ha. 2000. *Nuga kendi-reul moham henna: Bak in-ha-ui sunjeong manhwa madikke ilkgi* [Park In-ha's Tasteful Reading of Sunjeong Manhwa: Who Framed Candy?]. Seoul: Sallim Press.

Park, In-ha. 2003. Interview with John A. Lent. Seoul, August 17.

Park, In-ha. 2006. "A Short History of Manhwa." March 15. http://capcold.net/eng/blog/?p=11.

Park, In-ha. 2007. "Kim Dong-Hwa: Innovator of Korea's Comic Book Culture." *Koreana* (Winter): 40–45.

Park, Ji-won. 2021. "Sales of Graphic Novels Increase by 7 Times over Last 10 Years." *Korea Times*, March 22. https://www.koreatimes.co.kr/www/culture/2021/03/142_305679.html.

Park, Ki-jun. 1980. "Caricature and Comic Strips: Essential to Korean Journalism." *Asian Culture* (January): 4–5.

Park, Se-hyung. 2003. Interview with John A. Lent. Seoul, August 14.
Park, Si-soo. 2010. "Cartoonist Convicted of Defaming President." *Korea Times*, December 23. http://www.koreatimes.co.kr/www/news/nation/2010/12/113_78533.html.
Park, Su-dong. 1992. Interview with John A. Lent. Seoul, July 7.
Park, Yeong-kyun. 2009. "[Op-Ed] Comics on CEO Success Stories." *Dong-A Ilbo*, August 24.
Roh, Byung-sung. 1994. Interview with John A. Lent. Seoul, July 2.
Rowland, Ashley, and Hwang Hae-rym. 2009. "Teachers Feel Police Stepped over the Line with Pro-US Comic." *Stars and Stripes*, Pacific Edition, August 24. https://www.stripes.com/migration/teachers-feel-police-stepped-over-the-line-with-pro-u-s-comic-1.94190?=/&subcategory=478%7CVeterans.
Russell, Mark James. 2008. *Pop Goes Korea: Behind the Revolution in Movies, Music, and Internet Culture*. Berkeley, CA: Stone Bridge Press.
Seon, Jeong-u. 2003. Interview with John A. Lent. Seoul, August 17.
Simons, Dean. 2023. "Korean Publisher Investigated Following Suicide of *Black Rubber Shoes* Creator." *The Beat*, March 31. https://www.comicsbeat.com/Korean-publisher-investigated-following-suicide-of-black-rubber-shoes-creator/.
Smith, Kevin Michael. 2020. "The New Woman Arrives Again: A Review of the Museum of Modern and Contemporary Art, Korea's Exhibition on *Sin yŏsŏng*." *Cross-Currents: East Asian History and Culture Review* 33: 211–31.
Song, Dae-ho. 2003. Interview with John A. Lent. Seoul, August 16.
Sung, So-young. 2009. "Korean Comic Books Find Audiences in Africa." *Korea JoongAng Daily*, March 13. https://koreajoongangdaily.joins.com/2009/03/12/features/Korean-comic-books-find-audiences-in-Africa/2902197.html.
Sung, So-young. 2010. "Manhwa Industry Declines, but Movies Are Hits." *Korea JoongAng Daily*, May 20. https://koreajoongangdaily.joins.com/2010/05/20/artsDesign/Manhwa-industry-declines-but-movies-are-hits/2920748.html?detailWord=.
Thorn, Matt. 1995a. "Shoujo Manga: Comics by Women for Girls of All (1)." Epic World, September. http://matt-thorn.com/what_are_shoujo_manga.html.
Thorn, Matt. 1995b. "Shoujo Manga: Comics by Women for Girls of All (2)." Epic World, November. http://matt-thorn.com/what_are_shoujo_manga.html.
Toutenbd. 2004. "Focus on Korean Comics." November 6. https://www.toutenbd.com/dossiers/zoom-sur-la-coreenne/.
Van Gelder, Lawrence. 2007. "Korean Comic Book Is Deemed Anti-Semitic." *New York Times*, February 26.
VanVolkenburg, Matt. 2019. "Saving Children from Unhealthy Comics in 1960s." *Korea Times*, May 8. https://www.pressreader.com/korea-republic/the-korea-times/20190508/281930249415115.
Vergara, Vernieda. 2021. "Manhwa vs. Manga: What's the Difference?" Book Riot, July 2. https://bookriot.com/manhwa-vs-manga/.
Welsh, David. 2007. "Forget Manga. Here's Manhwa." Bloomberg, April 23. https://www.bloomberg.com/news/articles/2007-04-23/forget-manga-dot-heres-manhwabusinessweek-business-news-stock-market-and-financial-advice.
Wi, Tack-whan, and Chang Iou-chung. 2015. "Interview with Cartoonist Park Si-baek: Time Travel with Joseon Kings (Part One)." Korea.net, November 20. https://www.korea.net/NewsFocus/People/view?articleId=131046.
Wikipedia. N.d. "Cartoon Street." https://en.wikipedia.org/wiki/Cartoon_Street.
Yoon, Yong-ok. 1986. *The History of Korean Newspaper Cartoons*. Seoul: Yorhwadang.
Yoon, Yong-ok. 1992. Interview with John A. Lent. Seoul, July 3.
Young, Aah. 2010. "'Kkeoteongi' Creator Gil Chang-duk Dies." *Korea Herald*, January 31.

2011년 한국 영화의 아름다운 도전
마당을 나온 암탉

Compared to its East Asian neighbors, Korea was a latecomer to animation production. Japan's earliest domestic animation was in the 1910s; China's, the 1920s; while Korea's was not until the 1950s. Accounting for this wide time gap were the three-and-a-half-decade Japanese occupation of Korea and the Korean War; and later, beginning in the 1960s, domestic animation was sidelined by a preoccupation with the profitable offshore production for foreign studios and by four decades of dictatorial rule.

Ironically, the large offshore production industry boosted local animation when in 1994 the South Korean government, recognizing its export potential, pumped large amounts of money into building a strong infrastructure for the industry. The results of these dual operations are that South Korea is the world's third-largest producer of animation after the United States and Japan, a ranking it has maintained for decades; sports an assemblage of studios, educational programs, international competitions, festivals, museums, libraries, and professional organizations that are unique globally; and has produced award-winning animated films (see appendix III for a list of South Korean animated films, 1967–2023).

Chapter Four

Animation

The Beginnings[1]

As with China, the first commonly acknowledged animation in Korea came out of advertising, a black-and-white television commercial for Lucky Toothpaste, made for a new channel, HLKZ TV, in 1956. It was the creation of Mun Dal-bu, who, for want of an animation camera, took the photographs with a still camera. Mun's characters were based on the lovers in "Choonhyang-jeon," one of the country's most popular folktales. The relatively late start has been blamed on the Japanese occupation of Korea (1910–1945), an explanation that is justified for the most part, in that the colonized were prohibited from portraying their lives in their own voices and stories (Kim J-y 2006, 63). Korea under Japan presented a confusing scenario, according to Kim Joon-yang (2006, 63), because of Japan's contradictory policies of assimilation (*naisen ittai*) and discrimination (*furyo senjin*), in effect simultaneously,

4.1. Shin Dong-hun, creator of South Korea's first animated feature. Seoul, August 15, 1995. Photo by John A. Lent.

which could have affected whether Koreans were permitted to engage in animation production or were denied the privilege. It seems plausible that Koreans were involved in animation, just because other Asian colonies made animation while occupied by a foreign entity (India, under the British, as early as 1915; see Lent 2001, 199).

Other records indicate that Korean-made or -assisted animation predated the toothpaste commercial. In 1936, Kim Yong-woon and Im Seok-ki began to make an animation, *Gaeggum* (Dog Dreams), in their own studio; as an article in *Chosun Ilbo* on November 25, 1936, entitled "The Appearance of Chosun's First Talking Animation *Gaeggum*" proclaimed: "While the names of Mickey Mouse and Betty Boop are known throughout the world, there has not been an animated character created in Chosun. Now, thanks to Kim Yong-woon and Im Seok-ki, in association with the Jeongrim Movie Company, the production of *Gaeggum* has begun" (quoted in Giammarco 2005). Although *Chosun Ilbo* later reported that four hundred feet of film had been produced, it is unlikely that the animation was completed (Giammarco 2005; Heo 2002, 16–17).

During World War II, somehow, a Korean animator, Kim Yong-hwan (1912–1998), managed to work in the Japanese film company Shochiku, where he helped make the 1945 animated feature film *Momotaro, Umi-no Shinpei* (Momotaro, the Divine Soldier of the Sea), meant to justify Japan's taking over other Asian countries. Kim Joon-yang (2006, 65) writes that little knowledge exists about how many other Korean artists worked for the Japanese animated propaganda film organization. After settling in Seoul, Kim Yong-hwan established the Kim Yong-hwan Cartoon Movie Production Company, but it closed before making a film because of lack of celluloid and disinterest on the part of investors.

The Lucky Toothpaste animated advertisement was followed by others for soaps, pharmaceutical products, seasonings, cosmetics, and drinks. Other pioneer animators such as Nelson Shin (born Shin Neung-kyun, 1939), Han Seong-hak, and Shin Dong-hun (1927–2017), began their careers doing these commercials, initially for theater viewing and then for television (N. Shin 2009, 38). Han Seong-hak caused an uproar with an animated advertisement he created for an antacid when he used a Beethoven symphony as background music (Giammarco 2005). Nelson Shin, who had much to do with introducing Korea to service production for foreign studios, ran his own animated film commercial company for a decade in the 1960s.

In 1961, the first artistic animated film, *Gaemiwa Betzangi* (Ants and the Grasshopper), from Aesop's Fables, was made by Park Yeong-il, Jeong Do-bin, and Han Seong-hak at their own expense. Two years later, Park and Jeong collaborated on the six-minute public service animated film *I Am Water*, broadcast on American Forces Network Korea, and then a movie institute in the Ministry of Culture and Public Affairs sponsored the four-minute *Juireul Japja* (Let's Terminate Mice), featuring Kim Yong-hwan's strip character Kojubu (N. Shin 1996, 79).

Figuring prominently in early Korean animation was Shin Dong-hun, labeled the "father of Korean animation." In 1960, he made animated commercials for the Jinro Liquor Company and a soybean sauce while establishing a studio in his name. Throughout the 1960s, he was the most sought-after animator in Korea because of these two commercials, his having a studio, and his musical talent. The jingle he composed for the liquor commercial was catchy and remained in people's minds for a long time. Shin is most famously recognized for creating the country's first feature production in 1967, *Hong Gil Dong*, adapted from his brother Shin Dong-woo's strip *Punguna Hong Gil Dong* (The Boy of Wind and Cloud, Hong Gil Dong), which had appeared in the children's newspaper *Sonyeon Chosun Ilbo* (Chosun Daily Youth Newspaper) since 1965 (Yu 1999, 15). Shin's work was backed by Segi Sangsa, a film distributor.

Shin's life itself had the makings of a film script. Born in what is now North Korea, Shin dropped out of college, where he was studying architecture, at the beginning of the Korean War and ended up being a prisoner of war of both the North Koreans and the Americans. Besides the already mentioned works, Shin, also in 1967, finished a second feature animation, *Hopiwa & Chadolbawi* (The Man of Tiger Skin and the Body of Rock Stone), again with help from his brother. The film was known for its use of lip synchronization, another skill Shin picked up from his music interests. He headed the Universal Art Company from 1974 to 1980, a subcontractor for both Japanese and American animation that went bankrupt. Disenchanted, Shin spent the next three years as a free spirit, for half a year doing layout work at Nelvana in Toronto, then journeying for two years from "Texas to Alaska" and painting landscapes, which he sold to Korean Americans to have traveling money and "some to send home to my wife." When he returned to Seoul, Jung Wook, who had been one of his assistants earlier, appointed Shin honorary chairman of Daiwon Animation and soon after gave him an assignment to produce a daily children's animation show for the Munhwa Broadcasting Company, which he did until 1992, as he boasted, "single-handedly." Working independently under his own Shin Dong Hun Production Company, a privilege granted by Jung Wook, Shin said this was his "happiest time" (Shin D-h 1995). When I last saw Shin in 2003, he said the jingle he'd composed for the 1962 liquor advertisement was an idea that came to him while on a forty-day voyage across the Pacific Ocean: "I got the idea from the sea." He said his life in 2003 was the best: "drink a little, smoke a little, paint, and listen to music." His wife had told him to quit drinking and smoking, he said, to which he retorted, "I'm going to quit you" (Shin D-h 2003).

A "Miserable Story of Animation"

The arduous task of creating *Hong Gil Dong* was captured in commercials for the film upon its release and by reminiscences by Shin Dong-hun and co-animators. One advertisement proclaimed, "125,300 pictures drawn for one year by 400 people. If one person did it, it would take 400 years." Shin took much delight in relating the hardships animators suffered in Korea's animation beginnings, occasionally punctuating his repertoire with the rhetorical question, "You ever hear such a miserable story of animation?" (1995). He said that Korean animation grew out of three individuals (himself, his wife, and his brother[2]), who knew next to nothing about the field, improvised techniques such as double exposure and shadow effect through repeated experimentation and what Shin had learned from his hobbies, scavenged expired wide film from the US Eighth Army's base and chemically erased it for reuse, and hand-made a camera copied from one at the army base (Shin D-h 1995). Added to this "miserable story," according to Shin, was that he lost "big money" on some projects, his explanation being, "I'm suitable to be an artist, not a business tycoon like some of my juniors." He was referring to Jung Wook, Nelson Shin, Yu Seong-woong, and Kim Dae-jung, all of whom had worked with Shin Dong-hun and later started their own major studios: Daiwon, AKOM, Shinwon, and Seyoung, respectively.

Others reiterated the extreme conditions animators endured in the initial stages of the industry, such as cels sticking together during the rainy season (Jung Wook 1995), colors separating in the drying process of the salvaged air force surveillance film (see Kim I 1995, 49; Jeong 1996, 98–99; Kim S-p 1996, 98–99), film that had been cut in half for economic purposes and strung on laundry lines with clothespins (Jeong 1996, 98–99), and unheated and uncooled workplaces that inconvenienced the workers and damaged cels and equipment (Im 1996, 97). Jung Wook (1995) elaborated:

> When we started, we had trouble with the cels. It was the rainy season, and the cels stuck together and were damaged. We restarted in September 1966 and finished in January 1967. We did 125,000 cels; the film was 70–80 minutes long. We had no good cameras. We saw an animation camera at the US Eighth Army [base], but it was not to be removed from the premises. So, our cameraman went there and measured the stand and came back and made one like it. We then bought a camera and modified it for animation. This was very hard to do.

AKOM president Nelson Shin (1996, 79) said that animators were not paid reasonable rates but nevertheless trudged on, believing that they were being paid to study animation on the job.

Hong Gil Dong's success prompted Segi to produce other features between 1968 and 1971 such as *Sonogong* and *Golden Iron Man* (*Hwanggŭm Chorin*) in 1968, and *Treasure Island* (*Bomulseom*) in 1969, all directed by Park Yeong-il; and *The Prince Hodong and the Princess Nangnang* (*Wangja Hodonggwa Nangnang Gongju*) in 1971, directed by Yong Yu-su. *Golden Iron Man* was modeled after the Japanese superhero television series *The Golden Bat* (Ōgon Batto). Most early features emanated from legends and folk stories, but each carried a unique characteristic. Each new film faced dwindling audiences, who were becoming attracted to television. Much information about these and other early animated features is severely tarnished by the exaggerated claims or faulty memories of those who recalled them. Thomas Giammarco (2006) points out inconsistences in the claimed production time of *Hong Gil Dong*, eight months to more than two years; the number of people who worked on the film, from 106 to 8,032; and number of tickets sold, from under one hundred thousand to nearly four times that number. Similarly, Kang Tae-woong's *Heungbu and Nolbu* was Korea's first stop-motion animation but certainly not "the world's first full-length stop motion" as advertised. Also misleading were claims that *The Golden Bat* was a Korean-Japanese coproduction, when in reality it was a Japanese television series.[3] The latter practice was not uncommon as Korean television stations tried to get around the long-held regulations banning Japanese cultural products.

Most early studios did not last long; often, their first animated film was their last because of high production costs and small audiences, the latter attributable to the general belief that animation was low culture, meant for children (Whang 1990, 207). The few companies that did well, such as Segi Productions, owner of a number of theaters, succeeded in backing animators because of their heavy reliance on offshore contracts for animated and live-action films, and importing, profits from both of which were plowed back into domestic production.

4.2. The very successful science fiction animated film *Robot Taekwon V*, directed by Kim Cheong-gi in 1976, revolved around two scientists—one determined to dominate the world, the other to prevent this from happening by engaging a robot into battle.

From the 1970s to the 1990s, Korean feature animation production was erratic, with sixty-two features released between 1976 and 1985 but none in 1970, 1972–1975, or 1987–1993. The peak year was 1985 with nine works, followed by 1979, 1980, 1983, and 1984, each with seven; 1978 with six; 1981 and 1982, five each; 1976, 1977, 1986, and 1997, three each; 1967, 1968, 1969, and 1994, two each; and 1971, one (Han C-w 1995, 86–87; Rho 1995; Whang 1990; Yi 1994, 3–7). Most were copies of Japanese television robot animation.[4] In fact, the years of the 1970s and 1980s that yielded large numbers of features benefited from the establishment of Korean television stations, which required programming to fill children's program schedules. Aware of the success of science fiction animation in Japan, especially after the TV series *Mazinger Z* was aired by the Munhwa Broadcasting Company in 1975, Korean television took up this genre, mostly copying Japanese features. A result was that seventeen of the twenty animated features made in the 1970s were science fiction. Their popularity showed in box office receipts. Extremely successful was Kim Cheong-gi's *Robot Taekwon V*, later involved in a plagiarism scandal that went to court. The Robot Taekwon V Corporation sued a toy importer for violating copyright; the toy company responded that *Robot Taekwon V* itself had been stolen from *Mazinger Z*. Forty-two years after the animated film was released, in 2018, a court ruled that there was a striking difference between the two films' major characters and fined the toy manufacturer for breach of copyright.

4.3. Ahn Hyun-dong, an early president of Daiwon Animation. Seoul, July 6, 1992. Photo by John A. Lent.

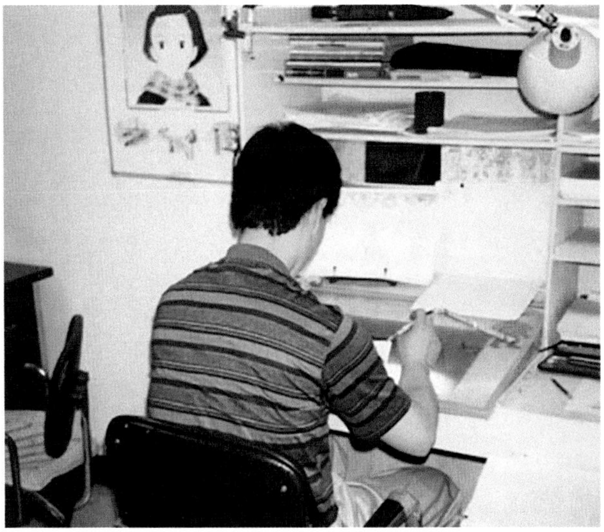

4.4. A checker at Daiwon Animation. Seoul, July 6, 1992. Photo by John A. Lent.

The prevalent, all-out copying was openly defiant of a 1945 government policy that banned the importation of all Japanese cultural products (Choi 1995, 147; see also Shin D-j 1994, 5). Obviously, the ban was not enforced. In 1980, the Korean authorities were able to slow down the making of Japanese-inspired robot animation with its Children's Protection Policy, which honed in on science fiction animation, calling it an "empty and meaningless illusion" for children (*Motion* 1997, 163). It is strange that the government had been lax in enforcing the 1945 ban of manga more aggressively, since it had been adverse to cartoons (most of which were Japanese) from at least 1967, when they were declared one of the six evils of Korean society, a phrase echoed by succeeding administrations.

As stated earlier, 1987 to 1993 were barren years for feature animation, one possible reason being that there was a shift of emphasis to televised series to satisfy the expected hordes of tourists coming to Seoul for the 1988 Olympics. Reasons given by Ahn Hyun-dong, president of Daiwon Animation, and researcher Kim Joon-yang are more likely: insufficient government support, tight censorship, lack of adult interest (Ahn 1992) because of the conventional thinking that animation is children's entertainment, and the expansion of new leisure activities such as professional sports, exhibitions, and amusement parks (Kim J-y 2006, 69). Kim further explains that the then-new military government wanted to divert attention away from the atrocities committed during the democratic uprising in Gwangju in 1980, while at the same time, a new technology, the VCR, allowed young people to see the latest Japanese animation through the pirate markets (Kim J-y 2006, 69–70).

Offshore Production

By 1992, about 100 to 110 animation companies existed in South Korea, according to Ahn (1992), whose Daiwon was the oldest (founded 1976) and largest. Most firms were in heavy competition to obtain North American and European clients; at the time, the production of those countries' animation was lucrative, bringing in US$50 to $60 million annually to the industry while producing a total of five hundred to six hundred episodes (Ahn 1992). In the case of Daiwon, Ahn said that 70 percent of its work was exported, 30 percent for domestic television and video. Daiwon and other of the largest ten companies began to switch to domestic production in the early 1990s, as they realized they could not compete with the cheaper labor of China and the Philippines, new entrants to offshore production. Daiwon also diversified into the infant industry of merchandising while beefing up its manhwa division (Ahn 1992, 1994). Its other media holdings included Daiwon Movie Company (1988), Daiwon Home Video Company (1989), and Daiwon Toy Company (1992).

To back up a bit, although Nelson Shin is often credited with introducing animation subcontracting to Korea in the late 1970s, others preceded him. In 1966, the Tongyang Broadcasting Company subcontracted for the Japanese animation show *The Golden Bat* (Jung Wook 1994, 5), and, according to Whang Seong-gil (1990, 207), International (Gukje) Art Production, under the wing of Jeong Yoon-song and Kim Tayk, did coloring work for US animators in 1969. With Korean American Steven (Sangho) Hahn, Kim Tayk started Dongseo Dongwha (East West Animation) in 1973 and was doing work for Ralph Bakshi. This studio served as a major player in the formative years of Korean subcontracting (Vallas 1997). Kim Tayk (1995) said that he made a two-minute demonstration film of *Felix the Cat* in 1973, after which Hahn approached him to work together. They produced portions of US films and later established Hanho Heung-Up, merging it with Dongseo Dongwha, which grew into a firm of five hundred employees (Kim Tayk 1995).

4.5. Nelson Shin (left), largely responsible for South Korea's emergence as one of the world's three largest producers of offshore animation. With John A. Lent and Jean-Louis Bompoint. AKOM Studio. Seoul, August 16, 1995. Photo courtesy of John A. Lent.

Actually, to understand the background of offshore animation production, one must go back to the days of animators Walt Disney, Fred Quimby, the Fleischer brothers, and Leon Schlesinger in the United States and recall the phrase that tied them to what occurred in Asia later in the twentieth century, namely "labor exploitation." From the 1920s through early 1940s, salaries at these studios and others were among the lowest in the entire film industry; at Fleischer in the 1930s, wages ranged from US$12 to $22 per forty-four-hour week, and at Disney they were comparable. Hours of work and footage quotas were staggering; talented animators were "utterly marginalized," endured "effronteries," and were treated vindictively, labeled as communists, and fired for attempting to unionize, as at Disney in the 1940s; and all the credit for the highly creative animation produced was stolen by these studio heads (Klein 1993, 93, 97, 183).

Different studios, predominantly Fleischer, Disney, Schlesinger, Warner, and MGM, either faced labor strikes or narrowly escaped them in the 1930s and 1940s, and in the 1950s, the US animation industry faced problems such as job insecurity, drops in play dates, skyrocketing production and exhibition costs, and marked changes in public habits because of consumer marketing (Lent 1998, 242). In fact, the entire film industry suffered, as many industries did in the 1960s, because of the collapse of movie chains and the gathering strength of television. The huge studios such as MGM closed their animation sections or rereleased old cartoons to cut corners.

Seeking inexpensive and union-free labor, US studios began to commission Japanese firms to carry out production functions, these being drawing the cels, coloring by hand, inking, painting, and doing camera work. Both the preproduction (script preparation, storyboarding, timing, and spacing) and postproduction (film editing, color timing, and sound) were accomplished stateside. In the 1970s, Taiwan, South Korea, and Australia became offshore animation producers.

US animation was first done in South Korea in 1969, followed by animation for a Japanese company, Golden Bell, in 1973. As Koreans learned US animation skills, they began to set up studios, the first of which was Daiwon, which was established in January 1974 by Jung Wook mainly to service Japanese studios. Claiming that his studio, Dongseo, was one of the rare ones dealing with US companies, Kim Tayk (1995) said that by the late 1970s he was processing first, theater, and then television animation for the Americans. A third pioneer in this area was Nelson Shin, who held many important contracts, including one for producing *The Simpsons* television show for nearly its entire long lifetime, and others with a North Korean studio and Marvel Productions. Shin (1995) told about how he came to work for Marvel. In 1980–1981, he met

4.6. Workers at AKOM Studio computer stations. Seoul, August 16, 1995. Photo by John A. Lent.

with Marvel executives, who inquired if he could produce a seventy-five-minute feature within two months. Shin told them that he would work it out upon returning to Seoul. He then hired "almost all the Korean animators" and finished the production within ten weeks, after which a flood of US business flowed his way.

To provide some insight about the scale of Korea's offshore animation operations at their near peak in the mid-1990s, I provide some data:

> Most animation workstations in Asia are, in fact, staffed by young people, many of whom are women. At Seoul Movie Co., Ltd., for example, 80% of the 300 employees are women, ostensibly hired for their "delicate touch"; their age range is from early 20s to 40s (Jun Chang-rok 1995). About 35% of the 500 employees at Seoul's Hanho Heung-Up Co. are in their 20s. Similar characteristics are found in the other offshore animation factories. At South Korea's Daiwon, 90% of all assistant animators are in their 20s, having joined the company directly from high school. (Lent 1998, 247)

Animators' wages were competitive with other sectors of the economy. At one time, according to the head of Hanho Heung-Up, animator wages exceeded those of other professions (Kim S-k 1995); at the Seoul Movie Company, salaries ranged from US$1,000 per month for the lowest-level colorist and cel cleaner to $4,000 to $13,000 monthly for top-notch animators (Jun 1995). In almost all cases, medical insurance and other fringe benefits were provided.

However, the whole scenario changed rather abruptly. A close observer of, and pioneer in, offshore animation, Nelson Shin (2003), said that in 1997, the US television networks ABC, CBS, and NBC reduced work orders to South Korea for their Saturday morning fare until they completely stopped in 1999. Disney, Dreamworks, and Warner Brothers also cut the quantity of orders after 1999, as well as limiting payment rates. Shin (2003) provided details:

> Before, US studios and networks paid good money, but not now. Warner Brothers used to pay US$200,000 for a show. Now, it is $100,000 or so. Digital people from Korea, Japan, the Philippines, India, all over, are targeting Los Angeles, trying to get subcontracts. From 1999, small studios sent emails and faxes to the US, offering to do their animation at half price. Competition is worse now and there is less work.

Shin put some of the blame for this deteriorating situation at the feet of foreign studio heads, saying: "The generations have changed, and younger people are in the head offices. They are not making money; they are spending money with much waste. A lot of the animation work in the world has shrunk." He said that his studio, AKOM, produced twenty half-hour shows a month in 1996, but by 2003 were given only five or six a month to do. Larger studios maintained work schedules by doing more domestic animation, Shin (2003) said, adding that some of the smaller ones had no work and made virtually no money; they survived by registering with the Korean Animation Producers Association and obtaining a venture enterprise certificate with which they received a government subsidy.

The precarious situation that some Korean animators found themselves in is illustrated by the career of Ahn Jae-hun. After completing his military service, Ahn joined a Korean animation company doing Japanese productions. A question that continually nagged him for years while drawing Japanese stories was, "Why are there no animated films that reflect Korean scenery or lives?" One day, he decided to do something to remedy this; he quit his job and, with his wife, started Studio Meditation with a Pencil—"pencil" because it is his preferred work tool. Ahn, at times, found it difficult to make ends meet and several times thought about closing his studio, but, as he said, he "unexpectedly would receive support and news about the success of animation deals done" (Park J-w 2020).

4.7. Some of the characters for which the Seoul Movie Company was responsible. Seoul, August 14, 1995. Photo by John A. Lent.

A Government-Inspired Change of Direction

The government's recognition of animation's economic value provided incentives in the mid-1990s, spurring studios to increasingly shift to domestic production. Even before this stimulus, Daiwon devoted 40 percent of its production to domestic shows, and the Seoul Movie Company already had a large domestic schedule. Other large producers of foreign animation such as AKOM and Hanho Heung-Up also began to take on more domestic work. Of course, a balance had to be maintained, as related by Jun Chang-rok (1995), who saw close links between domestic and foreign animation in that his studio, the Seoul Movie Company, had to depend on commercial revenue from foreign clients to pursue artistic domestic films and series.

Both Ahn and political cartoonist-cum-animator Park Jae-dong (born 1952) saw a brighter future for animation with the 1995 launch of cable television (with one channel devoted to cartoons) and with the prospect of strengthening the software skills of animators (Park J-d 1994). Three major problems of Korean animation that Ahn listed in 1992—lack of government support, "too tough" regulations by the ethics commission, and a lack of appreciation for animation—were about to be remedied by a never-seen-before (at least in Asia) government-supported thrust to upgrade the animation and comics industries and professions.

The propellant for this turnaround was a report of the Visual Products Development People's Committee (Yongsang Baljeon Mingan Hyeopeuiwhoe), set up in 1994, to look into the development and export of Korean visual products; to its surprise, the committee found that 98 percent of all visual products exported was animation. The government wasted no time in taking action to prime animation in 1995 by changing the industry's status from service to manufacturing, which triggered a 20 percent tax break (Shin H-s 1995); in effect, the government altered South Korea's economic policy by retreating from direct involvement in strategic industries such as electronics and automobiles in order to uphold and support cultural industries.

A Ministry of Culture, Sports, and Tourism official gave the rationale for this sudden about-face on the part of the government:

> The cartoon industry is a high value–added business which heavily affects other businesses such as video and computer games, records, character products, advertisements, and even tourism. In addition, it contributes to the promotion of Korean culture abroad.
>
> If drastic action is not taken, the domestic industry may fall to the state of permanent subcontractor for foreign major companies and eventually drop out of the competition altogether, just like the shoe and textile industries in the 1980s. (Quoted in Shin H-s 1995)

In the same year, government funding led to the establishment of the Seoul International Cartoon and Animation Festival (SICAF) and the annual Korean Animated Film Awards.[5] SICAF's goals to elevate the exposure of and bring prestige to Korean animation were met as 2,500 works from thirty-seven countries were screened or exhibited, nineteen prizes were awarded to Korean animators, and an international conference was held. More than 150,000 paying visitors attended the week-long event, comparable to

4.8. Jury members of the first SICAF, August 13, 1995. Left to right: Kim Seok-ki, Choi Min, John A. Lent, Shin Dong-hun, Jessica Langford, Park Se-hyung, and Im Kwon-taek. Courtesy of SICAF.

the largest comic-cons in the world. Other swift results of the government largesse were the release of three feature-length animated films in 1995; the creation of a twenty-four-hour cartoon cable network, Tooniverse, in late 1994; the establishment of other festivals; and the advancement of animation and comics education and training.

The development of educational programs in animation was extraordinarily swift after the government's initial commitment. From 1989 to 1994, animation and comics teaching only existed at Kongju National Junior College; by 1999, the number of universities, colleges, and institutes offering such curricula numbered nearly 20, and a few years later there were 156. Some were two-year programs, others four-year. There were even six high schools with full curricula in animation, something that is still unique anywhere in the world. These came about because of an amendment to a 1997 education law that permitted the establishment of specialized high schools. One high school, Korea Animation High School, had not only state-of-the-art facilities for its departments of cartoon production, animation production, film and directing, and computer game production but also its own dormitory for non-Seoul students.

The university and college programs carried a variety of names reflective of the different departments and schools they were under: the Hanseo University Department of Motion Graphics specialized in creative, experimental animation; Chungkang College of Cultural Industries had departments of comics and cartoon creation and animation; and Kyungmin College supported departments of digital cartoons and of animation in its Division of Design. There were departments and divisions with names associated with interactive multimedia arts in animation (Kyonggi University), design and animation (Kaywon School of Arts and Design), cartoon art (Kongju National University and Sonchon National University), animation design (Kongju Community Arts College), visual design/fancy and animation (Dongju College), visual multimedia design and 3-D animation (Byuksung College), cartoon/game notions graphics (Yewon Arts University), advanced imaging science, multimedia, and film (a graduate school at Chung-Ang University), and media design with a major in "epitome of animation" (Hansung University).

The names indicate the broad definition given to animation and the range of jobs graduates were likely to seek. Most graduates entered the workforce in an area of digital graphics, with few going directly into animation. Others were what Kim Byung-heon (2003) termed "underground" animators who did not pursue animation for commercial reasons; "they just like animation and don't expect to make money from it." As the amount of work for overseas clients dwindled, the animation industry became too small to absorb the large number of graduates yearly. Over the years, critics have pointed out the "wastage" of talent (Kim J-j 2003) and the improperly trained personnel whom animation programs had spawned. Others complained that the courses taught the mechanics (computer work) but not storytelling, character development, and the like (Park J-d 2003). Sunny Hong, a company CEO and graduate of an animation school, said: "In this stage of the industry's life, we need planning, development, and marketing people. There are no teachers of these areas; animation professors majored in fine arts and thus, Korean schools are only teaching drawing" (Hong 2003).

A second metamorphosis occurred in 1997, when the three major US television networks quit hiring out work to Korea and after the economic debacle that set back Korea and most of Asia. The government not only protected animation but also accelerated its growth, supporting and promoting it as a national strategic industry. Animation was listed as part of culture contents technology, one of six designated high-tech fields for the future. To coordinate cultural contents, the Korea Creative Content Agency

(KOCCA) was created in 1997 to handle animation, comics, film, television, music, and games. KOCCA had at its disposal US$10 million for animation's advancement and after 2002 began giving Star Project Awards yearly to support individual works with global promise. As an example, after earning the KOCCA honor in 2002, *Mask Man* was produced as thirty-nine half-hour episodes and was built into a substantial licensing program geared globally (Gurman 2006, 36).

Local governments and the private sector took notice of the national administration's financial support and got involved with animation. Seoul authorities fully supported the multipurpose Seoul Animation Center (SAC), outfitted with its training academy, museum, libraries, theaters, exhibition halls, festivals, and incentive awards programs for animators, and they pledged US$1 million annually for a decade to SICAF.[6]

Started in May 1999, the SAC had originated in a Seoul city government master plan two years earlier designed to help those software industries (animation included) that remained based in the city, as conventional companies moved out of the city. In 1998, the city government set up a foundation, the Seoul Industry Promotion Foundation, with five divisions, one of which was animation, to address the issue of industries abandoning Seoul. The SAC has maintained a number of facilities and events that are open to the public in addition to allocating funds to animators, cartoonists, and comic book writers ranging from twenty million won (US$16,666 at the time) to five million won ($4,166) (Kim J-j 2003). Director Kim Jae-jung (2003) delineated other services offered by the center: contests and awards; the Cartoon and Animation Academy, with courses in production and scriptwriting; at least three foreign animation festivals yearly with abundant screenings, exhibitions, workshops, and seminars; the Cartoon and Animation Information Center, containing two comic book and one video library with a mini-theater and viewing room; and the Seoul Cartoon Museum, with an exhibition room, Hall of Fame, and Cartoon History Center. The center was involved in other activities, Kim said, such as restoring cartoon classics, providing six production and two digital editing rooms for animators' use, offering offices to industry associates (e.g., the Korean Character Business Association), participating in international festivals such as Angoulême, Annecy, Hiroshima, Ottawa, and Zagreb, running an animation cinematheque, and renting theaters and exhibition halls inexpensively to the public (Kim J-j 2003).

In some instances, government awards were given directly to animation projects, examples being export promotion merits from the Ministry of Commerce and Industry and central government prizes for the ten best characters. At other times, the authorities channeled funds or awards through groups such as the SAC, KOCCA, the Korean Film Commission, and the Korea IT Industry Promotion Agency (KIPA). Kim Jae-jung (2003) explained the procedure at the SAC:

> The center is given government money to award cartoonists and senior writers. We announce our programs through our website and other publicity channels. Then filmmakers apply. We set up a jury board; the candidates go through a series of interviews, and we select a limited number of winners. We receive proposals for prework and select the superior projects. The jury gives proposals points, and funds are given to winners in installments. The last installment is given when the work is finished and screened. Although the government does not set stipulations, it does expect the animation to be a promising enterprise.

Asked how the animation community convinced the government to support animation so generously, Kim replied:

> The people who convinced the government of the importance of animation first studied the industry, knowing that government people are always on the lookout for programs and policies to support Korea. The government is easily convinced by success stories and was much impressed by Disney earning millions and millions of dollars from just one feature release. Authorities thought in terms of one Disney film being the same as maybe ten thousand Hyundai sedan cars.

Besides Seoul, the cities of Bucheon and Chuncheon also joined the national effort to elevate the status of animation and comics, both offering office rent and production costs

4.9. Statue of Hong Gil Dong at the Bucheon Cartoon Information Center, Bucheon. Photo by John A. Lent.

4.10. Poster for the animated film *Red Hawk*, released by Daiwon in 1995, a banner year for animated features after the barren period from 1987 to 1993.

to animation studios in their provinces. Bucheon actually rivaled Seoul as the country's comics city, going so far as to label itself "the best city of cartoons and film in Asia," with the goal of being the "cartoon city of the world" in its promotional material. The city is decked out with cartoon-themed streets (e.g., Street of Dooly) and a cartoon character park. By the 2000s, other locations, such as the city of Gwangju in southwestern Korea and the province of Chungnam, were engaged in the animation industry. Gwangju began funding computer-generated imagery in 2006 and in short order had a lineup of projects. In 2008, the Los Angeles talent management company Gotham partnered with Chungnam Province, a government-owned media center, and various Korean corporations and private investors to finance a series of animated features (Verrier 2008).

Despite the strong government initiatives, the chaebols kept their distance from animation production, with a few exceptions. In 1996, Cheil Foods and Chemicals, a split of the mammoth Samsung, bought 11 percent of Dreamworks SKG for US$300 million, confident enough about Korean animation to set up the first multiplexes in the country and to use revenue from the distribution of US films in Asia to produce domestic fare. Within months, Cheil established J Communications, an animation, film, and television company capable of making one or two animated features yearly (McDougall 1996, 20–27). A year later, another rare chaebol involvement in animation occurred when a consortium of the conglomerate SsangYong Group, Cine Dream, and Pilgrim Art Movie funded Park Hyeong-in's *The Last Warrior Ryan* (*Jeonsa Ryan*).

In the mid-1990s, after a void in production from 1987 to 1993, feature-length animation had a rejuvenation, no doubt because of the government stimulus. From 1994 to 1997, ten works were released, among them *Blue Seagull* (1994), Korea's first animated feature targeting adults; *Hong Gil Dong Returned* by the Stone Flower Company; *Red Hawk* by Daiwon; and *Hungry Best 5* by Yung Productions, all in 1995; and *Armageddon* by the Armageddon Committee and *Queen Esther*, both in 1996. *Hong Gil Dong Returned* was a remake of Shin Dong-hun's pioneer film, but this

4.11. *Hungry Best 5* (1995) was initially a strip in the *Daily Sports*. The film was severely criticized for being a copy of Japan's *Slam Dunk*. Courtesy of Nelson Shin and *Animatoon*.

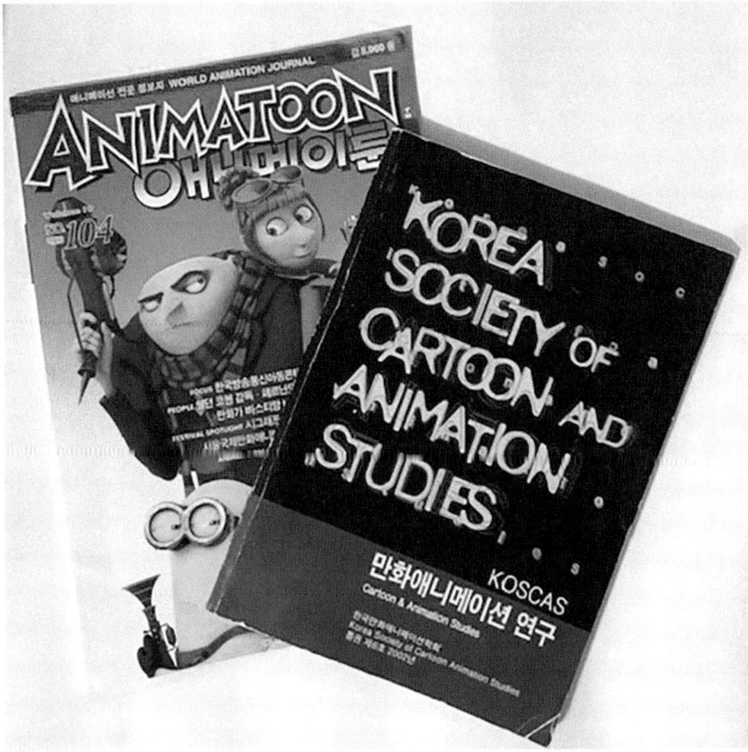

4.12. Two long-running animation periodicals: *Animatoon*, vol. 19, no. 104, 2013; and *Cartoon and Animation Studies*, no. 6, 2002. Courtesy of Nelson Shin.

time with a Japanese appearance that Nelson Shin (1995) characterized as "Samurai *Hong Gil Dong*"; *Red Hawk* was based on a manhwa series published in *Sonyeon Champ* that tells of two gang member brothers, one of whom (Red Hawk) must kill the other when the gang turns him into a weapon of death; and *Hungry Best 5*, first carried in the *Daily Sports*, was a copy of Japan's *Slam Dunk*, for which it was criticized. *Armageddon*, funded by a consortium of ten investors, did not meet expectations, mainly because of poor storytelling and inept adaptation from its comic book format. Three features of 1997 heeded the criticism heaped on their predecessors, but nevertheless they, too, failed miserably at the box office. The one successful film was *Baby Dinosaur Dooly: Adventure of Ice Planet* (1996), directed by Kim Su-jung, which benefited from a twelve-year built-in audience with its comic book and television show (*Animatoon* 1996, 86).

With such poor financial performances at the theaters, directors found it difficult to attract investors, and at least one toyed with alternative means to obtain funds. Park Jae-dong encouraged audiences to participate in the making of his film by purchasing cel drawings and paying for movie tickets in advance. Innovative as they were, Park's efforts fell far short of his goals (*Motion* 1997, 172).

The professionalization of animation proceeded at breakneck speed after 1997, with the establishment of animation-oriented agencies in three ministries in the national government, a number of professional associations, and the aforementioned 156 animation and cartoon schools and departments. Kim Jae-jung, the SAC's director, explained that agencies are of government initiation, while associations come from the industry (Kim J-j 2003). By 2003, Korea was inundated by associations and agencies, which Kim seemed hard pressed to explain, at one point saying, "It is a political thing," and at another, "That's Korean; people are very, very active" (2003). Animation agencies were located in the Ministry of Culture, Sports, and Tourism, the Ministry of Energy and Resources, and the Ministry of Telecommunications, a unique situation in itself. Character content (mainly licensing) was represented by KOCCA, registered in the Ministry of Energy and Resources and two other agencies in the Ministry of Culture, Sports, and Tourism (Kim J-j 2003). Among associations at the turn of the century were the Korean

Animation Producers Association (since December 1994), which dealt with studios; the Korean Animation Artists Association (since 1995), made up of individual animators; the Korean Alliance of Cartoonists and the Korea Cartoonists Association, consisting of junior and senior cartoonists, respectively; the Korean Society of Cartoon and Animation Studies (KSCAS); and others encompassing comic books. Kim Jae-jung (2003) said that an association of five of the major associations for animation was contemplated in 2003, a kind of governing/monitoring umbrella group.

Also coming out of the 1990s were the first animation periodicals. *Animatoon* appeared in time for distribution at the first SICAF in 1995. It was founded, published, and edited by Nelson Shin, mostly out of his own pocket. The full-color glossy quarterly features interviews, company profiles, technical information, film critiques, and news about Korean and other countries' animation. Some articles are in English. A second professional magazine, *Motion*, was published by Dongwha Publishing beginning in 1997. Besides these, there is the annual *Cartoon and Animation Studies*, a scholarly journal founded in 1997 by the Korean Society of Cartoon and Animation Studies.

The government's heavy subsidization; a quota system that was first enacted in 1998 by the Ministry of Culture, Sports, and Tourism and the Association of Broadcasting Systems requiring that 35 percent of all television animation be Korean (shortly afterward upped to 50 percent); and the downsizing of the overseas animation industry, directed most of the country's two hundred studios to switch to making Korean television series and to diversify their services.

Perhaps other reasons for the turn to television animation production had to do with the fact that feature films were very costly and that they had been flopping at the box office, some miserably, because of their imitation of Japanese anime, lack of a Korean identity, shoddy production (e.g., poorly drawn pictures, lack of synchronization of sound and movement, and unskilled colorization), and poor storytelling, the latter emphasized by Nelson Shin (2003) and Park Jae-dong (2003).[7]

Park Jae-dong regularly harped about the storytelling problem in Korean comics art, even declaring successful features such as *Hammerboy* and *Wonderful Days* to be weak stories. After telling of his own failure to come up with a good animation "scenario" after years of writing, Park said:

> I think the most important point of animation (and comics) is the story. In Korea, every part of animation grew up, but we still have to meet the problem of the story. We need writers with heart, who love people; this helps stories.
>
> Many Korean comics do not have varied themes. Themes must be spread to different topics—food, sports, science, plants, animals, stars, history, and so on. They must be spread to different generations—for children and older people. (Park J-d 2003)

Korea's first television animator was the Korea Broadcasting System (KBS) with *Wandering Kkachi* (*Tteodoro Kkachi*) in 1987; in the same year, KBS was joined by the Munhwa Broadcasting Company, then Tooniverse in 1995 and the Seoul Broadcasting System (SBS) in 1996. After *Wandering Kkachi*'s debut in 1987, forty other animated television programs sprouted from the stations in the next six years, altogether totaling 6,455 minutes. KBS led the pack, making 6,020 minutes of local animation from 1990 to 1997, or 74.2 percent of the nation's total during those seven years. Munhwa suspended making animation for about four years in 1993, after realizing that one of its series was more expensive to make and less popular with audiences than the station's drama shows. Despite this growth of domestically made television animation, at the turn of the century, 80 to 90 percent of all TV animation still was imported from Japan, the United States, and Europe. Competing with the imported (mostly Japanese) shows loomed large mainly because local producers could not match the low prices of these programs (Han S-h 1995). It was not a difficult decision to make—import works at US$2,500 to $6,250, or make them at $75,000 to $125,000 (N. Shin 1995).

Animation in Korea experienced a major reversal of operation because of the government's actions. Between 1999 and 2003, animation exports (mostly outsourced work) dropped from $160 million to $77.3 million, while

4.13. *Wandering Kkachi* (1987), the Korea Broadcasting System's first television animation, dealt with a young boy's difficulties accepting his stepmother and stepsister and his pleasure becoming a star baseball player.

4.14. *My Beautiful Girl Mari*, credited to Lee Sung-gang, was awarded the 2002 Grand Prix at Annecy.

exports of original Korean animation rose from 3 percent to 35 percent. Between 2000 and the first half of 2002, the share of subcontracting of total animation revenue decreased from 84.4 percent to 49.5 percent, while that of original productions (including coproductions) increased from 13.5 percent to 49.4 percent. (For more on animation subcontracting in Asia, see Lent 1998, 239–54.)

One of the reasons that Korea's homemade animation began to find an international market was the government and the profession having Korean animation screened and viewed at international festivals and competitions, and providing opportunities for foreign animators and industry officials to participate in SICAF seminars and similar Korean events. As examples, KOCCA sent forty Korean animation companies to the 2003 Cannes Film Festival, while the one-hundred-member Korean Independent Producers Association sent ten studios to the Korean Pavilion at Cannes (*Animation* 2003, 22). The same year, an animation retrospective made up part of a KOCCA-sponsored Korean comics exposition at the Angoulême International Comics Festival. Korea's *My Beautiful Girl Mari* (*Mari Iyagi*) won the grand prize for best animation at the Annecy International Animation Film Festival, while the stop-motion *Doggy Poo* took the Best Pilot Prize at the 2003 Tokyo International Anime Fair.

For years, the annual Seoul International Cartoon and Animation Festival set aside one large area for Korean and other countries' (particularly Chinese and Japanese) companies and centers to promote existing and planned shows and to seek foreign sales or production partners. In the 2003 *SICAF Promotion Plan Directory*, many listed studios sought to sell merchandising copyrights and licenses, promote investment, find business partners, "open up the China market," or "target the world market." As a result of these endeavors, Korean animation gradually found a small niche in the international market and partnered with some foreign producers and distributors.

Coproductions between different Korean companies and foreign studios became a common method to cut production costs, while upgrading the skills of Korean animators. All types of partnerships were put together involving Korean and/or foreign broadcasting systems, governmental and educational institutions, animation studios, toy and game developers, and digital graphics companies. In 2003–2004, Korea helped spearhead the establishment of a Northeast Asia consortium with Japan and China.[8] Together, they explored possibilities of working together in animation, such as the joint production and distribution of at least eight television series, the trading of festival exhibition space, and the extension of meetings for future cooperation. Animators from the three countries initially took pleasure in stating that all operational decisions and procedures and the division of credits had been executed democratically, allowing each company in these arrangements to reach its full potential.[9] The continuation of consortium talks seemed to peter out, perhaps because the organizers had no answer for a question Nelson Shin posed: "Where will the money come from?" (2003).

Independent Animation

A type of revolution that involved animation erupted in the Korean art world of the 1980s. Rebelling against the "oppressive and standardized Korean culture," small cultural groups made up of individuals whose diverse views could be traced back to their school days resisted norms of the existing art world and searched for alternatives. Song Seung-min, in an excellent overview of this movement relative to animation, termed it *min-joong* art (people's art), through which "artists criticized the existing estheticism and academicism in the art world, and took up the restoration of form as their theme. They emphasized strong ideological characteristics and direct contact with the populace through hanging pictures, woodblock prints, and folk paintings in public space" (Song S-m 2005, 352). *Min-joong* artists recognized the artistic importance of animation, not just its commercial value, and wanted to "resist Western cultures as well as the oppressive domestic political structure. . . . [T]he more important premise on which early Korean independent film was rooted was its expression of the depressing socio-political state. Korean independent films produced in this tumultuous period were accordingly rhetorical and inflammatory in their subjects" (Song S-m 2005, 352).

Many of the traits of *min-joong* art fall in line with those of independent filmmakers in China, Southeast Asia, and elsewhere; the underground comix movement of the 1960s and 1970s in the United States and parts of Europe; and later, the alternative comics of Indonesia, and the social conscientization thoughts expounded by the likes of Paulo Freire and E. F. Schumacher.

The first Korean independent animators were students who had been exposed to Western independent animation and, out of necessity, used rudimentary production techniques. For example, to make *The Screen* (*Bang Chung Mang*) in 1983, Choi Jung-hyun drew pictures on paper with pen and pencil and shot the individual sheets in 16 mm. The less-than-six-minutes film captured the chaos caused by demonstrators at a university in the 1980s. Choi followed up with *The Scar* (*Sangheun*) in 1984, expressing people's anger about the partitioning of Korea and the oppression of the superpowers (Seoul Cinema Group 1996, 190). Choi's pioneering work stirred artistic and social activist groups such as Labor News Production and Nemorami, and individuals such as Lee Yong-bae, Chon Seung-il, Park Myung-chon, and Lee Kwon-yong, to use animation to get their sentiments across and/or to bring awareness to certain social issues. Labor News Production produced the series *Laborer News*, into which they inserted the animation *Go, Mr. Strike* (*ChoolDong, ChongPaup-Gun*); there was also other labor movement animation such as *Now, We Are United* (*Ejeneun Hanada*) as well as unification propaganda animation such as *We Have to Meet* (*Urineun Mannaya Handa*). The art majors group at Hongik University, Nemorami, differed in its approach to animation, using diverse content and techniques, as Song Seung-min stated:

> [They] adopted refined and metaphorical expression even when dealing with social subjects. Their interests were aesthetical experimentation. . . . Most of the other contemporary independent animation artists strove to recover Korean sentiments and aesthetic consciousness. . . . However, in the cases of *Alice in Wonderland* [by Park Myung-chon] and *Badman*

4.15. *Dooly the Little Dinosaur*.

4.16. *Pororo the Little Penguin*, an eight-season television series that ran between 2003 and 2021, told about a penguin and his animal friends, the travails they faced, and the lessons they learned from them.

[by Lee Kwon-yong], these works, from the very first, start with a motif taken from a Western novel or movie. (2005, 356)

Entering the twenty-first century, Korean independent animation, to Song's thinking, was viewed as a stage preceding profit-making commercial animation; it had lost its way, was confused, and lacked its own identity and methodology (Song S-m 2005, 357).

The Twenty-First Century

Although the government had built a superstructure to support animation and comics, some shorts and features won international awards, new legislation favored the industry (i.e., the television quota system), and production shifted from overseas to domestic, box office success was elusive.

A few features and television series turned a profit in the late twentieth and early twenty-first centuries, largely on their brand value. For example, *Dooly the Little Dinosaur*, a megahit television show created by Kim Su-jung in 1987, made much of its profit when Kim started a company in 1995 and entered the character design industry. As of 2018, *Dooly the Little Dinosaur*'s related market had brought in US$1.7 to $2.7 million. The brand value of *Pororo the Little Penguin* (*Ppongpporong Ppororo*), which began on EBS, was worth the equivalent of $789.76 million in 2017.

Pororo the Little Penguin, a character often called "the president of children," amassed an unmatched audience globally for a Korean animated television series; it was aired in at least 127 countries between 2003 and 2021, spawned a theme park in Seoul, promoted much merchandise (everything from chopsticks and stick-on bandages to coffee mugs and cell phones), and boosted Iconix, the company that produced it, from 6 employees at its opening in 2001 to 160 by 2011 (Jung H-w 2011). In mid-2011, *Pororo the Little Penguin* was the subject of a political controversy when it was revealed that part of the animation was made

4.17. Poster for *Leafie, a Hen into the Wild* (2011), an animated feature megahit that broke the Korean box office record for most viewers, won awards abroad, and was viewed in at least nine countries.

in North Korea. For a while, there was concern that the United States would ban the showing of *Pororo*, but in July 2011, US Treasury officials consented to its importation (Park J-m 2011; Lee T-h 2011).

Strictly based on box office receipts, many quality animated films failed during this period. Among them were *My Beautiful Girl Mari* (*Mari Iyagi*) (2002) and *Oseam* (2003), both Grand Prix winners at Annecy; *Wonderful Days* (*Wondop ul Teiju*, aka *Sky Blue*) (2003), the then–largest budget production; *Flying Pig Pirate Mateo* (2004), a collaborated work of Korea, the United States, and Japan; *Life Is Cool* (2008), the first Korean full-length animated film to use rotoscoping; and *Empress Chung* (2005), produced in North and South Korea, and the first film released simultaneously in both countries.

Director Nelson Shin took great pains to perfect *Empress Chung*, spending eight years—three and a half in preproduction—working on it, using up a budget of US$6.5 million, and introducing special features, for example, recording characters' voices in both North and South Korea because of dialect differences. After its opening weekend, when it grossed a mere US$140,000, *Empress Chung* failed to get an international theatrical release, except for a few European screenings, or a home media release (Wikipedia n.d.).

Various reasons might be ventured for the box office shortfall, all of which had been heard in Korea and other Asian countries before: inroads into theater attendance made first by television and then by the internet and other new information technology; the dominance of American and Japanese animation; the continuation of the long worn-out belief that animation is a low-status medium meant for children; "the weak public awareness of Korean animation" (Kalbi 2017); and, less often mentioned, the shortcomings of local animation with respect to technology, character design, storytelling, and marketing. The "weak public awareness" reason is difficult to understand for the same reasons mentioned in chapter 3, countering cartoonists' complaint that the profession does not receive respect or prestige. Taking liberally from the Korean Digital Content 2002 report published by the Korea IT Industry Promotion Agency, Hyun Daiwon (2004, 331–39) gave his reasons why computer-generated animation seldom succeeded at that time. Hyun, then chair of the Digital Content Division of Korean IT New Growth Engines, detailed the problems as insufficient funds; not maximizing the worth of content by spinning it off into games, film, TV, goods, and other by-products; not taking full advantage of festivals and other promotional opportunities (Hyun 2004, 335); poor storytelling and low quality of design; and impediments to exporting, particularly to the United States, brought on by a "lack of smooth communication, as cultural and linguistic barriers get in the way" (338). Though making strides, Korean animation is relatively young in the area of marketing. For example, the producer of *Wonderful Days* acknowledged that the film was marketed poorly, being too difficult for children and targeted to teens without knowing what they like (Russell 2003). Sunny Hong emphatically said that Korean producers are "small, uneducated, have no marketing instruction; they are naive, innocent" (2003).

4.18. *Swimming to the Sea* (2012), a 3-D animated feature about two fish living in a sushi restaurant tank—one desperately attempting to escape, the other struggling to stay alive.

Some of these deficiencies seemed to be partially addressed by the 2010s. Animated features and television series improved their storylines, honing in on Korean values and traits; they concentrated heavily on preproduction, extended themselves into the merchandising and mobile game industries, and spent more time on "methodological marketing strategies (Kalbi 2017). Two resulting box office successes in 2011 were *Leafie, a Hen into the Wild* (*Madangeul Naon Amtak*) and *The King of Pigs* (*Dwaejiui Wang*). *Leafie, a Hen into the Wild* became the highest-grossing domestic animated feature in South Korean history, selling more than 2.2 million tickets, while receiving accolades abroad. The film, based on a popular children's book by Hwang Sun-mi, revolves around a hen who "escapes into the wild, hatches a duck's egg, and becomes the ensuing duckling's adoptive mother" (Witiw 2021). *The King of Pigs* is a thriller directed by Yeun Sang-ho (who later directed the animated zombie film *Seoul Station*); the storyline follows two middle school classmates who retrack their gloomy youth, when they both were bullied and sexually harassed (C. Lee 2011).

The following year, the annual publication *Korean Cinema* showcased two animated features—the 3-D film *Swimming to the Sea* (*Padak* or *Padakpadak*), which tells of two fish living in a Korean sushi restaurant tank, an ocean mackerel bent on escaping and her nemesis, a flatfish, struggling to stay alive as fellow tank occupants die (Korean Film Council 2012, 241); and *The Dearest* (*Eun Sil-i*), about the guilt and rage two friends feel when they learn that a mentally challenged childhood friend had been the plaything of the village and died while giving birth (242). There were two animated features in 2013 also: *The Fake* (*Saibi*), Yeun Sang-ho's fourth animated film, which satirizes organized religion, portraying a church minister who scams people in the face of a forecasted flood (Korean Film Council 2013, 73); and *Approved for Adoption* (*Pibusaek: Kkul*), an animated documentary partially based on the adoption experiences of the film's director, Jung Henin (41).

The year 2014 ushered in a significant growth of Korean animated features, both in the number made (eight) and the average length of the films (approximately eighty-five minutes). The plots were outerworldly, otherworldly, and not realistic. The fantasy *Ghost Messenger* (*Goseuteu Mesinjeo*) features a ghost returning to life who gets trapped in his own cell phone (Korean Film Council 2014, 79); *T-Pang Rescue* (*Ttwi-ttwi-ppang-ppang Gujodae Misyeon: Dungdung-i-reul Guhara!*) tells of the "best rescue team in town" and its struggle to find a baby bear who has gotten lost in a large amusement park that had metamorphized from a spaceship that had dropped from the sky (181); and *Timing* relates how a teacher envisions many people perched on the roof of the school building readying to commit suicide, while students with the ability to reverse or forward time engage in preventive efforts. *Timing* is based on a webtoon of the same name by Kang Full (178). Equally surreal, but real in the emotions captured, is *On the White Planet* (*Chang baek han Eolguldeok*), which tells of the bullying and isolation that a sole, yellow-skinned boy and his mother

4.19. *Timing*, a 2014 animated feature based on an early webtoon by Kang Full, portrays a group of people with supernatural powers related to time—for instance, they can freeze time, turn it back, predict the future, or have dreams that are premonitions.

face in a totally gray world devoid of any color (Korean Film Council 2014, 144). *The Crimson Whale* (*Hwasan gorae*), also far-fetched in plot, emits emotions of madness, pain, indecision, and betrayal, telling of a young girl, unbeknown to others, who can communicate with whales; she is persuaded by a ship's crew, all of whom have been victimized by whales, to hunt and kill them (56).

The other features of 2014 were *The Nut Job* (*Neot Jab: Ttang-kong Do duk deul*), about the challenges an outcast squirrel and his buddy rat face as they plan a heist of a nut store that is actually a front for bank robbers (Korean Film Council 2014, 140); *The Road Called Life* (*Maemilggot, Unsujoeunnal, Geurigo Bombom*), based on three famous Korean short stories, all dealing with real-life experiences (157); and *The Satellite Girl and Milk Cow* (*Wuribyeol Ilhowa Eol lukso*), a sort of romance saga complicated by a girl turned into a satellite, an aspiring musician who becomes a milk cow, a wizard who turns into toilet paper, the Incinerator, and an organ trafficker (162).

What might be concluded from the synopses of these eight works? None focus specifically on the contentious social issues and historical events that were favored areas for the film industry more generally in that time period, according to critic Darcy Paquet (2014, 23–24). Paquet writes that Korean thrillers were among the blockbusters, and perhaps one or two of the animated features of 2014 fit that category. Otherwise, the dominance of fantasy-oriented, surreal-adventure animated features that year might be explained as exploratory, a very expensive way to gauge a potential audience; as imitative, following trends elsewhere (perhaps Japan); or simply happenstance.

Succeeding years saw different genre configurations. The three animated features produced in 2017 lean toward robotics: *Power Battle Watch-Car: Return of Watch Mask* (*Pawobaeteul Wachika: Wachiga myeon ui Yeok-seup*) (Korean Film Council 2017, 83); *Tobot: Attack of the Robot Force* (*Geukjangpan Tobot: Robot gundanui Seup-gyeok*) (103); and *Turning Mecards W: Resurrection of the Black Mirror* (*Teoning mecadeu W: Beulraek mireoui Buchwal*) (103).

The next year, 2018, carried a varied assortment of genres: of eight animated films, four were listed as types of adventure (e.g., action), three as dramas (one each blended with comedy, tragedy, and eroticism), and one as fantasy. The films averaged 88.5 minutes each. Somewhat out of the norm for Korea is *My Bad Boss* (*Nabbeun Sangsa*), listed as an erotic drama. Conned by a friend, the main character resorts to working as a male escort for a while, after which he becomes a competent editor by day and a satisfier of all girls' desires at night. The story revolves around sex, seduction, and revenge (Korean Film Council 2018, 205).

Korean animation saw accrued rewards between 2015 and 2021 resulting from the government's heavy support beginning in the 1990s, the move from mostly outsourcing to domestic production, the resultant highly skilled animators' work pool, the creation of new types of platforms to distribute films, the increased emphasis on storyline and character development, and, perhaps, the prevalence of the notion that success breeds more success. Both the industry

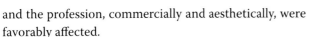

4.20. *My Bad Boss* (2018), a rare South Korean erotic drama revolving around sex, seduction, and revenge.

4.21. The Korean character Pucca, who appeared on a number of products for women and girls in seventy-two countries.

and the profession, commercially and aesthetically, were favorably affected.

In 2015, South Korea's Ministry of Culture, Sports, and Tourism made another push to enhance animation production, promising US$345.8 million during 2015–2019 (Kwan 2016). A couple of guesses about this generosity might be that the authorities took notice of the success of *Leafie, a Hen into the Wild* and *Pororo the Little Penguin*, and/or appreciated the phenomenal growth of the overall Korean content industry, of which animation was one of the eleven designated components.

The ministry had reasons to rejoice during the following six years. First of all, video on demand streaming pioneer Netflix entered Korea in 2016, investing in local content production, which generated an economic impact of nearly US$4.7 billion and created about sixteen thousand jobs within five years (Irwin-Hunt 2021). Streaming services in Korea and most of the world significantly boomed during the stay-at-home years of the COVID-19 pandemic, attracting Amazon Prime, Disney+, ESPN+, and Hulu to invest in local content production. A second reason was the perennial record-setting growth of Korean cultural content exports, for example up 16.3 percent to US$11.92 billion during 2019–2020 (Park G-y 2022).

Also on the positive side was viewership of animation. A 2022 Statista survey found that the number of respondents who watched animation "almost daily" jumped from 12.1 percent in 2016 to 19.3 percent the next year and climbed steadily, reaching 22.3 percent in 2021 (Statista Research Department 2022a).

Licensing and marketing strategies of Korean animation were improved in the twenty-first century. Between 2000 and 2006, retail sales of licensed goods in Korea rose by 10 percent yearly. In 2004 alone, retail sales of licensed materials in Korea totaled US$267 million, of which Korean characters accounted for more than 40 percent (Raugust 2006, 42). Already, companies were planning and

4.22a and 4.22b. *Tayo the Little Bus* animated character.

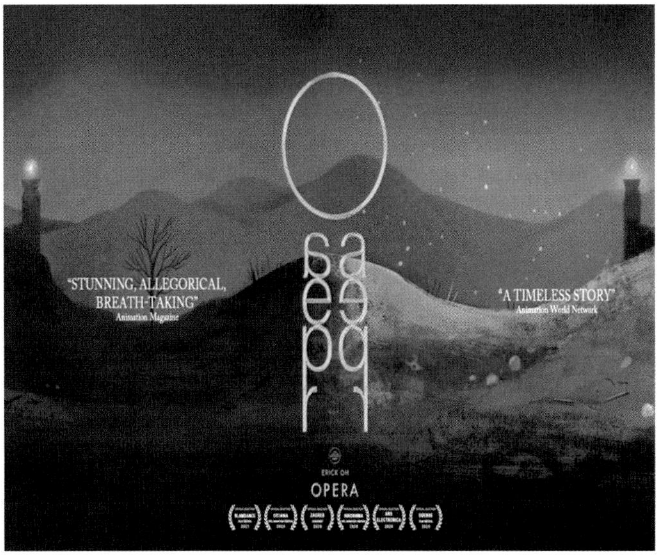

4.23. Erick Oh's *Opera*, a 2021 Academy Award nominee for best animated short, looked at aspects of humanity from a nonnarrative perspective.

developing properties that could adapt to more than one medium (animation, licensing, online, mobile).

Despite achieving this growth, producers and licensing firms recognized the limited size of the domestic market and started looking overseas for continued growth. One of the first characters to make foreign inroads was Pucca, whose image appeared on various products for women and girls in seventy-two countries of Asia and Europe (Raugust 2006, 40); another early character whose spin-off products made millions for its studio, the Seoul Movie Company, was Dooly the Little Dinosaur (Song J-a 2000, 66). Efforts by KOCCA and the industry were paying off as Korean animation characters became popular worldwide. A 2021 survey listed the most popular Korean characters in the world as Larva, Pororo, and Pucca (Statista 2022b).

One of the keys to effective marketing is visibility of product, a principle that seems to be guiding those attempting to advance animation. In 2014, the Seoul government, in alliance with Korean transportation authorities, fell into step with other cities such as Brussels, Hong Kong, and Taipei by placing replicas of popular animation and comics characters in public places. Statues of Larva, a popular character from a 2011 animated television series, and Pororo the Little Penguin were installed in a Seoul city park, at the same time that a subway line was based on a *Larva* character and some buses were designed as characters from *Tayo the Little Bus*, a 2010 production. The Tayo-decorated buses were actually a gimmick to increase public transportation ridership, which they did (Kwak 2015). Seoul is awash with other cartoon-related places, including a café that creates an optical illusion making customers feel that they have crossed dimensions into a cartoon world (Taggart 2018).

Artistically, Korean animation was hitting its stride entering the 2020s, increasingly chosen to be shown at overseas festivals and nominated for awards at prestigious international competitions. In 2021, Korean director Erick Oh's animated short *Opera* was nominated for an Oscar, while Cho Kyung-hun's *Beauty Water* (*Gigigoegoe Seonghyeon su*) won the best animated feature award at the Boston Science Fiction Film Festival, the oldest independent genre festival in the United States. *Boston Herald* reviewer James Verniere described *Opera* as being

> set in a pyramid-shaped, hierarchical world with moving parts and legions of inhabitants busily doing a variety of things, including feeding a giant, using a guillotine to decapitate prisoners, and meeting in conference rooms. Imagine an unbelievably elaborate, digital box. At the lowest level, which looks like this world's "outdoors," a war is waged between

> inhabitants of the left and right side of the pyramid. Oh says he was inspired by the artists Bosch, Michelangelo, and Botticelli among others. (Verniere 2021)

Beauty Water describes how a makeup artist's life is drastically changed when she discovers a beauty water that turns her into a very beautiful woman (Dong 2021). The story is an adaptation of a popular webcomic, *Tales of the Unusual*, by Oh Seong-dae. *Beauty Water*, along with *Motel Rose* and *The Shaman Sorceress*, were spotlighted at the Anima 2021 festival in Brussels. In 2020, Ahn Jae-hun became the first Korean animator to be invited twice to the Annecy International Animation Film Festival, for his animated musical *The Shaman Sorceress*, his fourth animated feature. He had been invited earlier in 2011 for *Green Days*.

Other well-done Korean animation appeared in 2021–2022, as Erick Oh completed *Tree* (*Namoo*), which depicts the "beautiful and heartbreaking moments of a painter's life, captured around a symbolic tree" (Desowitz 2021); Myung Films, producer of *Leafie, a Hen into the Wild*, continued dealing with social issues as it animated the life of labor activist Chun Tae-il (1948–1972) in time for the fiftieth anniversary of his self-immolation to raise awareness of poor labor conditions (Na 2021); and the 2021 Oscar-winning director Bong Joon-ho (for Best Picture and Best Director, *Parasite*), completed an animated feature about humans and deep-sea creatures (Frater 2021; see also Grater 2021).

The 2022 release of *Superdino* by SAMG Entertainment seems to indicate that Korean animation, as other K-content, has found the formula for success. The fifty-two-episode television series was specifically developed to enter the European and American markets; was made with a leading European content distributor with whom SAMG closely collaborated in every step of production; brought on board an award-winning writer to supervise story creation and telling; ensured cultural diversity by partnering with Sunac Culture; and developed a line of corresponding merchandise "enabling children to experience the joy of not only watching, but also playing with characters from the shows" (*Variety* 2022). The plot of the shows revolves around a rescue team of five "adorable" dinosaurs bent on saving their fellow dinosaurs when in dangerous situations.

Conclusion

South Korean animation owes much of its success to two factors: connections to the outside world and a very favorable relationship with the government. Since the 1960s, not long after the country's first domestic animation, Korea became engaged in offshore production for US and European studios. Eventually, the country became the world's third-largest animation producer as a result. Benefits were there for both sides as Korean studios became much more financially secure and better prepared for domestic production with the foreign revenue received and the skills that had been transferred, while the overseas firms received inexpensive and union-free labor. Later in its development, domestic animation joined in making coproductions with Western and East Asian countries, including North Korea.

Few governments in the world have been as supportive of animation and comics as that of South Korea. For a time between the mid-1990s and early 2000s, the government poured huge sums of money and other resources into animation, designated it as one of six high-tech fields for the future, found places for its agencies in three government ministries, and established a quota system that guaranteed at least 50 percent of television viewing time featuring animated programs to local animation shows. Following South Korea's lead, Chinese authorities boosted animation and comics in the 2000s and early 2010s.

South Korea shares common animation threads with other East and Southeast Asian countries, producing much offshore work (along with Japan, Taiwan, and China), working in coproductions (one example being the Northeast Consortium), starting as one-person operations (Thailand, the Philippines, Taiwan, and China [actually, for the latter, four brothers]), using handmade equipment under very adverse conditions, and sorely lacking good storytelling skills (China).

In a relatively brief period of existence (compared to India and Japan [both started in the 1910s] and China [1920s]), South Korean animation has earned high marks in overseas production, professional activity, and aesthetic quality; however, it has not always done as well at the box office.

Notes

1. For fuller histories in English, see Yu 1999 and Lent and Yu 2001.

2. Shin likely was referring to his studio, Shin Dong Hun Production Company, which when started in 1960 employed his immediate family members and was the first animation studio in Korea.

3. A 1967 animated television series featured *The Golden Bat*, aired by the Tongyang Broadcasting Company. This superhero character traces its origins in Japan to the 1930s, when street *kamishibai* (paper drama) storytellers drew movie and folklore stories (including *The Golden Bat*) on cardboard and related them to children for a small fee from the small theaters strapped to their bicycles. *Kamishibai* performed in colonial Korea, explaining children's duties to imperial Japan. The superhero was created in 1931 by Takeo Nagamatsu, predating Jerry Siegel and Joe Shuster's *Superman* (see Maliangkay 2015, 58–59).

4. These figures were compiled from Whang 1990, 191; Han S-h 1995, 86–87; Rho 1995; and Yoon 1995.

5. The author gave one of the major addresses and served on the jury of the first SICAF in 1995. He also gave a lecture at the 2003 SICAF, on August 13, and was an honorary committee member.

6. Normally, three-quarters of the SICAF budget came from the Seoul municipal government and one-quarter from admission fees, according to former SICAF director Park Se-hyung (2003).

7. This was true at the time. Although 105 Korean feature-length animation films were produced from the first one in 1967 until 1999, they were not successful at the box office. Claiming that "there has never been a box office hit" among animated features, Kim Jae-jung (2003) said possible reasons are that they did not attract older audiences, who think animation and comics are for little children; they had to compete with offshore animation in their studios' list of priorities; and they fell short in the preproduction realm. Stating that live-action film had the same problem until *Shiri* became a hit in 1999, Kim thought a similar cascading effect could occur if Korea came up with just one animation box office success.

8. The author participated in this discussion in Seoul on August 12, 2003, and in interviews with Chinese delegates Zhang Guoqiang and Yu Yan-yu in Seoul on August 13, 2003.

9. Kim Byung-heon, a manager at the Korean Film Commission, explained the allocation of credit: "In a joint project with China and Japan, if Korean animators do more than 30 percent of the work, it is called a Korean production" (2003).

References

Ahn, Hyun-dong. 1992. Interview with John A. Lent. Seoul, July 6.

Ahn, Hyun-dong. 1991. Interview with John A. Lent. Seoul, July [illegible]

Animation. 2003. "Korea Forms Healthy Alliances: The Country's Original Animation Pipelines Are Humming with New Co-Productions." *Animation* (October): 22–24.

Animatoon. 1996. "Agi Gongryong Dooly: Eoreum Byeol Moheom" [Baby Dinosaur Dooly: Adventure of Ice Planet]. *Animatoon* 2, no. 6: 86.

Cho, Kwan-je. 2003. Interview with John A. Lent. Seoul, August 16.

Choi, Peter. 1995. Interview with John A. Lent. Seoul, August 15.

Desowitz, Bill. 2021. "'Namoo': An Animated Short Explores the Tree of Life with Innovative VR." IndieWire, December 15. https://www.indiewire.com/2021/12/namoo-animated-short-erick-oh-1234685822/#!

Dong, Sun-hwa. 2021. "'Beauty Water' Becomes 1st Korean Animated Film to Win Award at Boston Sci-Fi Film Festival." *Korea Times*, February 20. https://www.koreatimes.co.kr//www/nation/2021/02/689_304498.html?fl.

Frater, Patrick. 2021. "Bong Joon Ho Working on Korean Animated Film about Deep-Sea Creatures." *Variety*, May 13. https://variety.com/2021/film/asia/bong-joon-ho-korean-animated-film-123497224/#!

Giammarco, Thomas. 2005. "A Brief History of Korean Animation, Part I, The Early Years." *Korean Film*, October 30. https://koreanfilm.org/ani-history.html.

Giammarco, Thomas. 2006. "A Brief History of Korean Animation, Part II, 1967–1972: The First Wave." *Korean Film*, January 29. https://koreanfilm.org/ani-history2.html.

Grater, Tom. 2021. "'Parasite' Filmmaker Bong Joon-Ho Helming Korean Animated Deep Sea Adventure." *Deadline*, May 13. https://deadline.com/2021/05/parasite-filmmaker-bong-joon-ho-korean-animated-deep-sea-adventure-1234755424/.

Gurman, Sarah. 2006. "A KOCCA Star Is Born." *Animation Magazine* 20, no. 4 (April): 36.

Han, Chang-wan. 1995. Interview with John A. Lent. Seoul, August 14.

Han, Seong-hak. 1995. "Animationgwaeni 40 Nyeon" [Forty Years with Animation]. *Animatoon* 1, no. 1: 86–87.

Heo, In-wook. 2002. *Hanguk Animation Yeonghwasa* [History of Korean Animated Film]. Seoul: Shinkan Media.

Hong, Sunny. 2003. Interview with John A. Lent. Seoul, August 14.

Hyun, Daiwon. 2004. "Promoting the Digital Content Industry in Korea, Focusing on Exporting Animation." *International Journal of Comic Art* 6, no. 1 (Spring): 329–39.

Im, Jeong-gyu. 1996. "Jakwhajireul Sseureonaemyeo Maeume Grimeul Grinda" [I Am Drawing in My Heart on Clean Drawing Paper]. *Animatoon* 2, no. 5: 97.

Irwin-Hunt, Alex. 2021. "Fresh Content: How Streaming Platforms Are Changing the Geography of Media Investment." *fDi Intelligence*, December 2021–January 2022. https://www.fdiintelligence.com/article/80490.

Jeong, Do-bin. 1996. "Cel 240 Maero Mandeun 'Gaemiwa Baetzangi'" ["The Ant and the Grasshopper" Made with 240 Cels]. *Animatoon* 2, no. 6: 98–99.

Jun, Chang-rok. 1995. Interview with John A. Lent. Seoul, August 14.
Jung, Ha-won. 2011. "S. Korea's Pororo Penguin Takes Flight Worldwide." Agence France-Presse, June 11. https://sg.news.yahoo.com/koreas-pororo-penguin-takes-flight-worldwide-033613427.html.
Jung, Wook. 1994. "Manhwayounghwa Saneobeui Hyeonwhang-gwa Jeonmang" [Current Situation and Prospects of the Animation Industry]. Paper presented at the Symposium for Animation Industry Development, Korean Ministry of Culture, Sports, and Tourism, Seoul, December 6.
Jung, Wook. 1995. Interview with John A. Lent. Seoul, August 14.
Kalbi. 2017. "K-Animation Series: A Brief History (21st Century)." Korean Culture Blog, August 6. https://koreancultureblog.com/2017/08/06/k-animation-series-a-brief-history-21st-century/.
Kim, Byung-heon. 2003. Interview with John A. Lent. Seoul, August 15.
Kim, Irang. 1995. "Umjigineun Manhwa-e Kkum" [Dreams of Moving Cartoons]. In *Hanguk Manhwa-e Seongujadeul* (Pioneers of Korean Cartoons), edited by Park Jae-dong. Seoul: Yorhwadang.
Kim, Jae-jung. 2003. Interview with John A. Lent. Seoul, August 15.
Kim, Joon-yang. 2006. "Critique of the New Historical Landscape of South Korean Animation." *Animation* 1, no. 1: 61–81.
Kim, Seok-ki. 1995. Interview with John A. Lent. Seoul, August 13.
Kim, Song-pil. 1996. "Cel-eul Ssiseo Animationeul Mandeuldeon Sijeol" [Those Days When We Made Animation by Washing the Cels]. *Animatoon* 2, no. 3: 98–99.
Kim, Tayk. 1995. Interview with John A. Lent and Yu Kie-un. Seoul, August 16.
Klein, Norman M. 1993. *7 Minutes: The Life and Death of the American Animated Cartoon*. London: Verso.
Korean Film Council. 2012. "Animation." In *Korean Cinema 2012*, 241–42. Seoul: Korean Film Council.
Korean Film Council. 2013. "Features." In *Korean Cinema 2013*, 41–73. Seoul: Korean Film Council.
Korean Film Council. 2014. "Features." In *Korean Cinema 2014*, 56, 79, 140, 144, 157, 162, 178, 181. Seoul: Korean Film Council.
Korean Film Council. 2017. "Theatrical Release." In *Korean Cinema 2017*, 83, 103, 105. Seoul: Korean Film Council.
Korean Film Council. 2018. "Theatrical Release." In *Korean Cinema 2018*, 46, 77, 138, 185, 204, 205, 221, 231. Seoul: Korean Film Council.
Kwak, Yoon-shin. 2015. "How South Korea's Cartoon Bus Increased Ridership." *The Urbanist*, March 13. https://www.theurbanist.org/2015/03/13/how-south-koreas-cartoon-bus-increased-ridership.
Kwan, Justin. 2016. "New Players in the Asian Animation Industry: Growth in China and South Korea." Asia Pacific Foundation of Canada, December 1. https://www.asiapacific.ca/blog/new-players-asian-animation-industry-growth-china-and-south.
Lee, Claire. 2011. "Animation Is the Future: Yeun Sang-ho." *Korea Herald*, November 21. https://www.koreaherald.com/view.php?ud=20111121000690.
Lee, Tae-hoon. 2011. "Will US Allow Import of Inter-Korean Cartoon?" *Korea Times*, June 29. http://www.koreatimes.co.kr/www/news/nation/2011/06/116_89865.html.
Lent, John A. 1998. "The Animation Industry and Its Offshore Factories." In *Global Productions: Labor in the Making of the "Information Society,"* edited by Gerald Sussman and John A. Lent, 239–54. Cresskill, NJ: Hampton Press.
Lent, John A., ed. 2001. *Animation in Asia and the Pacific*. Eastleigh, Hants., England: John Libbey; Bloomington: Indiana University Press.
Lent, John A., and Yu Kie-un. 2001. "Korean Animation: A Short but Robust Life." In *Animation in Asia and the Pacific*, edited by John A. Lent, 89–101. Eastleigh, Hants., England: John Libbey.
Maliangkay, Roald. 2015. "Embedding Nostalgia: The Political Appropriation of Foreign Comic Book Superheroes in Korea." *Situations* 8, no. 2: 49–65.
May, Kate Torgovnick. 2016. "A New Age of Animation." *Atlantic*, May 20. https://www.theatlantic.com/entertainment/archive/2016/05/a-new-age-of-animation/483342/.
McDougall, Lori. 1996. "Miky Lee Goes to Hollywood." *Asia, Inc.*, May, 20–27.
Motion. 1997. "Hanguk Animation Geungan Jomyeong" [Review of Recent Korean Animation]. June.
Na, Won-jeong. 2021. "'Chun Tae-il' May Be the Next Big Animated Movie." *Korea JoongAng Daily*, October 31. https://koreajoongangdaily.joins.com/2021/10/31/entertainment/movies/Chun-Taeil/20211031181440467.html.
Paquet, Darcy. 2014. "Review of Korean Films: A Serious Mood Descends on the Industry." In *Korean Cinema 2014*, 18–29. Seoul: Korean Film Council.
Park, Ga-young. 2022. "K-Content Industry Sets Another Export Record in 2020 at $11.92 Billion." *Korea Herald*, January 24. www.koreaherald.com/view.php?ud=20220124000809.
Park, Jae-dong. 1994. Interviews with John A. Lent. Seoul, July 3, 5.
Park, Jae-dong. 2003. Interview with John A. Lent. Seoul, August 15.
Park, Ji-won. 2020. "Director Seeks 'Koreanness' in Animated Film to Find Breakthrough." *Korea Times*, June 18. https://www.koreatimes.co.kr/www/art/2024/05/398_291438.html.
Park, Ju-min. 2011. "Iconic South Korean Penguin Character Actually Half–North Korean." Reuters, May 16. https://www.reuters.com/article/idUSTRE74F17V/.
Park, Se-hyung. 2003. Interview with John A. Lent. Seoul, August 14.
Raugust, Karen. 2006. "Crossing Borders: Korean Character and Animation Products Are Gaining Visibility Outside Their Homeland." *Animation Magazine* 20, no. 4 (April): 40, 42.
Rho, Gwang-woo. 1995. "Hankuk Manhwa Yeongwhaeui Gukjejeok Hacheonge Gwanhan Il Yeongu" [A Study of International

Subcontracting of Korean Animation]. Master's thesis, Korea University.
Russell, Mark. 2003. "Korean Animation Thrives, but Lacks Local Identity." *Hollywood Reporter*, August 25.
Seoul Cinema Group. 1996. *Byun Bang e Seo Jung ShimUe Ro* [From the Center to the Edge]. Seoul: Shi Gak Gwa Eon Eoh.
Shin, Dal-ja. 1994. "Imi Duk-eul Neomeo-on Ilbon Manhwa" [Overflowing Japanese Cartoons]. *Kyunghyang Shinmun*, March 5, 5.
Shin, Dong-hun. 1995. Interviews with John A. Lent. Seoul, August 13, 15.
Shin, Dong-hun. 2003. Interview with John A. Lent. Seoul, August 17.
Shin, Hye-son. 1995. "Korean Animation Industry Cashing In on World of Make-Believe: Still in Need of Investment into Original Production." *Korea Herald*, August 25.
Shin, Nelson. 1995. Interview with John A. Lent. Seoul, August 16.
Shin, Nelson. 1996. "Hanguk Animation-e Eojewa Oneul, Grigo Miraereul Wihan Je-eon" [Suggestions for Korean Animation's Yesterday, Today, and Tomorrow]. *Animatoon* 6, no. 5: 79.
Shin, Nelson. 2003. Interview with John A. Lent. Seoul, August 14.
Shin, Nelson. 2009. "History of Korean Animation." *ASIFA Magazine* (Summer): 38–41.
Song, Jung-a. 2000. "Dreams Come True." *Far Eastern Economic Review*, January 13, 66–67.
Song, Seung-min. 2005. "Korean Independent Animation: Its Origin and Meaning." *International Journal of Comic Art* 7, no. 1 (Spring): 351–59.
Statista. 2022a. "Share of Animation Consumers Watching It Almost Daily in South Korea 2016–2021." January 17. https://www.statista.com/statistics/1043637/south-korea-watching-animation-daily/.
Statista. 2022b. "Favorite South Korean Animation Characters Worldwide 2021." February 15. https://www.statista.com/statistics/999386/south-korean-favorite-korean-animation-characters-worldwide.
Taggart, Emma. 2018. "This Korean Café Makes Visitors Feel Like They've Stepped into a Cartoon." My Modern Met, September 24. https://mymodernmet.com/cartoon-world-coffee-shop-seoul/.
Vallas, Milt. 1997. "The Korean Animation Explosion." Animation World Network, September 1. https://www.awn.com/animationworld/korean-animation-explosion.
Variety. 2022. "South Korean Animators Aim to Contribute to the Region's Global Successes." February 23. https://variety.com/2022/biz/news/south-korean-animators-aim-to-contribute-to-the-regions-successes-1235184407/.
Verniere, James. 2021. "'Opera' Stands Out among Oscar-Nominated Animated Short Films." *Boston Herald*, April 2. https://www.bostonherald.com/2021/04/02/opera-stands-out-among-oscar-nominated-animated-short-films/.
Verrier, Richard. 2008. "Gotham Group Draws on South Korean Talent in Animation Partnership." *Los Angeles Times*, December 6.
Whang, Seong-gil. 1990. *Animation Yeongwhasa* [History of Animated Cartoons]. Seoul: Baeksousa.
Wikipedia. N.d. "*Empress Chung*." https://en.wikipedia.org/wiki/Empress_Chung.
Witiw, John. 2021. "10 Korean Animated Films You Need to See." CBR, February 4. https://www.cbr.com/korean-animated-films-need-to-see/.
Yi, Yong-bae. 1994. "Animation Jejak Productiondreui Choigun Donghyang" [Recent Situation of Animation Productions]. Paper presented at the Forum: Hanguk Animationeui Gilchatgi [Forum: Pathfinding of Korean Animation], Maru Youngsang Yonguwhoe [Maru Visual Arts Study Group], Sogukjang Oneul [Small Theaters Today], Seoul, December 3.
Yoon, Shinae. 1995. "Hanguk Animation Saneobe Gwanhan Yeongu" [A Study of the Korean Animation Industry]. Master's thesis, Yonsei University.
Yu Kie-un. 1999. "The Development of the Korean Animation Industry: Historical, Economic, and Cultural Perspectives." PhD dissertation, Temple University.

Vignette V

Nelson Shin

"Godfather" of Korean Animation

Nelson Shin is often called the "godfather" of Korean animation, an accolade well deserved, if the term refers to family-like caretaking. For more than a half century, Shin has taken great pains to ensure that Korean animation is well nourished and growing, and when it is ailing, to lend a hand in helping it recover.

First, Shin was at the forefront of both Korean offshore and domestic animation with co-pioneers Shin Dong-hun, Jung Wook, and Yu Seong-woong; in fact, he worked with Shin Dong-hun, as did the others. Second, Nelson Shin had a huge role in South Korea becoming the world's third-largest animation producer, maintaining contacts with studios in the United States and North Korea simultaneously, a mean task in itself. To expedite these maneuvers, he maintains a home and office in Los Angeles and has made many (nineteen at last count) trips to Pyongyang to work with the April 26 Children's Animation Film Studio.

A third major contribution Shin has made to his country's animation has to do with upgrading the profession, sometimes at a personal financial loss. Such has been the case with *Animatoon*, a glossy bimonthly magazine, which he founded in 1995 and of which he has published 108 issues as of August 2023. Shin said the purpose of *Animatoon* is "to spread knowledge to young people," but he added that "a lot of young people are not reading." In its first eight years of publication alone, the magazine cost Shin US$1.5 million, but he told me that he had no plans to discontinue its publication, because it would be "shameful" to do that. During the COVID-19 pandemic, Shin spent much time developing the Nelson Shin Animation–ART Museum, the touring of which was described as "going into a busy animation studio" (Cohn 2023). Other services he has given to the profession are teaching "a lot of students" at his studio and at Far East University in Chungbuk Province, and founding the International Animated Film Association (ASIFA) Korea in 1996; he was vice president, then president of ASIFA International from 2009 to 2013.

Fourth, Shin has played a major role in making Korean films and TV series known worldwide. After starting an animated commercial company in Seoul at the beginning of the 1960s, he moved to the United States in 1971, where he worked as an animator at DePatie-Freleng Enterprises.

Vig-V.1. Nelson Shin. Date unknown. Photo by John A. Lent.

Vig-V.2. Inaugural issue of *Animatoon*, August 1995, the premier periodical for the Korean animation profession, founded and sustained by Nelson Shin. Courtesy of Nelson Shin.

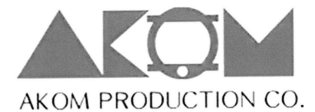

Vig-V.3. AKOM logo. Courtesy of Nelson Shin.

There until 1979, Shin was an animator on *Pink Panther*, *Daffy Duck*, *Mr. Magoo*, and *Dr. Seuss*, and he invented a way to animate the lightsaber in the live-action scenes of the original *Star Wars* film. In 1980, he went to Marvel Productions, where he was the producer for the televised series *The Transformers*; when the series became a movie, Shin made his directorial debut.

His producer and director roles mounted after he started AKOM Productions in Seoul in 1985, mainly to handle offshore productions. Major AKOM credits have been *The Simpsons*, *Batman: The Animated Series*, *X-Men*, *Invasion America*, and *Arthur*. When South Korea was producing about half of the world's animation in the mid-1990s, AKOM was the country's most prominent studio.

Shin was a trailblazer in still another dimension, not to the liking of some higher-ups in the United States; his *Empress Chung* animated feature was a coproduction between North and South Korea and was the first film released simultaneously in both countries. Shin claims that his intention was to culturally introduce both Koreas to the Korean diaspora through a film. He told me something similar in one of our interviews in 2003, before the release of *Empress Chung*. At that time, his hope was that the film would be seen as a good example of a Korean product and that it would prove wrong naysayers who thought that a folktale such as *Empress Chung* would not go over well; he pointed out that "Disney does folktales all the time." The film did not achieve the box office success that was expected, but it contributed to helping establish intercountry relations in divided Korea and exemplified excellent storytelling, a quality in short supply in South Korea in the early 2000s.

Approaching his mid-eighties (born December 20, 1939, in what later became North Korea), Nelson (Neung-kyun) Shin still exhibits the traits I have known him to possess in large quantities—perseverance and dogged determination.

Vig-V.4. Commemorative 2004 calendar promoting Nelson Shin's animated film *Empress Chung*. John A. Lent, personal collection, from Nelson Shin.

Vig-V.5. Personal greeting card designed and drawn by Nelson Shin in 2006, following the growth of AKOM Studio from its 1985 founding. John A. Lent, personal collection, from Nelson Shin.

He exhibited these traits in a letter he sent to me in December 2012, announcing the forthcoming one-hundredth number of *Animatoon*, the magazine that had cost him much time and money. He wrote, "As you may know, it is a very hard job to keep publishing [a] printed magazine, and especially it is more difficult for the animation magazine. But as an old man, . . . as a person who most cherish[es] the animation, I am hanging on to publish ANIMATOON with a call that this kind of magazine should exist in the animation field."

Shin has been a leader of South Korean animation nearly from its beginning, helping it grow by setting up and maintaining AKOM; nourishing it by involving overseas animation production, which brought in revenue and skills beneficial to the indigenous industry's growth; and providing a lending hand when the industry was ailing through teaching, seizing opportunities to cooperate with other nations, and adding significantly to animation's professionalism.

References

Cohn, Karl. 2023. "Meet Nelson Shin, the Godfather of South Korean Animation. He Has Created an Animation Studio in Seoul." *Newsletter ASIFA San Francisco* (August): 8–13.

Shin, Nelson. 2023. "An Animation Museum in Korea." International Animated Film Association, July 8. https://asifa.net/an-animation-museum-in-korea/.

Chapter 5

Webtoons

History and Features of Webtoons

In one of the very first academic studies on webtoons, Kwon Jae-woong defined the term, examined its status and main features, and told of its value in Korean society. Kwon divided web cartoons (he called them "essay cartoons") into book (paid service) and nonbook (free) types, and further separated the nonbook category into commercialized (newspaper sites, portal sites, and advertisements) and noncommercialized (independent sites, no advertisements) (Kwon 2005, 321).

An estimated 242 essay cartoons existed as of December 2004, according to Kwon (2005, 321). He broke them down by the lists provided by portal sites: Daum ranked first, although the number of essay cartoons was undetermined; Naver, second, with ninety-three; third, Yahoo! Korea, with eighty-seven; and fourth, Nate, with sixty-two (see appendix IV for a list of early essay cartoons in 2004). From his research, Kwon characterized essay cartoonists to be in their twenties, male (approximately 82 percent), unmarried, highly educated, and usually working in the fields of computers or internet services. As for the format of the early essay cartoons, Kwon (2005, 323–32) listed these characteristics:

1. Most essay cartoons are managed through their own websites.
2. Essay cartoons do not follow the typical style of comics; instead, they use a vertical length and do not find it vital to abide by the usual style of framing, speech balloons, and black-and-white drawing.
3. Most essay cartoons are presented as diaries.
4. Essay cartoons use diverse forms of characters; there are no fixed types of body shapes.
5. Computer technology frees cartoonists from the limitations of letter fonts and colors.
6. The way to reach readers differs with computers and networks, resulting in interactive communication in real time through essay cartoons.
7. More and more cartoons are mixing and composing different types of images, because image editing software is used by ordinary people.

5.1. *Snow Cat* was originally called *Cool Cat* when Kwon Yoon-ju used the character on her homepage in 1998, before turning it into a webcomic in 2001.

5.2. Kwon Yoon-ju (1969), creator of *Snow Cat*.

The specific features of essay cartoons delineated by Kwon are, first, topics are taken from daily life, such as mental stress, love, friendships in school and work environments, and relationships with friends, colleagues, and lovers; second, many essay cartoons show other media forms and genres that affect cartoonists or that they prefer to use; third, some cartoons are bizarre, weird, disgusting, and cruel; and fourth, several sites contain more than one cartoon (2005, 332–42). The benefits derived from essay cartoons, Kwon contended, are easy accessibility because of the widespread use of the internet in South Korea; a speedier way for cartoonists to enter the profession; and an opportunity for cartoonists to extend their online works to other media (books, television, or film) with the built-in audience they have already established (2005, 343).

Jane Yeahin Pyo, Minji Jang, and Tae-jin Yoon (2019, 2162) later went further, defining and showing the differences between various online manhwa. They pointed out that webtoons and digital comics are dissimilar in that a webtoon is "digitally produced from its very origin and is intended to be uploaded, circulated, and consumed online," whereas a digital comic is a scanned and uploaded version of a comic that has already been printed. They also distinguished between webtoons and webcomics, the former being longer in targeted period of serialization, thus requiring a longer narrative.

Crucial to a webtoon's format is its vertical layout, allowing the reader to scroll the comic in what Scott McCloud calls an "infinite canvas" (2010, 222). In the early days of Korean cartoonists using the internet (1999–2000), they posted their comics on portal sites such as N4 and Comics Today, fashioning horizontal pages to fit the landscape layout of a computer screen (Park I-h 2011, 69–70). The first to do a digital cartoon was Park Kwang-su with *Kwang-su's Thinking* in April 1997. Three years later, Chollian Webtoon was established to host what the site's creators called "webtoons," the first of which was *Invincible Hong Assistant Manager* by Hong Yun-pyo (Lee K-w 2000). The first three webcomics in vertical format were *Papepopo Memories* (2002) by Shim Seung-hyeon, *Snow Cat* (2000) by Kwon Yoon-ju, and *Marine Blues* (2001–2007) by Chung Chul-yeon. As Lynn Hyung-gu (2016a) writes, these works were "episodic, without overarching narratives, open to comments, free, and hosted on personal blogs and websites." Kwon originally used *Cool Cat* as the name of her homepage in 1998 but changed it to *Snow Cat* in 2000, before turning the page into a webcomic in 2001. *Marine Blues* started in 2001 and became one of the most famous Korean webcomics of all time (Lee D-w 2012). Other successful pioneering webtoons were Kim Chang-hwan's *Blackjelly* (2003), Seo Sang-hoon's *Bad Cartoon* (*Bulryang Manhwa*), and Kang Full's (Kang Do-young) *A Romance Comic* (*Sunjeong Manhwa*) (2003–2004), which Cho Heek-young (2016) credited with popularizing the vertical form.

In one of the most thorough articles about webtoons written at the time of their advent, Kwon Jae-woong (2005) provides specific information on 151 webtoons that he gathered and studied over three months, October–December 2004. The flexibility of webtoons stood out in Kwon's findings. Besides, or complementary to, the seven features already mentioned, webtoons can use color and letter fonts in various ways (to emphasize parts or separate real life from personal feelings); employ audio factors (as in *Choon Master*); make drawings look old-fashioned through the use of image editing (as in *Café Grapefruit*, *Life Is Good*, and *Krae-mong's Home*); and permit cartoonists to show their works whenever they want or can. Cartoons such as *Marine Blues* and *Snow Cat* seemed to compete in frequency of appearance, the former shown an average of twenty-one times monthly over a seven-month period (Kwon 2005, 326). Webtoon characters can be anything—a duck bill in *Ulzima*, a strawberry and a tangerine in *Kim Pyung*, a human shape that is not a human being in *Googims*, a cube and a cylinder in *Dandani + Moorni*. Chung of *Marine Blues* said that sometimes there is a motive behind the creation of these characters:

> To me who came up to the capital Seoul from the countryside, actually a seaside, marine products could be mostly compatible to me, I thought. At first, I thought of using fishes such as a dolphin and a mackerel. But, I changed my mind because it seems likely they have leading roles in the sea and, instead, I selected some peripheral characters such as a sea urchin, and a starfish, which looked more suitable to ordinary people. And the reason why I describe myself as a sea urchin is its shape. It is totally black and has so many sharp thorns giving the insinuation, "You'll be hurt, too, if you come closer to me." I liked that feeling as, frankly speaking, I broke up with someone and was so depressed for several private reasons around the time when I started *Marineblues*. In case of the cactus, which is delineated as a female, I bought one when I started living in Seoul to get over the feeling of loneliness. As time went by, however, I intentionally set up Ms. Cactus as my logo. (Chung 2004)

The cast of characters in *Marine Blues* includes Sea Urchin Boy, Cactus Girl, Starfish Boy, Octopus Girl, Baby Octopus Boy, and Baby Octopus Girl.

With the availability of image editing software, webtoonists play with mixing and composing different types of images, especially when they review movies and animated films. *Marine Blues*, for example, posted its movie critiques in cartoon form and also included actual scenes from the films (Kwon 2005, 331). Other artists create digitalized photo comics, in some cases making "meaningless photos," assembling them sequentially or mixing them with drawings and posting them on the internet. These possibilities increased the number of amateur cartoonists, so that in 2002, already more than one-half of newcomer artists had started their careers on internet sites, in more than a few cases making up for their lack of drawing skills by using photos, digital cameras, and internet programs, coupled with good ideas.

A second wave of webcartoonists rode to prominence in 2003–2004, as the print manhwa industry tailspun and some large internet portals established webtoon portals. Yahoo! Korea started its portal, Cartoon World, in March 2002, quickly followed by Daum's Manhwa World, SK Telecom's Nate Toons, and the KT Corporation's Paran Cartoon all in 2003, and then Empas Comics in early 2004 and Naver later that year (Lynn 2016a). Competition was intense, and the portal sector became overcrowded. Although webtoons were free at the start and were a financial loss, the portals, thinking of their low cost to produce and diversity of content, aimed to lure and keep visitors at their sites until they could find ways to make them profitable. Many cartoonists began to use these portals, some even receiving a small writer's fee. Most famous was Kang Full; his *Sunjeong Manhwa* averaged two million viewers daily on Daum, and because it was on such a huge portal and used vertical display, the Korea Creative Content Agency (2016) considered it the first manhwa webtoon. Unlike previous webtoons, which consisted of only a few episodes, *Sunjeong Manhwa* used the vertical scroll to keep the stream of stories moving. It was a huge success for Daum, which then generated printed books, Japanese versions, and a theater production.

In the second half of the 2000s, webcomics were distributed through multiple platforms and began to be adapted to other mass media, as in the case of *Sunjeong Manhwa*, which in 2008 became the film *Hello, Schoolgirl*.[1] Others

5.3. *Sunjeong Manhwa* (A Romance Comic) by Kang Full (Kang Do-young), who is credited with popularizing the vertical scroll.

5.4. Kang Full. Courtesy of Hancinema.

followed, including Kang Full's *Apartment*, about serial murders, and B-Class Dal-Gung's *Dasepo Naughty*, both in 2006; and Kang Full's *Fool* (*Ba Bo*), started in 2004 and made into a film in 2008. An advantage of webtoons as sources for films is their combining visual and textual elements; a disadvantage is their being too simple or complicated, requiring filmmakers to make major adjustments detrimental to the original story.

In 2006, Kang Full assured Seoul National University students that manhwa had not become boring. He said that it is "just that the center of culture has moved to the internet, which can offer more interesting content to people. To combat the diverse cultural content the internet can offer, comics must become funnier, wittier, and quicker" (Shin 2006). Kang's vertical scrolling certainly satisfied the "quick" requirement, while it also helped save, even revolutionize, the comics industry.

Kang's success led others to innovate new ways to use the portals. In January 2007, a webzine platform for webtoons, *Mankkik*, was started by a former editor of *IQ Jump* manhwa magazine, its major achievement before closing in 2008 being the webtoon debut of Yoon Tae-ho. Other publishers, for instance Korea House and Book Café 21, began to convert webtoons into books and vice versa.

The proliferation of "smart" phones after their development in South Korea in 2009 was a huge boost for webtoons, which grew nearly tenfold between 2010 and 2018. Coupled with South Korea's world-leading internet speeds, the "smart" phone made the webtoon the favorite vehicle for cartoons. By 2012, a little over a decade after its inception, the country's webtoon market was up to 6.2 million readers a day, involved 140,000 cartoonists, and was worth US$96 million (KT Economics and Management Research Institute, quoted in Kang 2014). Among the portals, Naver led with seventeen million readers a month and 175 registered professional cartoonists; it published 520 different webtoons from 2004 to 2012. Daum followed, having published 434 webtoons from 2003 to 2012. Other mobile operators entered the market, such as Lezhin Comics, with their sights on overseas sales (Kang 2014).

One of the most prolific webcartoonists about 2008–2012 was Yoon Tae-ho, who created *Moss* in 2008–2009, *Inside Men* in 2010, and *Misaeng* (Incomplete Life) in 2012–2013. The story of *Misaeng* fit the sociocultural landscape of Korea at the time, dealing as it did with the hopelessness of young people caught in the claustrophobic confines of office culture. The webcomic was published on Daum, where it racked up a billion readers; the nine-volume

5.5. Popular webtoonist Yoon Tae-ho (born 1969), author of *Moss* and *Incomplete Life* (*Misaeng*).

series claimed sales of nine hundred thousand copies. Its adaptation to tvN resulted in the second-highest rating of any cable network program in Korea (Baek 2014), and the series moved on to films and other television programs (see Jin 2019b).

Dal Yong Jin (2020) writes that people on the go who wanted their culture in short doses turned to webtoons on "smart" phones, resulting in what he calls "snack culture" and what I referred to as "fast food" content more than twenty years before.[2] Referring to sources such as Sohn Ji-young (2014) and his own earlier work (Jin 2015), Jin gives the reasons for the high popularity of webtoons as: (1) easy accessibility; (2) diverse genres and themes; (3) suitability for transference to other media because of their "diverse structures, conflicts, harmonies, and distinctive themes"; (4) briefness, fitting the public's changing habits of consuming popular culture, preferably to under ten minutes; and (5) fitting a "loser" syndrome prevalent among Korean youth. Jin explains that the "loser" syndrome is connected to "moron-taste," elaborating:

> For example, the webtoon written by Lee Mal-nyeon titled *Lee Mal-nyeon Series* is unrivaled in terms of being moron-like. To be specific, well-organized plots always have steps like introduction, development, turn, and conclusion in composition. In Lee's webtoon case, it has introduction, development, turn, and moron taste. The final step could result in either disaster of a whole story or unique charm. . . . His improvisation is likely to count on trends on the internet or funny things captured in society. As many Koreans have no jobs after college graduation, they feel like they are losers who pursue snack-like light humor and fun. Some webtoonists reflect this kind of social milieu in their webtoons, which make the contemporary webtoons popular. (Jin 2019a, 2103; see also Jin 2023)

Obviously, not every film adapted from a webtoon enjoyed box office success. As an example, taking three successful webtoons by prominent artists Kang Full and Yoon Tae-ho that were converted into films, Kang's *Apartment* flopped, ranking only forty-second in box office receipts in 2006, yet Yoon's *Moss* and *Inside Men* were blockbusters. Jin's (2019a) explanation for the disparity is that the latter two emphasized the characteristics and expanded the attractions of webtoons; in other words, they relied on the strengths of the webtoon.

Making maximum use of the verticality capacity of Korean webcomics is a key factor in their success. As late as 2016, Cho Heek-young writes, neither of the two dominant comics producers of the world, the United States and Japan, had completely and quickly broken away from the "inheritances" from print comics. One aspect of comics that Cho (2016) hones in on is the gutter, which in print comics is usually a "visually dull, monotonous space, usually a narrow, white space between panels" meant to denote a lapse of time or change of location, while in webtoons, the gutter serves the same functions but can also define the tone of the entire story. He illustrates his point using the webtoon *Papepopo*: "[E]ach episode . . . uses one long, pastel-toned gutter which embraces all panels within it, and its light-peach or pale-pink cover delivers the general impression of the story, which describes a young couple's sincere and lovely romance." A more poignant example Cho (2016) provides is the first episode of Ko Yeong-hun's *Rainy Season* (*Changma*, 2009–2010), in which the cartoonist uses elongated gutters of thick, straight, vertical lines denoting strong rain, connecting to other gutters and to

5.6. This part of Ko Yeong-hun's *Rainy Season* (*Changma*) uses the elongated gutter to depict strong rain, the long thick lines connecting to other gutters. Courtesy of the *Comics Journal* and Gary Groth.

the rain portrayed within the panels. The repeated image of rain in the darkened gutters creates a "feeling of fear or anxiety that hangs over the whole episode, in which the scene of a homicide is discovered," Cho (2016) explains.

In an excellent rundown of the advantages of vertical-scroll webtoons and their gutters, using Korean examples, Cho (2016) makes two other important points: the length of vertical panels gives a sense of time and space that cannot be conveniently expressed in print manhwa (e.g., in Yoon Tae-ho's *Pain* [A Country Pumpkin], a seemingly endless panel shows divers who traverse to the bottom of the sea to illegally recover antiques from a sunken ship); and the flexibility of webcomics gutters, with their expanded space, allows the relocation of text (captions, monologue, dialogue, narration, and words denoting sound or motion) to the gutter, freeing up space in the panels and allowing readers to focus more on the images. Cho (2016) writes that the deployment of the text to the gutter can give different effects; using Kang To-ha's *Great Catsby* (*Widaehan Kaetchubi*) as an example, he writes that "the main character's monologue at the beginning of the episode, explaining that he is unemployed and poor, is placed outside the panels. This external text housed in the gutter visually delivers the sense that the narrator 'I' is detached from the character 'I,' thus providing the reader with two presentations of the character that are sometimes in tension with one another."

Online manhwa creators seem not to exhaust the possibilities of the internet. In February 2017, many amateurs began uploading their short comics on Instagram. Termed "instatoons," the comics can be read by swiping the screen to move to the next frame, instead of scrolling. Instagram is open to anyone with an account, unlike Naver and Daum, which require fierce competition for entry. Most instatoons relate to light, everyday experiences, although some tackle social and political issues (Park J-y 2018).

Content

South Korea, having become one of the world's most industrialized newly emergent countries in a short period of time, harbors a society plagued with the maladies common to fast-paced populations: bigness for bigness's sake, instantaneousness, and suicide-prone competitiveness,[3] the latter both in the workplace and in schools. The hurriedness, coupled with people's shorter attention spans and their usually futile attempts at multitasking, necessitate that they receive their information and entertainment in bite-size portions, quickly gotten and digested, similar to fast food or a snack. Webtoons have become a convenient vendor of this type of fare.

Webtoons are no different from other comics art forms or mass media in that they give priority to content based on popularity, which, of course, is not an accurate gauge of artistic quality. Kim Bong-seok (2020) captured this sentiment, saying, "In extreme cases, cartoons with subpar quality but surefire appeal factors like trendy humor thrived. At other times, plots or other core traits of an ongoing series fluctuated in response to reader requests or reactions." Webtoons that draw wide audiences usually have themes of humor, fantasy, and daily life, Kim (2020) continued, but those "artistically exceptional but not exactly mainstream are rarely given exposure by a platform."

Content in the early years of webtoons featured humor, fantasy, and daily life, as Kim said above, but also love and mystery thrillers, which Kang Full debuted with, such as *Fool* (*Ba Bo*) (2004), a love story about a boy who is accidentally poisoned and becomes mentally challenged, and *I Love You* (*Geudaereul saranghapnida*) (2007), about two elderly couples whose love survives many challenges. Kang Full is also known for his mysteries, three of which deal with serial murders: *Apartment* (2004–2008), *Neighbor* (*Iutsaram*) (2008), and *Timing* (2005).

Throughout their history, webtoons have borne traces of realism. Kang Full's *26 Years*, serialized in 2006, relates to the 1980 uprising in Gwangju, instigated when the Korean army fired upon civilians. In Kang's story, revenge is sought on the person responsible for the massacre, referred to as "that man" but who was actually the dictator President Chun Doo-hwan. Researcher Alyssa Kim provides other examples of webtoons based on actual events and situations or that touch on sensitive Korean topics in an offhand manner (2016, 423–33). *The Insiders* by Yoon Tae-ho is a mystery thriller with oblique meanings, at least in some readers' minds, especially when Yoon said that he would not complete the serial in the middle of the story. *The Insiders* is about the connection between a fictional newspaper, *Choguk Ilbo* (referring to the widely circulated right-wing newspaper *Chosun Ilbo*), and politicians of South Korea's conservative party, to whom the newspaper's editor provided "black money."

Alyssa Kim (2016, 424–26) saw other allusions to Korean sociopolitical issues in *Secretly, Greatly* (*Eunmilhagae, Widaehagae*) (2010–2011) by Hun; *Along with the Gods* (*Singwahamkke*) (2010–2012) by Ju Ho-min; *Misaeng* (2012–2013) by Yoon Tae-ho; and *Songgot* ("awl") (2013), *100 Degrees Celsius* (*100 dossi*) (2009), and *Lawyers for Workers* (*Byeonhosadeul 1*) (2012), all by Choi Kyu-seok.[4] Although fictional, *Secretly, Greatly* deals with the

5.7. A page from Choi Kyu-seok's graphic novel/webtoon *100 Degrees Celsius*, about one family's travails during the Chun Doo-hwan era. Permission of Choi Kyu-seok.

two-Koreas scenario, while *Along with the Gods* is a comics treatment of Dante's *Inferno*, but to Kim's thinking, the story is built on the Korean problems of suspicious deaths in the military and the deaths of overworked men (A. Kim 2016, 425). The already discussed *Misaeng* openly confronts discrimination at work and temporary workers' plight, while Choi's *100 Degrees Celsius* relates the June 1987 democratic uprising through the lives of one family caught up in the turmoil of the Chun Doo-hwan period; *Songgot* fictionizes the true story of the friction that led to a 512-day strike by workers of the French-owned Carrefour retail company and its sale to the E-Land Company and its subsidiary, Homever; and *Lawyers for Workers* tells of ten important incidents that shaped the Korean labor movement (432). Kim concludes that realism-based webtoons are not only popular but also combine commercialism with social awareness and indirectly give voices to people who are not able to speak out in real life (433).

Another matter that webtoons have given an open and sometimes fierce voice to is Korean feminism and the status of young women. In 2015, the radical feminist website Megalia first appeared, different from previous peaceful and academic platforms in that it employs a "mirroring" method that imitates the derogatory language that men have used against women over the ages. Both Naver and Daum created websites with webtoons that portray the lives of young Korean women—*My ID Is Gangnam Beauty!* (*Nae IDneun Gangnam Miin!*) (2016–2017) and *Mask Girl* (2015–2018) on Naver, and *There Is No Areum in the Engineering College* on Daum (Yoon 2017). Written by Kee Maeng-kee, *My ID Is Gangnam Beauty!* was impactful for the social issues it raised such as beauty standards, insecurities, and other aspects affecting young women's lives. In some ways, *Cheese in the Trap*, first written in 2010 by Soonkki and appearing over seven years, fit in with these stories in dealing with young women's issues. The 180-chapter webcomic, which became a television hit in 2016, follows college student Hong Seol and her relationship with a model male student who she suspects has a darker side. The story takes on the harsh reality of college life, the injustices of group work, and a young woman's confrontation with others' expectations of how she should behave.

Throughout the brief existence of webtoons, creators have extended their reach to encompass a wide swath of viewers/readers, as seen in the example of Megalia with its feminist twist; at the same time, they have tried out different story styles and genres, sometimes through technical touches, other times reviving characteristics of manhwa, and occasionally mixing styles or genres and coming up with something different or even unique. An example of the latter are *isekai manhwa*, formulaic stories focusing on an average person being reincarnated in a fantasy setting and becoming a protagonist, and its subgenre, *otome isekai*, in which a young woman is reincarnated into the world of an *otome* (maiden) dating game, but as a villainess (Freedman 2020). *Otome isekai*, a webnovel form, became popular in Korea in about 2013, as webnovels were converted into webtoons. Korean *otome isekai* webtoons soon became popular in Japan with Piccoma, a manhwa app made by Kakao Entertainment for the Japanese market, which predominantly featured Korean webtoons. Among the titles are *Solo Leveling*, *Death Is the Only Ending for the Villainess*, and *Omniscient Reader*.

In the earliest days, webtoons were basically collages of lighthearted drawings; however, by the 2010s, they often were high-tech with sound, movement, vibration, and other special effects. In July 2011, artist Horang introduced 3-D effects in his short horror webtoon *OK-su Station Ghost*, released on Naver. In one scene, the hand of a ghost seems to jump off the screen as if to grab viewers. The next month, Horang's *Bongcheon dong Ghost* carried a scene in which a "horrific bloody face of a ghost seemed to fly towards the viewers as it made a creepy, riveting sound" (Ko 2015).

Ko Dong-hwan (2015) gives other examples of advanced technology used in Korean webtoons, mainly in horror stories with the intention of frightening audiences. Among them are "smarttoons," which breathe life into static drawings; a few examples Ko gives involve a vibrating phone synchronized with a viewer's "smart" phone to ring at the same time, and "voicetoons" that use voice actors to speak the dialogue. These gimmicks may have stirred public interest for a brief time, as did *byeong-mat* ("a taste of mind-numbing stupidity") content, introduced by the already mentioned Lee Mal-nyeon. But to have commercial success, namely having webtoons adaptable to television or film, webtoonists knew they needed genre-based webtoons of high quality with strong plots. Ko (2015) identified Han Dong-woo as one of the leaders of a genre-based content movement with *My Nights*, an R-rated, politically charged thriller based on the true story of a hostess, Jeong In-suk, who had an affair with Prime Minister Chung Il-kwon and was killed on a Seoul street by an unknown gunman. After Han's short-story version was published to much acclaim in Japan's *Grand Jump* magazine in 2011, he released it on Daum as a series in 2012, where it became the portal's top webtoon. Other high-quality stories followed that broke online readership records or made it to television or movies including *Joseon Kingdom Annals Talk* by Byun Ji-min, *Prince of Prince* by JAEA and SE, *Burning Hell* by Youn In-wan and Yang Kyoung-il, and *Along with the Gods: The Two Worlds* by Ju Ho-min.

5.8. *Squid Game* scene.

Along with the Gods is an example of the "treasure trove of original stories" that emanated from webtoons in increasing numbers during the 2010s. A blend of melodrama, fantasy, humor, satire, action, and folklore, the story revolves around a dead man who is judged in seven hells by various gods in the afterlife. The film version was released in December 2019 and became the second-highest-grossing Korean movie of any kind and the highest among those that evolved from a webtoon (Jin 2020). As with most transmedia operations, the webtoon-turned-film required tweaks because of narrative complexity and different audiences.

Jin Dal Yong (2020) analyzed *Along with the Gods*, looking at features of webtoons that lead to good moviemaking:

1. "Webtoons reflect various real lives that many people are able to easily sympathize with";
2. They have the potential to turn into long, novel-length literature even though webcartoonists publish only a few pages at a time;
3. They demonstrate that Korea can create webtoon movies heavily dependent on computer-generated imagery; and
4. They use "timely and desirable" values and mores.

Along with the Gods was turned into eight books, and the movie version had 2,300 shots with visual effects; the story focuses on family values and filial piety.

Building stories around the lives of real people with problems to which others can relate has led to some highly profitable and award-winning webtoons, an example being the violent *Squid Game* (2021). The plot of this survival drama, created by Hwang Dong-hyuk with a nearly all-Korean cast, revolves around the economic despair felt by many young Koreans in a country with one of the highest suicide rates in the world. *Squid Game* provides a last-ditch solution in which debt-ridden individuals play children's games that could be fatal, for a chance to win more than US$38 million (Park K 2021). Funded by Netflix, the nine-episode television series gained international fame as the world's most-watched show and garnered many awards and nominations, such as a Golden Globe, a Screen Actors Guild Award, and a Primetime Emmy. The series was renewed for a 2024 release.

The Business of Webtoons[5]

It is safe to say that at the launch of the 2020s, webtoons ranked atop or near the top of all South Korean media forms in acceleration of the industry's growth, estimated future growth rate, expansion of transmedia and transnational connections, the start-up of new companies and platforms, and acquisitions and mergers among older platforms. Webtoons had become big business within the span of a generation.

Growth Rates

The phenomenal speed at which South Korean webtoons developed can be viewed from the industry's overall figures and individual platforms' growth rates. In 2020, the market size of Korean webtoons amounted to about one trillion Korean won (US$855 million, at a rate of US$1 to 1,183 won), up from 584.5 billion won (US$494 million) in 2016. Figures for 2019 showed that the total revenue from the top ten Korean webtoon platforms was 289.4 billion won (US$245 million), led by Naver with 93.4 billion won (US$79 million) and followed by Kakao Page, 52.2 billion won (US$44 million); Toptoon, 40.4 billion won (US$34.1 million); and Lezhin Comics, 37.4 billion won (US$31.6 million) (Park E-m and Lee 2019). The webtoon market reached 1.05 trillion won in 2020, according to the Korea Creative Content Agency. A later figure had Naver with gross merchandise volume ("a metric for the amount of money spent by users within the app") of US$900 million in 2021, up from $492 million in 2019, a 46 percent jump. That same year, Naver consisted of an astounding 750,000 creators with eighty-two million active monthly users. Also impressive was Piccoma's monthly revenue of $96 million in January 2021, making it the second-top-grossing non-gaming app worldwide. Piccoma is the Japanese webtoon affiliate of Korea's Kakao Corporation (72.9 percent owner) and Kakao Entertainment (18.2 percent) (Davies and Song 2022; see also Lee M-j and Hyuga 2022; Kim Soo 2022). In August 2022, Piccoma postponed plans to go public on the Tokyo Stock Exchange because of slumping tech valuations, hoping to maintain its 2021 valuation of US$6.2 million. (Lee M-j and Hyuga 2022).

Much of the growth has been attributed to the entry and quick rise of new and midsize online publishers in the 2010s that focused on content for adults with purchasing power and foreign markets. A couple of examples support these points. By breaking into the US market, Lezhin Comics became South Korea's fourth-largest platform in just six years, from its 2013 founding until 2019, with 946 content items compared to number one Naver Webtoon's 1,025 (Park E-m and Lee 2019). Perhaps a more remarkable success story is that of Postype and its creator, Shin Gyu-seub. A software engineer and heavy consumer of online content, Shin decided to do something about what he considered to be low-quality webtoons, in 2015 creating Postype, "a content open market platform" (quoted in Song J-a 2022). With a compound annual growth rate of 92 percent from 2017 to 2020, Postype placed 108th in the 2022 *Financial Times* ranking of high-growth Asia-Pacific companies. At that time, the company had more than 4.8 million monthly active users and more than 330,000 writers. The platform attracts creators because it allows amateurs and professionals to upload their work and make money; does not screen their work; does not require the signing of a contract or charging readers a fee; and helps to find funding and to build a fan base for webtoonists' stories (Song J-a 2022).

The larger platforms stayed apace in expansion, primarily through adaptations and going global. Webtoons lend themselves to offshoots to television and cinema because each series has weekly updates, providing a large amount of source material to draw from, and at much lower costs, keep series and sequels alive. To give an idea of the wealth of story material that is available: in 2021, South Korea had more than 14,000 webtoons made by 9,900 creators (J. Lee 2021).

Future Prospects

Webtoons were not considered "flash-in-the-pan" media forms; in 2022, they were forecast to grow worldwide by a rate of 31 percent annually from 2022 to 2028, from a market size of US$3.7 billion in 2021 to $26.2 billion by 2028. The Asia-Pacific region was the largest market with about 71 percent, followed by North America with 14 percent and Europe, 11 percent (*Digital Journal* 2022).

Predictions for South Korean webtoons were also very positive as records continued to topple by large numbers for the number of creators and users, market size and share of the market, the number of adaptations to other media, and international reach. Newspapers and other periodicals regularly headlined articles that claimed webtoons were "shaping the future of global media" (*Forbes*; J. MacDonald 2021), driving the "K-drama craze" (the *Indian Express*; PTI News Agency 2022), "riding the Wave" (the *Los Angeles Review of Books*; McKinney 2020), "taking over the world" (the *Hustle*; Litterst 2022), becoming mainstream, going global (the *Korea Herald*; Choi 2020), hitting "unicorn status" (*Forbes*; Wang 2022), leveraging "low-cost stories with potential huge upside" (Reuters; J. Lee 2021), and witnessing "significant growth until 2025" (TechSci Research 2021). The TechSci Research report expected the South Korean webtoon market to grow at an "impressive" rate until 2025, with romance and comedy being the dominant genres. Research Director Karan Chechi said,

> [The] South Korea webtoons market is expected to grow significantly owing to their growing popularity not only in the country but also across the globe. The effect of [the] Korean wave is clearly visible across the globe especially among . . . countries such as China, India, Indonesia, Vietnam, Singapore, among others in the Asia Pacific region. This is in turn expected to positively influence the market growth through 2025. Furthermore, the emergence of various webtoon developer countries and freelancers is expected to further bolster the market growth over the next few years. (TechSci Research 2021)

Korean webtoons seem to have very few limits, even benefiting from the global COVID-19 pandemic. A KOCCA survey of forty-three webtoon companies and 625 webcartoonists for the period of 2019 and the first half of 2020 revealed that the readership of webtoons increased by 37.4 percent because of COVID-19, with 63.4 percent of survey respondents answering that they read webtoons at least once a week. One half of the companies credited COVID-19 with boosting sales (Yoon 2020), understandable during long periods of lockdown.[6] As an example, Tapas, a division of Kakao Entertainment, had a ten times year-over-year revenue boost in 2021, much of it credited to COVID-19 (Griepp 2022b). A Korean Film Council report showed that webtoon viewing outpaced movie theater attendance by an astronomical percentage over the course of a year because of the pandemic (Kwak 2020).

Acquisitions, Mergers, Startups

The practices of acquiring more properties, merging with other firms, and signing deals with still others to handle auxiliary aspects, all with the intention to grow, perhaps into conglomerates, raised heads in the Korean webtoon industry in the early 2020s. Webtoons seemed on the verge of joining a large segment of the world's mass media that are owned by conglomerates such as Disney.

One of the initial huge transactions was Korea's largest platform, Naver, purchasing Toronto-based Wattpad in early 2021 for more than US$600 million in cash and stocks. Wattpad, an online social writing and reading platform with more than five million writers and ninety million users, was to align with Naver's Webtoon and provide stories for young adult readers online and in print (Nawotka 2021). In November 2021, Webtoon started a new graphic novel imprint, Webtoon Unscrolled, to be published under the Wattpad umbrella.

Just a few months later, Kakao Entertainment purchased Los Angeles–based Tapas Media for US$510 million in cash, intensifying the competition with Naver for the North American webtoon market. At the time, Tapas was one of North America's fastest-growing webtoon platforms, with 500 percent growth in year-over-year revenues in 2020, generated from its 96,000 original series of comics and prose novels. Prior to this move, Kakao announced its intention to spend $889 million on new assets (Salkowitz 2021). In May 2022, Kakao merged Tapas with the digital prose platform Radish, valued at $440 million, which it had bought in 2021, forming a venue for the Asian fantasy fiction platform Wuxiaworld, which it had purchased in December 2021 for $37.5 million. Kakao, which took credit for developing the webnovel-to-webtoon model, planned to use the merged firm as a "pipeline of intellectual property from webnovel to webtoon and other media including films, television, and gaming" (Griepp 2022b). Kakao also acquired Neobazar, an Indonesian webtoon and games producer.

In late July 2022, Tapas Media sent shockwaves throughout the webtoon industry, shifting to more user-generated content (UGC) and away from its acquisition of "new content from new and established creators" (H. MacDonald 2022a), and merging Tapas, Radish, and Wuxiaworld under CEO Chang Kim. The shift away from original content was particularly surprising, according to *The Beat* staffer Heidi MacDonald (2022a), because Tapas "had been positioning itself as a place for creators to bring original content, hoping to tap into the lucrative but highly selective world of top webcomics like Lore Olympus." She speculated that the "softening of the tech/streaming market left these companies less valuable by a huge factor." Getting rid of the gatekeepers and relying more on readers for the direction that webcomic content will take, Tapas also announced that 30 percent of the overall staff of the three companies would be laid off, 80 percent from Radish alone. These layoffs included high-ranking executives and large chunks of the editorial staff. The Tapas webcomic creator base is very young in age (between seventeen and twenty-five) and very female-centric (two-thirds of the readers), and they desire topics that young people can directly relate to, according to a company vice president.

In August 2022, CEO Chang Kim explained the Tapas "ramp-down" of in-house originals and the mass layoff as efforts to "optimize" the business. He said that developing stories in-house is "nice," but it is the "most time-consuming, resource-heavy approach," and thus, Tapas decided to scale back. Instead, Chang Kim said that Tapas will "double down on the community" for story ideas, and independent creators will continue to be offered different ways to monetize, for instance tipping, merchandising options, and a monthly stipend (Salkowitz 2022b). Seven months later, Kakao Entertainment announced the closure of its Korean branch of Tapas to zero in on the advancement of the company's North American and other global interests (H. MacDonald 2023).

Rival Webtoon had cut editorial staff earlier, after precipitating a surge of original content for the US market and then going to a UGC Korean model. Webtoon vice president for content David Lee explained the company's monetization program in the United States as made up of two groups, its "Originals," who are offered contracts, and its "Canvas," which allows a place for independent creators to self-publish. Key features of the plan are its advertising revenue sharing, whereby Webtoon creators with a thousand subscribers and forty thousand monthly page views can receive 50 percent of revenue from ads placed on their content; its allowing Originals creators to own copyright control of their work; and its offering Originals creators contract advances and revenue sharing on paid content (Stanley 2022).

Large businesses are known for gathering into their fold auxiliary companies that provide products and services necessary for their own maintenance or enhancement. This practice is not new; almost a century ago, US publishing mogul Samuel I. Newhouse owned a paper mill that helped supply newsprint for his chain of newspapers and magazines (see Lent 1966). With webtoons, the products and services are stories and licensing, merchandising, and film and television opportunities.

Korean webtoon companies were relatively slow in soliciting help from such service firms. Possible reasons may have been that they were not large enough to require or afford outside help in their early stages, that they did not recognize the huge potential of webtoons until the late 2010s and early 2020s, or that they followed the pattern of Korean animation, which also was a latecomer in adopting licensing and merchandising as part of its business plan. LINE Webtoon, launched worldwide by Naver in July 2014, was an exception, signing with the Creative Artists Agency (CAA) in 2016 to represent its manhwa titles for film and television opportunities in the United States (Spangler 2016). In 2021, Naver Webtoon signed a deal with DC Comics and HYBE (the biggest entertainment company in Korea), giving the latter an exclusive license to use characters owned or managed by the companies in its webtoons and to create new plots (Yoon 2021). The following year, Webtoon worked out an arrangement with a brand management firm, Surge Licensing, to handle the licensing and merchandising of its intellectual properties and create a brand strategy (Alverson 2022).

Among the many startups in the late 2010s and early 2020s is Ize Press, an imprint of Yen Press (which itself is part of the behemoth Hachette), dedicated to Korean material. Ize Press's chief function is to publish print editions of popular Korean webtoons. Of its initial titles, seven are from Webtoon and two from Tapas (Griepp 2022a). A leading e-reading platform, Ridi Corporation, started a subscription-based webtoon app, Manta, in 2020; and the streaming platform Watcha (started in 2011 as Watcha Pedia, a data platform, from which Watcha was launched in 2016) expanded to include webtoons in 2022 (Song S-h 2022). In 2018, Kenaz began as a webtoon production startup company, and by the time it sold a 40 percent share to a domestic hedge fund in 2022, it was leading the field (Kim J-w 2022). In December 2022, Kenaz signed a three-year contract with Apple to supply webtoons to its global-reaching Books app (Lee M-j, Lee, and Bloomberg 2023).

Piracy and Labor Issues

Piracy has been a piercing thorn to South Korean comics art from its post–World War II rejuvenation, usually pertaining to manga during the more than half century when Japanese cultural forms were banned in Korea. Webtoons were not spared despite coming onto the scene after the ban was lifted. File sharing of Korean hardback manhwa dates to about 2000, when a few online sites existed. Scanned comics really took off in 2003–2004, when the prices of scanners dropped considerably. The Korea Cartoonists Association reported that the manhwa industry lost sixty billion won (US$60 million) in 2006, only ten billion won short of the country's entire industry (Kim K-t 2006). Fifteen years later, Lee Hae-rin, reporting in the *Korea Times*, wrote that illegal scanlation (a portmanteau of "scan" and "translation") of webcomics abroad was still growing rampantly and "causing growing financial and psychological damage to Korean creators" (Lee H-r 2021b) According to the Korean Foundation for International Cultural Exchange, more than 1,300 scanlation aggregate websites exist in more than thirty countries, hosting unlicensed and amateur translations of webcomics from Korea and other countries in forty-plus languages and yielding 334.8 billion page views in 2020. Nearly every Korean webcomic is illegally scanlated and shared online, the head of the Korean Webtoon Creators Union, Kim Dong-hoon, said. The scanlators contend that the cost, quality, and speed of releases on legal platforms are unsatisfactory and that the creators should be flattered by the global reach their works get through scanlations. On the other hand, 92 percent of surveyed Korean webtoon creators said that illegal scanlations make it difficult for them to work, and more than 50 percent had considered retirement because of the piracy. The latest information (before publication of this book) shows that as the country's webtoon industry continued to post bullish growth with sales of US$1.27 billion in 2021 (48.6 percent over 2020), so did the illegal distribution of webtoons, up 53.6 percent from the previous year (Park H-s 2023).

In April 2020, the Korean government and Interpol started a three-year investigation with the intent of arresting individuals engaging in the illegal distribution of Korean contents. The next year, a group of boys' love webtoon artists began a campaign against piracy sites, claiming that, because a large number of views were through piracy, their revenues suffered. Others said that up to 70 percent of their income can be lost to piracy, that to issue takedowns of the illegal material takes time and creates stress, and that many illegal sites expose adult material to children (Morrissy 2021).

A major issue of Korean animation when the industry was a world leader in offshore production was labor exploitation, a problem that has also come up at times with webtoons. However, a crucial difference is creativity—offshore animation was based on doing finishing work on stories conceived, plotted, and sketched in non-Korean studios, whereas webtoons involve content creation at all stages.

A question that webtoon platform operators have faced is, how is value produced? Compounding the question is that early webtoonists, and many still yet, make webcomics for personal enjoyment and do not expect financial compensation; so, creative labor is associated with pleasure.

In a very comprehensive article, Kim Ji-hyeon and Yu Jun (2019) provide an overview of how the evolving platformizing of webtoons affects Korean creative and digital labor, which is summarized here. They point out the differences between manhwa and webtoon work practices and the benefits and criticisms of webtoon labor: manhwa creators start out as apprentices to senior cartoonists, usually work under editors, are prone to be censored or guided, expect to be rewarded financially, and often have to be loyal to one publisher. Webtoonists normally do not experience intervention by platform operators; have a sense of autonomy; own their works; are not wedded to economic capital, technical training, or expert advice; and are free in nearly all parts of the creative process, which Kim and Yu believe is beneficial to amateur webtoonists and leads to more diversity of genres and production methods, or what they term "mass amateurization." Under these new norms, it is necessary that artists adapt to digitalization, be disciplined and self-taught, and not expect payment unless commissioned.

Almost all webtoon platforms operate three-tier competitions to determine who is commissioned, advancement depends on user feedback and ratings—in other words, popularity. Criticisms about the tier system have been frequent over the years, according to Kim and Yu (2019), because only a few winners from the top tier benefit. For example, of Naver's 120,000 amateurs who uploaded to the site, only 0.03 percent were commissioned. Lucrative adaptations are also rare in that selling copyrights is limited to the famous and popular artists; only 1.8 percent of webtoonists receive the majority of their annual income from copyright sales (Kim J-h and Yu 2019).

Much of Kim and Yu's information comes from a survey they conducted with fourteen anonymous webtoonists affiliated with Naver and Daum (Kakao) from 2015 to 2017. What they found was that the average monthly compensation for amateurs was a mere US$360, which some scholars call "exploitative and precarious" (Jin 2015, 201). One respondent who had won the three-tier competition said that the platforms did not "reflect the popularity (during the competition) when it comes to budgeting the cost of our work" (Jin-Ah [pseud.], quoted in Kim J-h and Yu 2019). Other concerns expressed were that webtoonists do not share information with one another about their relationships with platform operators and are discouraged from doing so; platforms have the power to choose which webtoons are commissioned, using popularity as the most decisive factor; and the choosing is done "informally, irregularly," and in an unfair way, all of this leading to "platform imperialism." At one point, Kim and Yu (2019) equate these actions with "digital capitalism . . . which seeks to colonize all the domains of webtoon-related activities."

In another survey reported in 2019, of four Korean webtoon creators, four company producers, and the CEO of Korea's major webtoon service, reactions to labor issues were mixed. The creators acknowledged that the webtoon industry provided them with "opportunities and benefits" but described their relationships with platform companies as "not always amicable"—a "tug of war" (Pyo, Jang, and Yoon 2019, 2170). They expressed discontent with unfair income, excessive workloads (of as many as eighty cuts per week), strict policies on late submission, and "required modifications of their contents," the latter necessitating "compromise by sacrificing quality" (Pyo, Jang, and Yoon 2019, 2170). Interviewed producers said they interacted with creators and understood their gripes, but, as representatives of the platform companies, they stood by the "commercial side," ready to enforce rules and "prevent creators' power outgrowing their own" (Pyo, Jang, and Yoon 2019, 2172).

Platform companies have made adjustments benefiting webtoonists, especially small and medium-size platforms that have formulated more "creator-centered incubator" policies such as scouting for outstanding amateurs able to operate at basic and second-tier levels (Kim J-h and Yu 2019). Naver and Daum introduced creator-friendly policies in about 2012, partly reacting to the introduction of other platforms and the public criticism of webtoonists' working conditions. KOCCA reported in 2016 that these two major platforms "increased the minimum monthly wage for all commissioned webtoonists to US$1,800, and in 2013, they launched 'competitive compensation' programs such as a Page Profit Share (PPS) strategy, which maximizes the exposure of character products and paid content created by particular webtoonists and gives 70% of the revenue generated to corresponding webtoonists" (Korea Creative Content Agency 2016, 17–21, abstracted in Kim J-h and Yu 2019). Platforms over the years modified other policies to benefit webtoonists in the second tier, such as Naver and Daum permitting them to insert advertisements into their pages, from which they receive half of the revenues; or LINE Webtoon organizing a crowdfunding program through which audiences can donate money directly to the amateur webtoonists, or webtoon platforms in general, adopting "competitive crowdsourcing" in which "digital collaboration occurs in the format of idea contests" (Kim J-h and Yu 2019).

By the 2020s, Naver Webtoon showed pride in how it treated creators, occasionally releasing payment information to the press and the public. In mid-2022, the company boasted that its payments to English-language creators had surpassed US$27 million since 2020, an average of more than $1 million a month and nearly a 75 percent increase since starting its creator monetization program in the United States in 2019 (Salkowitz 2022a). In South Korea, the top Naver Webtoon creator was paid more than $9 million in 2021.

Taking into account the "power curve where a few top features account for a majority of revenue, views, and subscribers, with a long tail of material that generates significantly less," still, on average, some South Korean creators made six figures (in US dollars) in 2021 (Salkowitz 2022a). Naver Webtoon also reported its gross merchandise volume in 2021 as $900 million.

Apparently, the modifications by platform companies made a difference. In 2021, webtoonists made double the average annual income in Korea, according to KOCCA, pulling in an average of 81.2 million won (US$73,080 at the 2021 exchange rate) if they worked all year round. The average annual income in 2021 was 38.3 million won ($34,470). Of course, this average for webtoonists is spiked by the incomes of a few top creators such as Kian84, Lee Mal-nyeon, and Yaongi, who each bring in roughly US$1 million in a year.[7] Nevertheless, in 2020, "webtoonist" was one of the top ten dream jobs of Korean elementary school students (Yoon 2022).

Other points Kim and Yu (2019) deducted from their survey and readings include: platform staff, who still make decisions about which webtoonists are promoted or commissioned, usually have no expertise as in the manhwa industry; criteria for evaluating webtoons are not based on narrative, aesthetics, and drawing skills but on what is fun and popular and what delivers user satisfaction; capturing an audience's attention has become a form of capital; popularity as a barometer is a "direct proxy for whether or not a webtoonist is qualified enough to be successful"; platforms "scarcely" protect webtoonists from the physical and emotional stress that can result from directly interacting with audiences; the webtoonist-platform relationship is more complex than that between cartoonists and a sole proprietor; and there is a "critical ambivalence" of free labor in the digital context, meaning that labor is "unwaged . . . and exploited," but also "voluntarily given and . . . enjoyed" (Terranova 2000, 36, quoted in Kim J-h and Yu 2019).

Transmedia and Transnational Surges

Pyo, Jang, and Yoon (2019, 2162) describe webtoons as "outstanding" examples of hybridization and convergence culture, embodying transmedia tendencies and aspirations ("delivery of a similar story across different media") and transnationalism (dispatching versions of webtoons to other countries).

This is an apt portrayal of South Korean webtoons as they existed in the mid-2010s and after, as television and cinema directors more fully recognized the rich reservoir of stories in webtoons; as genres or stories were merged, sometimes creating hybrids in the process; and as platforms and webtoonists increasingly tapped the lucrative international market with fare altered to be clearly translated, easily understood, and culturally aware and sensitive—in other words, made glocal.

Transmedia webtoons took off in about 2018 and continued onward; during the 2010s, there were twenty-six webtoon adaptations on television, and more than half of those appeared in the last two years of the decade. That ten-year total nearly doubled in 2022 alone, when Kpopmap confirmed that forty-eight dramas based on webtoons were forthcoming.

Webtoons are rich sources of storylines suitable for adaptation, offering perks not available with printed novels and short stories, nor with original scripts. *Forbes* journalist Joan MacDonald mentions a few of these benefits:

> [T]he creativity the format inspires . . . [is] a boon for novice writers who have innovative ideas and previously had limited platforms. Because they don't have any limitations on imagination, webtoons can deliver interesting and unusual stories. . . . [T]hey save the time and energy a drama or film would otherwise spend developing a story line. (J. MacDonald 2019)

Furthermore, webtoon adaptations are relatively inexpensive, cutting out some costly stages such as developing a story; they possess a built-in audience and have a one-source, multiuse capability. Coupled with the already mentioned advantageous features of webtoons generally, it is not surprising that they have become the most sought-after pool of abundant storylines for Korean film and television conversions.

The Korean government is very much aware of webtoons' success, the Ministry of Culture, Sports, and Tourism posting an article on its website in August 2020 declaring that Korean webtoons showed the potential to become "the next big genre" boosting *hallyu* (Kim Soo 2022). The national government provided indirect support for the industry years before through "public subsidy and investment programs, abolition of unnecessary regulations, and provision of translating service for foreign webtoon markets . . . establishing a policy for reducing pirate or illegal websites from 10% of total market in 2013 to 5% of the market by 2018" (Lynn 2016a, 10). More direct support came when the government backed Busan International Film Festival, as early as 2011, launched a market program, Book to Film, to help publishers connect with filmmakers, after which the number of webtoon titles grew "significantly" (Lee H-w 2017).

Many webtoon-originated films and television series have been of a high standard, attracting star-studded casts of actors and actresses who have performed in blockbuster films such as the crime classic *Old Boy* and the Oscar-winning *Parasite* (Best Picture and Best Director, plus two others), and receiving high recognition in Korea and abroad. For example, *Squid Game* won a Golden Globe; *D. P.* made the *New York Times* Best International Shows list of 2021; and others were nominated for Screen Actors Guild Awards, Eisner Awards, and other prestigious honors.

Their success was followed by other high-grossing films and series that emanated from webtoons. The supernatural apocalyptic drama *Hellbound* broke all records as the most-streamed non-English series in its first weekend in November 2021, chalking up more than forty-three million viewing hours; in 2022, the romantic comedy *Business Proposal* appeared among the top ten shows on the Netflix TV chart, at the same time that its webtoon origin, *The Office Blind Date*, had 160 million views in Korea and a total of 450 million views worldwide, reaching number one in sales in Taiwan, Thailand, and Indonesia; while the zombie apocalypse Netflix-streamed drama *All of Us Are Dead* quickly had 560.8 million hours of viewing while its original webtoon, *Now at Our School*, shot up eighty-fold in online views and fifty-nine-fold in sales in February 2022 (Kim B 2022). The immense popularity of television adaptations of webcomics definitely spurred sales of their originals.

The ready adaptability of webtoons lends itself to other entertainment forms besides cinema, television, and books. For example, at one point, the very popular K-pop band BTS released a webtoon on Naver titled *Save Me*, featuring the band members' "adventures . . . with a little time travel thrown into the plot" (J. MacDonald 2019).

Webtoons followed the trajectory of other Korean Wave (*hallyu*) entertainment, weaving their way into Japan, Southeast Asia, the United States, and Europe, in the process becoming a global popular culture form. Webtoons were relative latecomers to the Korean Wave, as Korean dramas were exported to more than eighty countries and K-pop music had in excess of fifty billion views and downloads on YouTube by 2015 (Jang and Lee 2016, 6). This cultural spread was greatly enhanced by the many instances of foreign consumers of Korean Wave cultural products turning themselves into producers of localized versions; for example, a Vietnamese K-pop-style group emerged after the Korean idol band 365 performed in the country. Called "glocalization," this phenomenon creates a "balance between the hybridity of global factors and local characteristics" (Jang and Song 2017, 170). The term came out of the Japanese business field of the 1980s.

Initially, webtoons were not immediate hits in foreign markets—first of all, because readers were accustomed to consuming comics through books and magazines, not a scrolling screen, and second, because of the lack of availability of good translations. The Naver platform initially provided webtoons only in English but by 2017 had added other languages such as Chinese, Taiwanese, Thai, and Bahasa Indonesia; a few months earlier, in 2014, Kakao's Daum Webtoon offered webtoons in English and Chinese (Lynn 2016a, 4–5).

Lynn Hyung-gu (2016b) includes translation among three potential hurdles to exporting webtoons, the other two being infrastructure and branding. Although Korea is at or near the top in the world in all categories of infrastructure, other emerging markets such as India, Indonesia, and the Philippines are not. As for branding, Lynn writes that crediting webtoons as Korean has "stuck"; however, quality of translation varies. Because translated titles are selected from a large pool, they are "the best," according to Lynn, but "maintaining consistence in translations of individual titles, not just in terms of fidelity to the original but culturally contextualized renderings, remains a challenge, especially for English versions" (2016b). Another obstacle webtoon platform operators have worked on alleviating in recent years is the strong Korean cultural environment embedded in Korean webtoon stories, often misunderstood or not relevant to foreigners. For example, the very successful dramatized TV webtoon *Misaeng*, about struggling Korean rookie office workers, did not resonate with Chinese audiences well, because of China's less stressful office settings (Doo 2017). Individuals in the industry have been aware of this dilemma for years. At a KOCCA conference in 2022, speakers addressed the need for a continuing supply of stories acceptable worldwide, suggesting the expansion of stories already developed, to meet the high demand of the burgeoning rise of platforms (Lee G-l 2022).

In the 2010s, Korean webtoon platforms began their services overseas. Comico, the webtoon platform of NHN Comico, opened in Japan in 2013; LINE Webtoon had Japanese, English, and Chinese services the following year, and not long after, Bahasa Indonesia and Thai. Japanese manga publishers, whose titles for years dominated large parts of Asia, including South Korea in the 1990s, began to take notice as sales of their comics magazines trended downward, and Korean webtoons made significant inroads. By 2019, the Line Corporation's LINE Manga had twenty-three million users in Japan, mainly reading manga titles that had first appeared in print. Increasingly, Korea-originated stories appeared among LINE Manga's offerings, and just as had happened in Korea in the 1980s and 1990s (only reversed), Japanese consumers likely were not aware of these webtoons' origins. Taking the analogy further, neutralizing all aspects of "South Koreanness" from these webtoons became an important strategy to quell reader backlash. A difference was that South Korean manhwa publishers hid the fact that their books were translations of manga because of their government's longtime ban of Japanese cultural products, while Japanese webtoon platform operators did so because of reader pride in manga's premier role in the world, and their disdain for foreign (particularly Korean) comics (Osaki 2019). Comparatively, the webtoon culture in Japan remained underdeveloped for a while, with a few exceptions, one being ReLIFE, a vertical comic by Japanese webtoonist So Yayoi, later converted to anime and live-action film. Kakao's Piccoma did well in sales, its trading volume increasing 2.3 times year-on-year in 2019 and more than doubling for the third consecutive year (Park M-j 2020) while becoming Japan's second-largest manga app, but 98 percent of its content consisted of Japanese-style horizontal manga and 2 percent, webtoons (Osaki 2019). By 2021, Piccoma and LINE Manga had become the highest-grossing nongaming mobile apps in Japanese app stores.

Korean webtoons swept other parts of Asia to different degrees. India took to Korean Wave cultural products, including webtoons, during the pandemic lockdowns of 2020 onward. Kross Komics, headquartered in Seoul and cofounded by Kim Hyunwoo Thomas, pioneered the webcomic format for the Indian market, bringing out about one hundred titles in December 2019. Kim said that Korean website stories were very different from what Indian readers were used to, namely the *Amar Chitra Katha* books full of mythologies and superheroes; in contrast, webtoons talk about "love, dating, romance and just everyday life" (quoted in Gowri 2021). Translations in the early stages were in Hindi and Telugu (and, of course, English), but Kim planned to expand into at least eleven other Indian languages in a few years. In 2021, daily readership was between sixty thousand and one hundred thousand—70 percent in English, 25 percent in Hindi, and 5 percent, Telugu (Gowri 2021).

Naver Webtoon and Comico opened the Southeast Asia market with original webtoons and translated titles in Indonesia and Thailand, while translated titles of Daum and Mr. Blue were used in Vietnam's first webtoon portal, Vinatoon. Naver Webtoon dominated in Thailand, Indonesia, and Taiwan, with more than thirteen million monthly active users in 2022. Significant growth was very evident in the figures for the three countries: year-on-year, weekly transaction volume reached new highs, increasing by about 68 percent, and monthly transactions rose by approximately 55 percent year-on-year. More impressive was that local

5.9. The New York City subway advertisement for webtoon strips that caused some uproar. Photo by Heidi MacDonald.

folktale webtoons topped sales charts in Indonesia and Thailand (P. Lee 2022).

After Japan, the second-largest comic book pool to tap with webtoons is that of the United States. Korean manhwa in printed version attracted US-based manga publishers such as Tokyopop, Dark Horse, Central Park Media, and Drama Queen, and Korean publishers Ice Kunion and Netcomics, around 2005. The American publishers saw manhwa as a "fresh source of potentially lucrative properties"; the Koreans saw their export as an opportunity to reinvigorate faltering domestic sales (Lee Sunyoung 2007). At a time when other manhwa companies had not figured out how to use the internet to sell their titles, Netcomics and its parent company, Ecomix, in 2006 began paying webtoonists a per-page rate for their stories and devised a pay-per-view system for its English-speaking audiences. By the end of 2006, Netcomics was offering fifty-eight volumes of twenty-five manhwa series in horizontal form online (Lee Sunyoung 2007).

The vertically scrolling story format, pioneered by Naver's Webtoon, debuted in the United States in 2014, and by 2020 that single platform, Webtoon, rivaled the revenue of the entire US comics industry—"periodicals, graphic novels and digital across all publishers, genres and channels" (Salkowitz 2021). Naver Webtoon, founded by Kim Jun-koo in 2004, was the world's largest platform in 2022, hosting 750,000 creators and eighty-two million active monthly users (Davies and Song 2022), operating in more than sixty countries. There were no signs that the firm was about to rest on its achievements as it continued marketing relentlessly, for instance in mid-2022 plastering the New York City subway with splashy advertisements for Webtoon (e.g., *We Basically Invented Doom-Scrolling*) and some of its most successful shows, such as *Everything Is Fine* (forty-three million views), *Homesick* (fifty-six million views), and *Lore Olympus* (1.1 billion views). Taking over an entire New York City subway station with advertisements is pricey, well into six figures in US dollars (H. MacDonald 2022). One of Webtoon's subway advertisements, for *Lore Olympus*, raised the ire of some creators, who took offense that their work was reduced to a "side-hustle" as stated in the text: "Comics are literature's fun side-hustle." Webtoon immediately issued an apology and promised to change the advertisement (Drum 2022).

Many of the most popular shows on US streamers were adaptations of Korean webtoons. On Netflix, there were the fantasy horror drama *Sweet Home* (2020), the Golden Globe and Emmy Award winner *Squid Game* (*Ojingeo Game*) (2021), *All of Us Are Dead* (*Jigeum Uri Hakgyoneun*) (2022), *Hellbound* (*Jiok*) (2021), *D. P.* (Deserter Pursuit) (2021), and others; Disney+ had its first Korean series, *Snowdrop* (*Seolganghwa*), in December 2021, the same month Apple+ released its initial K-drama series, *Dr. Brain*. The largest streaming service for Asian content in the United States, Rakuten Viki, housed more than forty webtoon-inspired K-dramas and films in 2022, with top-ranking *True Beauty*

(*Yeosin Gangrim*) (2020); *My Roommate Is a Gumiho* (*Gan Ddeoleojineun Donggeo*) and *So I Married an Anti-Fan* (*Graeseo Naneun Anti-fan'gwa Gyeolhonhaetda*), both 2021; and *What's Wrong with Secretary Kim* (*Kimbiseoga Oegreolkka*) (2018) (see Kim Soo 2022).

Korean webtoons found their way into Europe, primarily France, in the 2010s. The Francophone webtoon portal site Delitoon was started in 2009 by the leading French-language comics publisher, Casterman. In the beginning, Delitoon merely scanned printed comics; actual webtoon-style comics appeared later, and from 2015 to 2017 the platform hosted forty Korean webtoons in addition to three French webtoons created by local artists (Jang and Song 2017, 181). In 2022, Naver Webtoon opened Webtoon EU in France to oversee its webtoon services in France, Germany, and Spain and to explore other possibilities in Europe. Naver's German service began in 2021; the following year, the company started an open webtoon platform, Canvas, to nurture German amateur webtoonists (Byun 2022). Its French and Spanish webtoon services date to 2019. Naver added new creators and series in 2022—about two hundred new series in French and one hundred in German, both locally created and translated titles from top webtoonists in Korea, Japan, and the United States. In February 2022, Naver Webtoon's French and German services ranked first in monthly sales and active users among webtoon/comics apps on Google Play and the Apple App Store (Hume 2022). A 2020 survey by the Korea Trade-Investment Promotion Agency (KOTRA) showed that 7 out of 10 French respondents (out of a total of 580 respondents) had never heard of webtoons, but another 20 percent read them daily. Bound to inflate that number considerably was the installation of free Wi-Fi in the Paris metro in 2020 (Lee H-r 2021a).

Conclusion

Undoubtedly, webtoons are South Korea's major contribution to the world of comics art—a platform that has changed how comics are created, distributed, and read, and that allowed a much broader section of the population to participate in their production. With webtoons, both professional and amateur artists and writers have significantly changed comics with different technology ("smart" phones), stories, genres (e.g., *isekai* and *otome isekai*), and techniques (3-D, sound, vertical movement, vibration, and other special effects).

The rapid progression of webtoons gained much from their welcomed reception, initially in Japan and the United States, and then Southeast Asia, Europe, and elsewhere, in their original form or hybridized to more facilely meet local lifestyles and values; the eagerness of investors to create platforms; and the Korean government's recognition of their potential to shape the future of global media by abolishing some regulations and providing subsidies and services.

Socioculturally, the many realistic-oriented webtoons have given a voice to those who previously lacked outlets, for instance young women and feminists, and alluded to or reported on topics often avoided by mainstream media, such as the two Koreas policy, suspicious deaths in the military, work discrimination, and the labor movement.

Webtoons, by providing a different way of enjoying comics, have rescued the medium during a time when readers were pulled away by the internet and its attractions. The webtoon is not only Korea's unique contribution to global entertainment, but perhaps also the savior of manhwa.

Notes

1. Daum Webtoon reported that of the 500 webtoons on its service from its founding in 2003 to May 2018, 280 had been adapted into films, dramas, musicals, or novels.

2. I used the fast-food analogy relating to rushed, low-quality media content as early as the 1990s. One of the first instances of my usage of the term in a public presentation was in a major lecture in Seoul, September 7, 2001, at the International Symposium on Cultural Content, sponsored by the Korea Creative Content Agency. The title of the lecture was "Asian Media Content: Fast Food or a Cultural Banquet? Some Policy Implications."

3. South Korea has had the highest suicide rate among developed nations since the turn of the twenty-first century—24.6 suicides per 100,000 people in 2019. Older adults die by suicide because of poverty and isolation, young people because of lack

of employment possibilities, "constant pressure and endless competition," and the need to cope with the widening gap between the haves and have-nots. Between 2018 and 2019, the number of under-forty Koreans who committed suicide rose by 10 percent (K. Park 2021).

4. Choi Kyu-seok's work is also mentioned in the "Investigative Cartooning" section of chapter 2 of this book and treated more fully in Lent 2018, 90–109.

5. This section contains financial information that will be dated by the time this manuscript goes through the editing and production process; this is the case with all books. The data here are as current as possible at the time of writing, spring and early summer 2022. The information is valuable in establishing a timeline for comparative and contrastive purposes, and in adding to the historical record.

6. Other information from the survey that is not related to COVID-19 is provided in appendix V; such surveys are seldom conducted or publicly reported or are out of the financial reach of academia.

7. The split of all webtoon revenues allocates an average of 30 percent to the webtoon platform; the remaining 70 percent is divided equally by the agency and creator (Yoon 2022).

References

Alverson, Brigid. 2022. "Webtoon Signs with Surge Licensing." ICv2, May 12. https://icv2.com/articles/news/view/51170/webtoon-signs-with-surge-licensing.

Baek, Byung-yeul. 2014. "'Misaeng' Cartoonist Shares Advice for Success." *Korea Times*, December 8. https://www.koreatimes.co.kr/www/art/2024/05/398_169462.html.

Byun, Hye-jin. 2022. "Naver Webtoon to Set Up Branch in France." *Korea Herald*, March 21. http://www.koreaherald.com/view.php?ud=20220321000600.

Cho, Heek-young. 2016. "The Webtoon: A New Form for Graphic Narrative." *Comics Journal*, July 18. http://www.tcj.com/the-webtoon-a-new-form-for-graphic-narrative/.

Choi, Ji-won. 2020. "K-Webtoons Become Mainstream, Go Global." *Korea Herald*, May 6. https://www.koreaherald.com/view.php?ud=20200506000728&ACE_SEARCH=1.

Chung, Chul-yeon. 2004. Email interviews with Kwon Jae-woong. December 17, 29.

Davies, Christian, and Song Jung-a. 2022. "South Korea's Webtoon Companies Target Global Takeover." *Irish Times*, March 31. https://www.irishtimes.com/business/innovation/south-korea-s-webtoon-companies-target-global-takeover-1.4838395.

Digital Journal. 2022. "Webtoons Market Size, Share, Growth Factors, New Business Development, Top Leading Players, and Recent Developments, CAGR Status 2022 to 2028." April 5. https://www.digitaljournal.com/pr/webtoons-market-size-share-growth-factors-new-business-development-top-leading-players-and-recent-developments-cagr-status-2022-to-2028.

Doo, Rumy. 2017. "Korean Webtoon Readership Growing, Themes Need Diversifying: A Report." *Korea Herald*, February 5. https://www.koreaherald.com/view.php?ud=20170205000176.

Drum, Nicole. 2022. "WebToon Issues Apology after Controversial Ad Calls Comics a 'Side Hustle.'" ComicBook, June 15. https://comicbook.com/comics/news/webtoon-issues-apology-after-controversial-ad-calls-comics-a-side-hustle/.

Freedman, Maxwell. 2020. "Otome Isekai Is the Isekai Sub-Genre No One Saw Coming." CBR, May 23. https://www.cbr.com/otome-isekai-sub-genre-villainess/.

Ghana Report. 2022. "After Squid Game and Kpop, Korean Webtoons Get Moment in the Sun." January 31. https://www.theghanareport.com/after-squid-game-and-kpop-korean-webtoons-get-moment-in-the-sun/.

Gowri, S. 2021. "Addicted to K-Drama or K-Pop? Now, Dive into Korean Digital Comics or K-Webtoons in Indian Languages." *The Hindu*, September 2. https://www.thehindu.com/entertainment/korean-digital-comics-find-stronghold-in-india-after-kpop-kdrama/article36243995.ece.

Griepp, Milton. 2022a. "Yen Doubles Down on Korean Webtoons." ICv2, April 18. https://icv2.com/articles/news/view/50950/yen-doubles-down-korean-webtoons.

Griepp, Milton. 2022b. "Tapas Merges with Prose Platform." ICv2, May 20. https://icv2.com/articles/news/view/51228/tapas-merges-prose-platform.

Hume, Kiel. 2022. "Webtoon to Establish a New European Corporation, Solidifying the Company's Position as the European Market Leader in Digital Comics." *Business Wire*, March 21. https://www.businesswire.com/news/home/20220321005363/en/.

Jang, Won-ho, and Lee Byung-min. 2016. "The Glocalizing Dynamics of the Korean Wave." *Korean Regional Sociology* 17, no. 2: 5–19.

Jang, Won-ho, and Song Eun-jung. 2017. "Webtoons as a New Korean Wave in the Process of Glocalization." *Kritika Kultura* 29: 168–87.

Jin, Dal Yong. 2015 "Digital Convergence of Korea's Webtoons: Transmedia Storytelling." *Communication Research and Practice* 1, no. 3: 193–209.

Jin, Dal Yong. 2019a. "Snack Culture's Dream of Big-Screen Culture: Korean Webtoons' Transmedia Storytelling." *International Journal of Communication* 13: 2094–115.

Jin, Dal Yong. 2019b. "Korean Webtoonist Yoon Tae-ho: History, Webtoon Industry, and Transmedia Storytelling." *International Journal of Communication* 13: 2216–30.

Jin, Dal Yong, ed. 2020. *Transmedia Storytelling in East Asia: The Age of Digital Media*. Abingdon, Oxon., England: Routledge.

Jin, Dal Yong. 2023. *Understanding Korean Webtoon Culture: Transmedia Storytelling, Digital Platforms, and Genres*. Cambridge, MA: Harvard University Press.
Kang, Tae-jun. 2014. "South Korea's Webtoons: Going Global." *Financial Times*, July 28. https://www.ft.com/content/3b5a3b59-6aae-3c90-bf96-8ace895f32cf.
Kim, Alyssa. 2016. "How Realism Is Shaping Korean Webtoons." *International Journal of Comic Art* 18, no. 2 (Fall–Winter): 421–36.
Kim, Bong-seok. 2020. "How Webtoons Swept Korea." *Korea Webzine*, November. https://www.kocis.go.kr/eng/webzine/202011/sub01.html.
Kim, Boram. 2022. "Popularity of Korean TV Series Drives Sales of Original Web Comics." Yonhap News Agency, March 17. https://en.yna.co.kr/view/AEN20220317003700315.
Kim, Ji-hyeon, and Yu Jun. 2019. "Platformizing Webtoons: The Impact on Creative and Digital Labor in South Korea." *Social Media+ Society*, November 21. https://journals.sagepub.com/doi/full/10.1177/2056305119880174.
Kim, Joo-wan. 2022. "Korean Webtoon Startup Kenaz Acquired by Hedge Fund." *Korea Economic Daily*, June 15. https://www.kedglobal.com/mergers-acquisitions/newsView/ked202206150008.
Kim, Ki-hong. 2012. "Gatekeeping the Webtoons: A Study on the Internet-Based Cartoon Culture in Korea." *International Journal of Comic Art* 14, no. 2 (Fall): 464–71.
Kim, Ki-tae. 2006. "Internet Sharing Hits Comics Market in Korea." *Korea Times*, February 17.
Kim, Soo. 2022. "How Korean Webtoons Are Taking Over the K-Drama and Streaming Worlds." *Newsweek*, January 14. https://www.newsweek.com/k-drama-korean-webtoons-netflix-streaming-television-south-korea-1669402.
Kim, Subin. 2022. "After Squid Game and Kpop, Korean Webtoons Get Moment in the Sun." Al Jazeera, January 31. https://www.aljazeera.com/economy/2022/1/31/korean-webtoons.
Ko, Dong-hwan. 2015. "Korean 'Webtoons' Turn to Technology, Genre-Based Stories." *Korea Times*, November 2. https://www.koreatimes.co.kr/www/news/culture/2015/11/148_189995.html#.
Korea Creative Content Agency. 2016. *2016 Content Industry Outlook*. Naju-si.
Korea Tech Today. 2021. "South Korean Webtoon Firms Excel in Japanese Manga App Industry." March 4. https://www.koreatechtoday.com/south-korean-webtoon-firms-excel-in-japanese-manga-app-industry/.
Kwak, Yeon-soo. 2020. "Interest in OTT Services Surges as Pandemic Forces People to Stay Home." *Korea Times*, May 4. https://www.koreatimes.co.kr/www/art/2020/04/398_288778.html.
Kwon, Jae-woong. 2005. "New Type of Popular Culture in the Internet Age: An Analysis of the Korean Essay Cartoon." *International Journal of Comic Art* 7, no. 1 (Spring): 320–50.
Lee, D.-w. 2012. "Marine Blues Turned into a Go-Stop Game." ZDNet, June 12. http://www.zdnet.com.kr/news/news_view.asp?article_id=20120612182001.
Lee, Gyu-lee. 2022. "K-Content Storytelling Needs to Continue to Evolve to Target Global Audiences: Industry." *Korea Times*, May 3. https://www.koreatimes.co.kr/www/art/2024/05/398_328227.html.
Lee, Hae-rin. 2021a. "Global Comics Market Transforming in Favor of Korean Webtoons." *Korea Times*, July 8. https://www.koreatimes.co.kr/www/culture/2021/07/703_311789.html.
Lee, Hae-rin. 2021b. "Illegal 'Scanlation' of Web Comics Overseas Frustrates Korean Creators." *Korea Times*, August 28. https://www.koreatimes.co.kr/www/culture/2021/08/703_314538.html.
Lee, Hyo-won. 2017. "Why South Korean Filmmakers Are Adapting Local Webtoons into Movies and TV Shows." *Hollywood Reporter*, November 3. https://www.hollywoodreporter.com/news/general-news/why-south-korean-filmmakers-are-adapting-local-webtoons-movies-tv-shows-1054466/.
Lee, Joyce. 2021. "S. Korea 'Webtoon' Firms Leverage Low-Cost Stories with Potential Huge Upside." Reuters, December 8. https://www.reuters.com/business/media-telecom/skorea-webtoon-firms-leverage-low-cost-stories-with-potential-huge-upside-2021-12-08/.
Lee, K.-w. 2000. "Chollian, Manhwa Special Site Webtoon." ET News, August 9.
Lee, Min-jeong, and Takahiko Hyuga. 2022. "Popular Manga App Seeks 2023 IPO in Tokyo at $6 Billion Value." Bloomberg, August 22. https://www.bloomberg.com/news/articles/2022-08-22/popular-manga-app-seeks-2023-ipo-in-tokyo-at-6-billion-value.
Lee, Min-jeong, Lee Youkyung, and Bloomberg. 2023. "Apple Turns to South Korea's 'Webtoons'—Short, Vertically Read, and Made for Small Screens—to Revive Its Books App." *Fortune*, May 6. https://fortune.com/2023/05/06/apple-books-app-webtoons-south-korea-kenaz-entertainment/.
Lee, Philip. 2022. "Local and Korean Webtoons Are Being Loved in Southeast Asia." *Pickool*, March 17. https://pickool.net/locally-korean-webtoons-are-being-loved-in-southeast-asia/.
Lee, Sunyoung. 2007. "The Koreans Are Coming: Manhwa in America." *Publishers Weekly*, January 2. https://www.publishersweekly.com/pw/by-topic/industry-news/comics/article/11971-the-koreans-are-coming-manhwa-in-america.html.
Lent, John A. 1966. *Newhouse, Newspapers, Nuisances: Highlights in the Growth of a Communications Empire*. New York: Exposition Press.
Lent, John A. 2018. "The New Wave of Investigative Cartooning in South Korea." *International Journal of Comic Art* 20, no. 2 (Fall–Winter): 90–109.
Litterst, Rob. 2022. "Webtoons Are Taking Over the World. Is the US Next?" *The Hustle*, March 30. https://thehustle.co/03302022-webtoons.

Lynn, Hyung-gu. 2016a. "Korean Webtoons: Explaining Growth." *Institute of Korean Studies Annual* 16, no. 1: 1–13.

Lynn, Hyung-gu. 2016b. "South Korean Webtoons: Challenges of Translating the Domestic to the Global." *Asia Pacific Memo*, no. 366 (February 26). https://apm.iar.ubc.ca/korean-webtoons-challenges/.

MacDonald, Heidi. 2022a. "Major Layoffs and Reported New Direction at Tapas Media." *The Beat*, July 28. https://www.comicsbeat.com/major-layoffs-and-reported-new-direction-at-tapas-media/.

MacDonald, Heidi. 2022b. "Webtoon Ads Take Over New York City's Hippest Subway Station." *The Beat*, June 13. https://www.comicsbeat.com/webtoon-ads-take-over-new-york-citys-hippest-subway-station/.

MacDonald, Heidi. 2023. "Kakao Entertainment Closes Korean Office of Tapas, amid Layoffs and Consolidation." *The Beat*, March 14. https://www.comicsbeat.com/kakao-entertainment-tapas-layoffs/.

MacDonald, Joan. 2019. "Webtoons Provide Abundant Storylines for Korean Film and Drama Adaptations." *Forbes*, February 12. https://www.forbes.com/sites/joanmacdonald/2019/02/12/webtoons-provide-abundant-storylines-for-korean-film-and-drama-adaptations/?sh=5645d17.

MacDonald, Joan. 2021. "Kakao Entertainment Sees Webtoons Shaping the Future of Global Media." *Forbes*, November 10. https://www.forbes.com/sites/joanmacdonald/2021/11/10/kakao-entertainment-sees-webtoons-shaping-the-future-of-global-media/?sh=5e9559916c3a.

McCloud, Scott. 2010. *Reinventing Comics: How Imagination and Technology Are Revolutionizing an Art Form*. New York: HarperCollins.

McKinney, D. W. 2020. "Riding the Wave: The Steady Rise of Korean Manhwa." *Los Angeles Review of Books*. October 24. https://lareviewofbooks.org/article/riding-the-wave-the-steady-rise-of-korean-manhwa/.

Morrissy, Kim. 2021. "How Does Piracy Affect Korean Webtoon Artists?" Anime News Network, August 22. https://www.animenewsnetwork.com/feature/2021-08-22/how-does-piracy-affect-korean-webtoon-artists/.176285.

Na, Won-jeong. 2018. "The Age of New Players: The Globalizing of Korean Films Gets a Boost." *Korean Cinema Today* 32 (October): 60–63.

Nam, Kyung-don. 2022. "S. Korean Webtoon Market Jumps to Top W1tr in Sales." *Korea Herald*, January 14. https://www.koreaherald.com/view.php?ud=20220113000855.

Nawotka, Ed. 2021. "South Korea's Naver to Acquire Wattpad for $600 Million." *Publishers Weekly*, January 19. https://www.publishersweekly.com/pw/by-topic/international/international-deals/article/85348-south-korea-s-naver-to-acquire-wattpad-for-600-million.html.

Osaki, Tomohiro. 2019. "South Korea's Booming 'Webtoons' Put Japan's Print Manga on Notice." *Japan Times*, May 5. https://www.japantimes.co.jp/news/2019/05/05/business/tech/south-koreas-booming-webtoons-put-japans-print-manga-notice/.

Park, Eui-myung, and Lee Ha-yeon. 2019. "Webcomics Pose as New Power behind K-Wave with Revenue to Near $1 Bn Next Year." *Pulse*, October 28. https://pulse.mk.co.kr/news/english/9040444.

Park, Han-sol. 2023. "Major Webtoon Platforms' Fight against Piracy." *Korea Times*, February 2. https://www.koreatimes.co.kr/www/art/2023/02/398_344709.html.

Park, In-ha. 2011. "Hanguk Dijitai Manhwa Ui Yoksa wa Pal Chon Panghyangsong Yongu [A Study on the History of Korean Digital Comics and Its Future Directions]. *Aenimeisyŏn Yongu* 7, no. 2 (June): 64–82.

Park, Ju-young. 2018. "Amateur Cartoonists Rush to Instagram in Search of New Path." *Korea Herald*, July 11. www.koreaherald.com/view.php?ud=20180711000624.

Park, Katrin. 2021. "South Korea Is No Country for Young People." *Foreign Policy*, November 5. https://foreignpolicy.com/2021/11/05/south-korea-suicide-rates-mental-illness-squid-game/.

Park, Min-je. 2020. "Webtoons, Big in Japan, Are Korea's Latest K-Export." *Korea JoongAng Daily*, April 20. https://koreajoongangdaily.joins.com/2020/04/20/industry/Webtoons-big-in-Japan-are-Koreas-latest-Kexport/3076275.html.

Press Trust of India. 2022. "'All of Us Are Dead' to 'Itaewon Class': A Look at the K-Dramas Inspired by Webtoons." *Republic World*, February 26. https://www.republicworld.com/world-news/all-of-us-are-dead-to-itaewon-class-a-look-at-the-k-dramas-inspired-by-webtoons-articleshow/?amp=1.

PTI News Agency. 2022. "From *Itaewon Class* to *A Business Proposal*, Webtoons Drive K-Drama Craze." *Indian Express*, February 27. https://indianexpress.com/article/entertainment/entertainment-others/from-itaewon-class-to-a-business-proposal-webtoons-drive-k-drama-craze-7793354/.

Pyo, Jane Yeahin, Jang Minji, and Yoon Tae-jin. 2019. "Dynamics between Agents in the New Webtoon Ecosystem in Korea: Responses to Waves of Transmedia and Transnationalism." *International Journal of Communication* 13: 2161–78.

Salkowitz, Rob. 2021. "Webtoon CEO Sees Massive Growth and New Opportunities in U.S. Market." *Forbes*, November 2. https://www.forbes.com/sites/robsalkowitz/2021/11/02/webtoon-ceo-sees-massive-growth-and-new-opportunities-in-us-market/?sh=7e759777707a.

Salkowitz, Rob. 2022a. "Webtoon Is Paying Its Creators Millions to Make Mobile Comics." *Forbes*, July 18. https://www.forbes.com/sites/robsalkowitz/2022/07/18/webtoon-is-paying-its-creators-millions-to-make-mobile-comics/?sh=6eee8a0f1369.

Salkowitz, Rob. 2022b. "Tapas CEO Chang Kim on the Company's Layoffs and Abrupt Pivot Away from Original Content. ICv2,

August 5. https://icv2.com/articles/columns/view/51821/tapas-ceo-chang-kim-companys-layoffs-abrupt-pivot-away.
Shin, Hae-in. 2006. "Korean Cartoonist Kang Full Turns New Page for Comics." *Korea Herald*, February 7.
Sohn, Ji-young. 2014. "Korean Webtoons Going Global." *Korea Herald*, May 25.
Song, Jung-a. 2022. "South Korean Webtoon Platform's Pitch for Global Fans." *Financial Times*, April 6. https://www.ft.com/content/905928c3-5bbc-4c93-89b7-5933082f79f2.
Song, Seung-hyun. 2022. "Korean Startup Watcha to Offer Webtoons, Music Streaming This Year." *Korea Herald*, February 22. https://www.koreaherald.com/view.php?ud=20220222000764&ACE_SEARCH=1.
Spangler, Todd. 2016. "Korea's LINE Webtoon Digital-Comics Publisher Signs with CAA for TV and Film Projects." *Variety*, August 31. http://variety.com/2016/digital/news/line-webtoon-comics-caa-tv-film-1201847907/.
Stanley, Grace. 2022. "Webtoon's Vice President of Content David Lee Shares How Creators Can Monetize Their Comics." *Daily Dot*, July 28. https://www.dailydot.com/unclick/webtoon-david-lee-interview/.
TechSci Research. 2021. "South Korea Webtoons Market to Witness Significant Growth until 2025." https://techsciblog.com/south-korea-webtoons-market-to-witness-significant-growth-until-2025/.
Terranova, Tiziana. 2000. "Free Labor: Producing Culture for the Digital Economy." *Social Text* 18, no. 2 (Summer): 33–58.
Wang, Catherine. 2022. "Korean Webcomic Platform RIDI Hits Unicorn Status with GIC-Led Round." *Forbes*, March 2. https://www.forbes.com/sites/catherinewang/2022/03/02/korean-webcomic-platform-ridi-hits-unicorn-status-with-gic-led-round/.
Yoon, So-yeon. 2017. "Webtoons Offer Space for Female-Led Narratives: Stories Highlight Harsh Realities Young Women Face in Modern Society." *Korea JoongAng Daily*, July 5. https://koreajoongangdaily.joins.com/2017/07/05/features/Webtoons-offer-space-for-femaleled-narratives-Stories-highlight-harsh-realities-young-women-face-in-modern-society/3035514.html.
Yoon, So-yeon. 2020. "Korea's Webtoon Industry Continues to Thrive in Spite of Pandemic." *Korea JoongAng Daily*, December 23. https://koreajoongangdaily.joins.com/2020/12/23/culture/gamesWebtoons/webtoon-covid19-coronavirus/20201223183300524.html.
Yoon, So-yeon. 2021. "Naver Webtoon Signs Deals with DC Comics and HYBE." *Korea JoongAng Daily*, August 18. https://koreajoongangdaily.joins.com/2021/08/18/business/tech/Naver-Webtoon-Kim-Junkoo-CEO/20210818162100465.html.
Yoon, So-yeon. 2022. "[WHY] The Rise of Webtoons Means Fat Pay Checks, but Only for a Few." *Korea JoongAng Daily*, April 2. https://koreajoongangdaily.joins.com/2022/04/02/business/industry/webtoon-webtoonist-Naver/20220402070019357.html.

그림책
그림 리철근

Chapter 6

North Korea

Comics *(Kurimchaek)*

One thing that is certain is, there seems to be no certainty in defining North Korean comics. This is evident in the sparse writing (especially in English) about the subject. The foremost Western researcher of North Korean print comics, Martin Petersen of Denmark, spent considerable wordage attempting to sort out differences between the labels "children's illustrations," "*kurimchaek*," "comics," and "graphic novels," seemingly to little avail; in the end, he uses the terms interchangeably and even arbitrarily (Petersen 2019, 8–17).

Jacco Zwetsloot (2015, 7–10) faced the same dilemma, as indicated in his labeling of two pertinent sections of his thesis as "Defining Comic Books—Problematic" and "Defining Comic Books in North Korea—More Problematic." He relies on North Korean sources for clarification, mainly *Joseon Daebaekkwasajeon* (Korea Encyclopedia, 1995), *Munhak Yesul Sajeon* (Dictionary of Literature and Art, 1972), and "Dear Leader" Kim Jong-il's *On Fine Art* (1991). The encyclopedia and dictionary, and a writer named Han Sang-jeong, associate manhwa with negative parody and satire of social conditions. Han (2011, 23–28) writes that no books have used "manhwa" in their title since 1998. As for the term "*kurimchaek*," the Korea Encyclopedia provides these traits: such works are based on pictures for easy understanding, use subject matter that is novel and educational, possess persuasive power that allows readers "to see directly with their eyes and to feel [the message]," serve a broad readership with a wide variety of content and format, and provide "workers, youths, and children" with knowledge of nature and society. Zwetsloot (9) points out that the definition fails to mention any common elements of a comic (multiple sequential panels, speech balloons, etc.).

In his treatise, Kim Jong-il (1941–2011) listed eight forms of art in North Korea.[1] The third he enumerated, *chulpan misul*, which literally means "published or printed art," came to mean "graphic arts." Calling for illustrations to be diverse with colorful bindings, and for the comic strip to be developed, Kim identified the word "comic strip" as *ryŏnsok-kŭrim-hyŏngshik*, literally "sequential picture format." "Manhwa" was not mentioned at all. Zwetsloot

(9) claims that this was the only time in all of the works of Kim Il-sung (1912–1994) and Kim Jong-il that comics were treated; yet, the "Dear Leader" declaring that they needed to be developed granted them "the top seal of approval."

Taking into account these delineations, this chapter uses the term "*kurimchaek*" interchangeably with "comics" and "graphic novels," to mean continuously connected panels that tell an entire story at once or spread out over an extended time, incorporating any or all of the characteristics of humor, satire, fantasy, adventure, and education, and espousing national ideological beliefs and values, and the causes of loyalty, revolution, morality, patriotism, class issues, and counterespionage (Petersen 2019, 16).

Kurimchaek usually appear as books, varying from 32 to 256 pages; since the advent of the twenty-first century, they are increasingly in color. They come in four different dimensions, aligned with the target groups of early elementary school, elementary school, middle school, and high school, usually made up of stories by "Great Leader" Kim Il-sung, Kim Jong-il, or Kim Jong-suk (Kim Jong-il's mother, 1917–1949). Zwetsloot (2015, 11) points out that a clear division of labor exists between writer, illustrator, editor, cover illustrator, proofreader, and computer layout worker.

Production is carried out by sixteen publishers; six account for 80 percent of all *kurimchaek*. The largest two, the Kumsong Youth Publishing House[2] and Literature and Arts Publishing House, bring out 46 percent and 16.2 percent, respectively, of the total. All publishers are owned by the government in one form or other, and nearly all *kurimchaek* are printed by the Pyongyang Integrated Print Factory 1 or 2. In more recent years, *kurimchaek* have been printed for domestic audiences on low-quality paper and carrying a price, and for international readers on higher-quality paper minus a price.

In North Korea, the principle of "art for art's sake" cannot take precedence over art's ideological significance—its mission to educate, motivate, and inform the people, as declared by Kim Jong-il (1991, 110–15). All artworks (including *kurimchaek*) must be inspected and approved by the publishing company involved and the Publications Inspection Bureau (Chulpan Geomyeolguk) to ensure that themes are appropriate and handled correctly. There have been occasional crossovers and adaptations of *kurimchaek* to animation, film, or merchandise, or vice versa (Zwetsloot 2015, 12–16).

Two of the very few North Korean works written about *kurimchaek* leave much to be desired with respect to what *kurimchaek* are, according to Zwetsloot (16–17), who describes Kim Yong-il and Ri Chae-il's *A New Turn in Graphic Arts* (2003) as a "dead end" and Ri Chang-hyeok's 2010 *Joseon Yeseul* (Korean Art) article "Illustrations of the Sequential Picture Format and Their Types" as also suffering from arbitrary and unclear distinctions. What also irked Zwetsloot were the "half-hearted" definitions given, the lack of mention of key elements (e.g., speech balloons), and the sense of confusion surrounding what constituted *kurimchaek* (17). He did acknowledge that Ri Chang-hyeok in a second article (2010a), and Cheong Hyeon-ho in a separate *Joseon Yeseul* article (2011), subsequently moved forward in deconstructing *kurimchaek*—Ri, by introducing the speech balloon as a necessary element, encouraging irregularly shaped and sized panels, and stressing dialogue as a key driver of a story; Cheong, by distinguishing sequential *kurimchaek* from children's *kurimchaek*, specifying that "moments of a story are shown in sequential 'cuts' that are close to each other in time" and suggesting the use of *insangpyogi-kŭl* (his neologism), likely meaning title and panel letters written or drawn in calligraphic style to express certain emotions and impressions (Ri 2010a; Cheong 2011; both cited in Zwetsloot 2015, 18–19).

Although the Korean peninsula has a comics art tradition dating to the early twentieth century, the part north of the thirty-eighth parallel, North Korea, is treated here after its split as a separate country in 1945. Comics or *kurimchaek* came about as "Great Leader" Kim Il-sung aimed for the mobilization and enlightenment of the new nation, perhaps first in wall newspapers (*pyŏkpo*) that he personally made.

Quickly after independence, in August 1946, North Korea published an illustrated satire magazine, *Horangi* (Tiger), which changed its name to *Hwalsal* (The Arrow) in January 1948. *Hwalsal* was modeled after the Soviet Union's *Krokodil* (Crocodile) and in its beginning years frequently reprinted material from its Soviet counterpart. Likewise,

Hwalsal's cartoons were reprinted throughout North Korea (Mironenko 2014, 60). Dmitry Mironenko, leaning on Alenka Zupančič's "surplus-satisfaction" theory (2008, 132), wrote that, in *Hwalsal* cartoon representations, the trivial, familiar, and mundane were turned into something funny through artistic simplification and exaggeration.

Hwalsal brought "play into the public domain" as it solicited satirical cartoons on everyday life from its readers and carried a series of articles in the 1950s teaching them how to make effective cartoons for workplace wall newspapers (Mironenko 2014, 63). Wall newspapers were also common in the Soviet Union (called *stengazeta*) and China (*dazebao*) at the time. Often, *pyŏkpo* used *Hwalsal*'s satirical cartoons.

Overreaching all of this was what Mironenko said was an "all-out satirical offensive" in 1950s North Korea, where the working masses often gathered in public spaces and improvised pranks, tricks, and other disorderly conduct as amateur "street jesters" (2014, 67). *Hwalsal* turned this street play into social satire and for a while had a regular special section, Rogeumsil (Recording Studio), "documenting instances of disorderly public behavior in the form of satire" (65).

Martin Petersen, who traced five volumes of *Hwalsal*, said the sixteen-page magazine consisted primarily of "satirical and agitating" cartoons, comic strips, and illustrated texts, "one-frame and full-page political cartoons, juxtaposing life in the North and South—the socialist and the imperialist-capitalist worlds. In many cases, this juxtaposition was accentuated by rendering self and other, right and wrong, in disparate graphic styles" (2019, 28).

To gauge the contents, a look at volume 16 (April 28, 1950, less than two months before the commencement of the Korean War) reveals "satirical caricatures of U.S., Japanese and Korean adversaries in the South; sympathetic and pitying portrayals of the impoverished, exploited, and suffering people in the South; heroic appraisals of guerilla units; peasants, workers, union women and soldiers in the North; and Soviet Russians" (Petersen 2019, 96).

Petersen (2019, 96–97) hones in on the revolutionary heroism portrayed in the sequential visual narrative *Comrade Han Kilseok! May Our Comrade's Name*

6.1. Cover of volume 16 of illustrated political satire magazine *Hwalsal*. Courtesy of Martin Petersen (2019, 29).

Shine Forever! (*Han Kilseok tongmu! Tongmuui ereumeun yongwonhi bitnarira!*), published in volume 16 of *Hwalsal*, pointing out that it was rare for recent *kurimchaek* to depict so explicitly the "intimidation, gruesome torture and finally execution" of any person, in this case Comrade Han.

The early volumes of *Hwalsal* focused on foreign influences and connections, carried editorial cartoons as "Soviet manhwa," and strongly acknowledged the dominant role played by Soviet occupation forces in North Korea. Kim Il-sung was not the central focus in these initial volumes (Petersen 2019, 28–29).

The 1950s witnessed a continuing escalation of newspapers, magazines, books, and brochures in North Korea, some of which lent themselves to the use of cartoons and comics. Even throughout the Korean War (1950–1953), called the Fatherland Liberation War in the North, the number of publications steadily climbed, increasing from 213 book titles in 1946 and 487 in 1949 to 522 book and brochure titles in 1953, with a total print run of 9,227,060 copies (Mayorov 1954, cited in Mironenko 2014, 41).

Besides *Hwalsal*, other notable examples of North Korean comics art from the 1940s through the 1960s were the cartoon-laden Satire and Humor section of *Cho-Sso Chinseon* (Korean-Soviet Friendship), an organ of the Korean-Soviet Friendship Society that reprinted cartoons from Soviet periodicals; *kurimchaek* that appeared in *Cheollima*

(Thousand Miles Horse); and a continuing strip, *Kildoli: The Destiny of a South Korean Orphan* (*Kildoli: Namjoseonui han koaui unmyeong*). *Cheollima* was a monthly cultural journal founded in 1959, a year after the start of the Cheollima movement. Its image and text contents included illustrated stories, comic strips, and manhwa. Surveying volumes 2–7 of 1964, Petersen (2019, 35–36) identified five illustrated stories, namely *Cho Hŏn and the Seven Hundred Martyrs, Why Did I Escape South Korea?* (*Naneun wae Namjoseoui talchul haetneunga?*), *Things Go from Bad to Worse: South Vietnam and US Imperialism* (*Kalsurok shimhan nambu wollamgwa mije*), *Phoenix* (*Pulsajo*), and *Latin American March* (*Ratin Amerika haengjngok*). The plots featured historical accounts of Korean battles during the Hideyoshi invasion (1592–1598) and a Korean independence fight against the Japanese in 1937; satires of the plight of South Korean society, showing President Park Chung-hee as a dog on a leash held by a US soldier, and the US involvement in Vietnam, depicting President Lyndon B. Johnson recumbent in despair; and illustrated lyrics to "Latin American March," a song of Cuban origin that calls for struggle against US imperialism across Latin America.

The two comic strips in Petersen's sample are *America by Day*, four panels about a burglar caught by the police, who "[h]alf indignantly, half admiringly . . . exclaims: Humph. They are one level above me"; and *Old Man Teokpo* (*Teokpo ryeonggam*), six panels by Hong Chong-ho of a man escaping prison who takes the time to address readers directly: "Long time no see."

A serial manhwa that appeared during Petersen's surveyed six months of 1964 was the fourteen-panel *Kildoli: The Destiny of a South Korean Orphan*. The orphan Kildoli is an escapee from a harsh prison in the South, a down-and-out street urchin who lives by his wits. He often is the victim of abuse and neglect dished out by adults, yet he performs acts of bravery to aid adults. He also does what he can to support his country, for example, surreptitiously and daringly jumping on a truck driven by a US official and scattering pamphlets declaring, "Get out, US Army! Let's drive out the US Army!" When Kildoli witnesses an armed American soldier trying to rob an elderly Korean man, he fashions a "scarecrow" [*sic*] and bravely overcomes the soldier (Petersen 2019, 36). The character and his farcical exploits are similar to other Asian child vagrants, such as Zhang Leping's *Sanmao*, created in 1935 in China, and Rafiqun Nabi's (Ranabi) *Tokai*, started in 1977 in Bangladesh (Lent 2012, 35–50). As with Kildoli, Sanmao carries out unbelievable (even absurd) actions while defending China against Japan's invasion; in one episode, he manages to lift his heavy gun and kill four Japanese soldiers with one bullet (Lent 2015, 45).

The monolithic ideology of the Party (*yuil sasang*) and the "struggle to advance the victory of socialism," as they developed in the late 1960s, had far-reaching impacts on the trends, formats, and distribution of *kurimchaek* in the 1970s. The clear messages derived from a speech by Kim Il-sung and an editorial in the *Literary Gazette* emphasized "the predominance of only the leader's ideology in the Party" and the need for children's literature to function as an ideological educator and nurturer of a new generation of revolutionaries "proud to live for the Leader . . . without a moment's hesitation," respectively (Smith 2015, 117; Won 2012, 301; both quoted in Petersen 2019, 39).

Examining seven *kurimchaek* of the 1970s, Petersen (2019, 43) fit all of them into the themes of an editorial in the *Literary Gazette* of October 24, 1967, titled "Let Us Further Improve the Revolutionary Spirit," which listed "the colonial period independence struggle, the struggle during the glorious Fatherland Liberation War, and the life and struggle of the children in the South." Petersen contended that these seven *kurimchaek*, in print runs of either one hundred or two hundred thousand, a number of copies of which were distributed to libraries, were accessible to the majority of North Korean children.

A "golden age" of *kurimchaek*, especially the sequential image–format variety, was reached in the 1980s. Ri Chang-hyeok describes the changes that contributed to this rich period for *kurimchaek*: "In illustrations in sequential image *kurimchaek* format, brief dialogue and panels are weaved into sequential scenes and have diverse changes in the size and format of panels according to events; moment by moment in new panels, the content is developed in an amusing way resulting in a unique illustration format that evokes the interest of readers" (Ri 2010b, 62, quoted

6.2. *The Strange Guest Who Came to an Empty House*. Ho Seong-pil, 1983. Courtesy of Martin Petersen (2019, 50).

6.3. *Whistle in the Misty Mountains*. Kim Sang-bok and Kim Ryong, 2003. Courtesy of Martin Petersen (2019, 123).

in Petersen 2019, 43). Ri mentions five titles published between 1980 and 1992 as being memorable because of their framing, layout, coloring, rhythm, and space, all comparable to English-language comics of the West. Past genres were enriched with "notable stylistic and thematic changes," and new genres appeared, such as "contemporary society anti-spy stories and war-time stories about patriots behind enemy lines" (Petersen 2019, 43).

Singling out seven antispy *kurimchaek—Signal Flare over the Stony Mountains (Tolbaksane oreun sinhotan: Kurimchaek)* (1980), *Sharp Eyes* (*Yerihan nunchori*) (1980), *The Strange Hair* (*Isanghan meorikarak*) (1980), *Dark Shadow in the Mirror* (*Keoule bichin keomun kurimja*) (1981), *The Strange Guest Who Came to an Empty House* (*Pinjibe chajaon isanghan sonnim*) (1983), *Lost Letter* (*Ireojin pyeonji*) (1985), and *Trace Left by Nut-Brown Shoes* (*Pamsaekkudue namgin heunjeok*) (1986)—Petersen writes that they have universal features, one of which is "emphasis on vigilance, awareness and protection of The Fatherland" (2019, 48). Also commonplace, in Petersen's phrasing, is "[t]he conflict resolution and the harmonious finale with children and public security officers summing up the moral lesson of love for Fatherland, hatred for the enemy and heightened awareness" (48). Children are often the spy catchers, and the enemy appears from inside and outside of North Korea.

From five war story comics (*Secret of the Black Cup* [*Keomeun keopui bimil*] [1986, 1987], *The Onrush Scouts* [*Tolchin chongchi aicho*] [1980], *Looking for "Black Dragon"* [*Keomeun yongeul chajaseo*] [1985], *Until the Final Explosion Has Roared* [*Majimak pogeomi ullil ttae kkaji*] [1986], and *The Tankman and the Two Boys* [*Ttangkeo pyeong kwa tu sonyeon*] [1980]), Petersen deduces themes of undercover heroes on missions to the South; generally, the life of patriots on enemy soil; the life and activities of Korean children during the Korean War; and anti-Japanese conflicts during the colonial period (53).

War-themed *kurimchaek* continued into the 1990s, particularly through the works of Kim Sang-bok and Choe Hyok (born 1958). Kim authored a number of wartime *kurimchaek*, among them *The Awaited Agent* (*Kidarideon ryeollagwon*) (1991) and *The Broken "Poisoned Needle"* (*Bureojin dokbaneul*) (1991), both about the anti-Japanese independence struggle and unconventional in panel arrangement and frame shapes, as well as the Korean War stories *Island in the Mist* (*Angae teopin seom*) (2002), the already-mentioned *Looking for "Black Dragon"* and *Secret of the Black Cup*, and the antispy comic book *Lost Letter*.

Kim continued to write and edit comics into the twenty-first century, including the story of a North Korean family of traitors who attempt to sabotage a train, *Whistle in the Misty Mountains* (*Angaeryeongeui kijeoksori*) (2003). A fine example of "Military First–era revolutionary realism," the story tells how a young female soldier on patrol recognizes a would-be saboteur, defeats him and his family, and halts the train just before derailment; after denouncing these class enemies, she rallies train personnel and passengers to reassemble the damaged railroad tracks (Petersen 2019, 123).

Choe Hyok's penchant for wartime stories came naturally, as his parents were Korean People's Army volunteers and Korean War veterans; as a child, he liked to draw "exclusively soldiers and similar subject matter" (Zwetsloot 2015, 22). After his own military service, followed by his graduation from Pyongyang University of Fine Arts in 1988, Choe worked for six years as a journalist at the Korean Fine Arts Publishing House. His first comic book was *A Brilliant Exploit* (*Wilhun*), published in 1980 when he was twenty-two years old, followed by others such as *A Military Coup* (*Panbyeon*) (1984), *The Target* (*Pyojeok*), *The Satellite Reports* (*Wiseongeun bogohanda*), and *Dagger* (*Dangeoŏm*) (1986–1988), successively. His *The Human Bomb* (*Yuktan*) came out in two volumes in 2005; like so many of his *kurimchaek*, it tells a Korean War story, and as all of them was both written and illustrated solely by Choe.

In a careful analysis of Choe's books, Zwetsloot (2015, 21–23) finds that he was creatively experimental, using diagonal frames, cloud-shaped panels to indicate flashbacks, and characters and speech balloons breaking panel frames; giving equal weight to characters and backgrounds; employing techniques of hatching, cross-hatching, stippling, and screentones; and using varied, but usually higher than average, numbers of panels per page. About Choe's visual language in *kurimchaek*, Zwetsloot (2015, 24) concludes that it has its own dialect that immediately discloses the good and bad characters, and was drawn realistically, portraying foreign antagonists with "pointier features, dark, hollow eyes, impassive, expressionless faces, a facial scar, full dark beards and sunglasses, an eye patch, and, occasionally, large, beaked noses" (25). American soldiers appear larger and stronger than Korean soldiers, but the latter's cunning leads to their victories in Choe's stories, which also allow "antagonist women to appear sexualized such as less than fully dressed, or having a shapely figure, or behaving coquettishly with men" (25).

6.4. *The True Identity of "Pear Blossom."* Kim Yong-hyon and Choe Chu-sop, 2004. Courtesy of Martin Petersen (2019, 168).

Much of what Choe was doing with framing, characters, and visual language was pioneering in North Korea, as was his use of morphology, narrative grammar, and reading order conventions. Among visual morphemes in Choe's *kurimchaek* are carriers (speech balloons, thought bubbles), indexical lines (motion lines, zooming effects), impact stars (e.g., when a person is hit), and upfixes (e.g., a light bulb above a person's head to indicate an idea). Choe did not hesitate to make use of morphemes, again, not a regular practice among North Korean cartoonists.

Choe's Operation series appears more than a few times in the scant literature about *kurimchaek*. Consisting of *Special Operation* (*Teuksu Jakjeon*) (2001), *Operation Meteor* (also *Operation Shooting Star*) (*Ryuseong Jakjeon*) (2002), *Operation Typhoon* (*Taepeung Jakjeon*) (2003), and *Operation Daggar* (*Tangeom Jakjeon*) (1993), the books varied

6.5. *Guard the Cradle*. Chin Yong-hun and Kim Hye-kyeong, 2008. Courtesy of Martin Petersen (2019, 55).

from 150 to 192 pages, likely were completed long before their publication dates, and indicated high-level research of their textual and graphic narratives.

Other notable *kurimchaek* includes *The True Identity of "Pear Blossom"* (*Baekkotui jeongche*, hereafter *Pear Blossom*) (2004), *They Came Back* (*Geudeuleun dolawatda*) (2001), *Guard the Cradle* (*Yorameul jikyeo*) (2008–2009), and *Quiet Outpost* (*Goyohan jeonchojeon*) (2006).

Petersen labels *Pear Blossom* as a "representative example" of North Korean graphic novels published in the 2000s (2012c, 29). Brought out by a four-member team, including writer Kim Yong-hyon and artist Choe Chu-sop, and the Kumsong Youth Publishing House, the eighty-page black-and-white graphic novel is a spy story with a focus on the meaning of family and its strengths and weaknesses in North Korea. The plot revolves around an undercover spy bent on destroying her alleged son's project for the Fatherland's national defense industry. The mother, Paek Ri-hwa (a CIA agent, alias Pear Blossom), is caught by her granddaughter, Chong-ok, listening to foreign music one night while smoking cigarettes, and Chong-ok becomes suspicious. (In North Korea, women portrayed smoking is a negative signifier in comics and film.) Paek succeeds in having her granddaughter committed to a psychiatric hospital. In the end, Chong-ok is released from the hospital; her father, Sung-u, discovers what his mother has been doing and as a "true son of the nation" leaves the house with his daughter "singing a patriotic song" on their way to the party office to report the matter. There, he pleads, "Deal with me, please, that is, after I have completed P-9" (the project). The message is clear, according to Petersen (2012c, 34): "North Korean parents should always uphold the interests of the nation and state, even when this seems to be to the detriment of their own family."

A few key characteristics of contemporary North Korean graphic novels that Petersen (2012c) identifies, based on his analyses of *Pear Blossom*, are: the graphic artwork and spatio-topical system are regular, with very little artistic experimentation; a relatively high importance is given to words (a trend in the first decade of the 2000s) (37); and the placement of slogan posters in panels of *Pear Blossom* for "supportive" purposes is not unusual (50).

The North Korean concept of "adapt to the circumstances" plays out in five Korean War–themed *kurimchaek* that Petersen (2013) studied—the already mentioned *They Came Back*, *Guard the Cradle*, *Quiet Outpost*, *Operation Shooting Star* (or *Meteor*), and *Operation Typhoon*. These titles show a succession of North Korean patriots sent to South Korea on undercover missions to battle American aggressors and their southern bedfellows, their competence to pass as South Koreans and adapt to enemy culture outweighing their competence to fight (Peterson 2013, 372).

Cartoonists use metaphors to make points in these *kurimchaek*, according to Petersen (2013, 375–76). In *They Came Back*, two female undercover heroes, about to be sent on a mission, are compared to flowers, in that flowers bloom for a while and then wither. In the same sense, though not always depicted visually in *kurimchaek*, Kim Il-sung always "accompanied" the patriots on their missions to South Korea, transcending "spatial and temporal divides and unif[ying] visual and verbal tracks" (377). In *Operation Shooting Star*, Kim is compared to the sun, and the character who prevents an attack by sacrificing his life becomes a star of the Eternal Sun.

Some war-themed graphic novels portray South Koreans infiltrating the North with the goal of unsettling socialism, an example being *Quiet Outpost*, in which the seemingly affectionate caretaker of the hero's daughter turns out to be a "ruthless South Korean spy for the Americans and the daughter of a secret service officer who served the Japanese Empire" (Petersen 2013, 380). Americans in *kurimchaek* are shown as "radical and racial Others," instigators of military confrontation, dispensers of harmful, decadent culture, and murderers and predators high on methamphetamines (383; see also Petersen's analyses of *kurimchaek* on family background [2012a] and food issues [2012b]).

North Korean comics and graphic novels are not entirely war and spy related; other genres such as fables, adventure, current issues, and history exist, all with the goal to instill Kim Il-sung's philosophy of juche (self-reliance) and otherwise promote the nation and its brand of socialism. Plots of *kurimchaek* have been labeled "wacky" (Cain 2010), and "outlandish" and "unabashedly propagandistic" (Strangio 2011), which they are, as are American superhero comics, especially those tampered with by the US government during the Cold War (see Hirsch 2021).

A *kurimchaek* that deals with fables and legends is the *Dangun* series of 2001, a detailed account of the mythical founding king of the first Korean kingdom. The character Dangun, related to a she-bear on his mother's side and a god on his father's, is known on both sides of the thirty-eighth parallel, the difference being that in the North, he is depicted as real, his bones supposedly found by Kim Il-sung in the early 1990s (James 2012). Kim Il-sung, though not physically visible, also figures prominently in a famous adventure comic, *Blizzard in the Jungle* (*Yoltaerim ŭi nunbora*, 2001). When a plane carrying North Korean agents is downed in an African jungle by Mafia gangsters determined to steal secret documents on board, the hero, Kim Yeong-hwan, leads the survivors to safety by employing the wisdom of Kim Il-sung's juche philosophy and the strength provided by ginseng. Two Americans, exercising their individualism, separate from the other passengers and are eaten by crocodiles (Strangio 2011).

6.6. *Blizzard in the Jungle* (2001) tells about a plane carrying North Koreans and Americans that crashes in an African jungle; the Americans abandon the group only to be eaten by crocodiles in a nearby river.

Perhaps not a genre per se, "North Korea as world savior" *kurimchaek* have appeared from time to time. An example that appeared in 1994, the year of Kim Il-sung's death and a period of the severe drought and famine, is *The Secret of Frequency A: An Incredible Disaster*, based on a fringe conspiracy theory claiming that American military research projects at the onset of World War II introduced 440Hz A tuning as an instrument for climate control warfare and mind control, and to cause "greater aggression, psychosocial agitation, and emotional distress" (Heinz Insu Fenkl, quoted in Strangio 2011; see also Eom and Ko 2011). The comic tells of North Korean teenagers and their professor who save an African nation from a plague of locusts engineered by Americans in cahoots with a Nazi criminal and Japanese acoustical engineer, who used a particular frequency of the note *A* to advance imperialist interests in Africa.

Kurimchaek that relate to current events in North Korea usually do so obliquely. A poignant example is *Great General Mighty Wing*, published in 1994, when a devastating

6.7. *Great General Mighty Wing*. 1994. One of North Korea's most popular children's comic books, the story promotes working collectively for the benefit of all people.

6.8. Inside page of *Great General Mighty Wing*.

drought and famine were severely damaging the landscape and economy, killing about six hundred thousand people. A moralistic story, *Great General Mighty Wing* features a honeybee general who leads his hive in a successful effort to ward off an alliance of wasps and spiders bent on seizing the honeybees' Garden of 1,000 Flowers. A traitor among the honeybees misallocates labor resources designated to build a much-needed aqueduct to prevent future flooding, instead sending off workers to build a summer home for the Queen Bee. To drive home the allusion to the drought, after fighting off the traitorous wasps and their secret airborne "missile" (bow and arrow), Mighty Wing manages to organize the bees into a workers' collective and build an irrigation canal that will serve all of the bees, not only the powerful ones, and increase honey production (Strangio 2011). Not coincidentally, the North Korean government was building a large irrigation canal at the time *Great General Mighty Wing* was very popular (Cain 2010). Accompanying the action, the margin of each page carries a revolutionary saying, for example "Wings That Beat Stronger than the Storm Wind Can Never Be Broken," "Though the Enemy May Be No More than a Mosquito, Consider Him No Less than an Elephant," "Never Think of the Enemy as a Lamb—Always Consider Him a Jackal," "The Enemy of a Friend or the Friend of an Enemy—Be Equally Wary of Both," and "Radicals and Idiots Are Both Mentally Deficient."

By late 1998, the North Korean government was trying to placate the citizenry that the crisis was over and began calling the previous period "Arduous March," after Kim Il-sung's 1938–1939 guerrilla movement. In the meantime, the country's literary and arts communities took up themes associated with issues stemming from the Arduous March, including those of food. A *kurimchaek* of this type is *A Strange Letter* (*Isanghan pyŏnji*, Kumsong Youth Publishing House, 2001), which tells how a foreign attempt to poison North Korean military food supplies is foiled, and why it almost succeeded. Petersen, in a talk at the University of London, School of Oriental and African Studies, on November 25, 2011, said that *A Strange Letter* explains what went wrong in the mid- to late 1990s, what was expected of the people to remedy the situation, and what the citizens could expect of the regime.

Crude political satire also saturates *kurimchaek* dealing with contemporary issues and people, as found in *General Loser and the Gnats*, published in 2005 when George W. Bush was the US president. In one part of the book, Bush asks cabinet members about his popularity and is told that people named "Bush" are changing their names, and soldiers who take his name in his honor do so only after being bribed (Strangio 2011).

The history genre remains important in the twenty-first century as a means of reimagining North Korea's past and proudly retelling its dynastic era and the Communists' "heroic struggle against Japanese imperialism" (Strangio 2011), thus serving educational and propagandistic purposes. A historical *kurimchaek* example that exhibits both nationalistic pride and propaganda goals is *World Professional Wrestling King*, a biography of North Korean wrestler Kim Sin-nak, who won world fame on the Japanese circuit in the 1950s despite the problems he faced in a harsh, discriminating foreign society.

In his analysis of more than two hundred *kurimchaek*, researcher Heinz Insu Fenkl concludes that overall, the books are of low production quality; have well-developed aesthetics, a dearth of humor, "a surprising level of conceptual complexity," principles of composition like those of the social realism of the Stalin years, and a "fairly representational" style; and exhibit far-reaching research (Fenkl, quoted in Strangio 2011; see also Cain 2010).

Animation

Animation early in North Korea (1947–1961) was considered as just another film form subsiding in the Motion Picture Studio for Film and Art (est. 1947). Much of the animation initiated in the 1950s and the first half of the 1960s was experimental, learned through trial and error and by imitating other works frame by frame, and implemented in a primitive manner making do with whatever was available or "invented" on the spot. It was a scenario very much like what Shin Dong-hun and other animation pioneers were enduring about the same time in South Korea. Among the first animation were two paper-cut animation shorts, *Marvelous Peach* and *Pleasant Rice Field*, which appeared in 1952 (Lee Y-b 2001; Lee J and Lee 2004).

A major spark for the further development of animation was Pyongyang's hosting a week of Czechoslovak animation in summer 1957, featuring some of that country's world-renowned animators, who stayed long enough to conduct a workshop. Exposure to the Czechoslovak animation was the impetus for the development of national children's film (Mironenko 2014, 194; see also Mironenko 2007), for, on February 7, 1958, the Executive Committee of the Korean Workers' Party Central Committee passed a resolution, "On Further Developing the Film Industry," that called for the production of films promoting "patriotic socialist" education among children and youth through live-action and animated works (Mironenko 2014, 193). Shortly after, also in 1958, the National Film Studio established the experimental Institution of Animation and Film, manned by painters, sculptors, and plastic artists with no experience at all in animation.

The institution team lacked textbooks and necessary equipment but trudged on, learning the basics and how to utilize them by studying others' works frame by frame and using trial and error methods, according to Cho Kyu-seop, a member of the team (Cho 1966, 22). Under those conditions, they produced their initial animated short, *Our Hill* (*Uri tongsan*).

Increasingly, North Korean authorities saw the potential importance of animation as a propaganda tool as they reinforced national identity based on their own brand of social communism, separate from that of the Soviet Union, called *Juchaesasang*. Major changes occurred between 1962 and 1972 when Kim Il-sung actively promoted children's film. Disguised in these children's cartoons were anti-US messages. Katherine Lam describes a propaganda animation released in the 1960s as showing "schoolchildren in battles with the U.S. Navy, firing pencil-like missiles to blow up aircraft carriers" (2017). The cartoon appears to be educational, Lam writes, with the children using a protractor to measure the rockets' launch angles, "but the message is clear—the 'imperial' U.S. is trying to invade North Korea."

In 1965, the North Korean Film Studio for Children was established as the first full studio specializing exclusively in producing children's film and animation. In 1997, the April 26 Children's Animation Film Studio was moved from the Art and Film School, where it had resided from its beginnings on September 7, 1957, to the Scientific and Educational Film Studio Korea (SEK), focusing solely on children's animation (Jang 1995; Lee Y-b 2001; Yun 2001).

Mironenko (2014, 196) elaborates on the growing pains of the early years of North Korean animation, ascribing them to issues of "medium specificity and child psychology." He gives considerable attention to the latter, stating that filmmakers were not aware of children's cognitive development and, therefore, could not capture their *tongsim* (child-heart) or *heungmi* (interest). In the 1960s, filmmakers began to realize that they had to "gain the love and admiration of the child spectator [so that he or she] would take away precisely what the authors intended" (196), and that children need their own stories in understandable language built on tropes with which they are familiar (197). In the beginning, producers were transferring live-action film theories and techniques to animation without success, not knowing, for example, that the laws of realism do not apply with the same rigor to animation, itself founded on exaggeration and fantasy (211).

It seems that North Korean animators were in hit-or-miss (mostly miss) situations during the 1960s. When they portrayed the fantastic abject, as in *Boy Artist* (*Kkoma hwaga*) and *Two Boy Scouts* (*Tu adongdanwon*), the result was "unwelcome parodying and mimicry" among children (Mironenko 2014, 213); as they inserted *Juchaesasang* messages, they were criticized for overmoralizing and being ignorant of child psychology. The institution team gradually found solutions to their problems. To capture and convey continuity of movement, they used live models to show locomotion (Cho 1966, 22); to offset the labor, time, capital, and technology intensiveness of using celluloid sheets that had to be imported, they converted to stop motion with puppets and paper cut. The first paper-cut animation was *Black Rabbit* (*Kkamjang tokki*) (1963). The rise of animation during the early 1960s necessitated the development of supporting industries, which North Korea did not possess. For example, the institution team did not even have a stop-motion camera and had to devise and build one from "scratch." Most materials made locally were inferior, resulting in animation "not always up to par" (Mironenko 2014, 217–18).

Mironenko (2014, 217–22) describes the stop-motion animation as "cumbersome, awkward and klutzy" with a "grotesque appearance," and uncanny in that puppets were missing a finger or two, their lip movements were not synchronized, music and sound effects were not harmonized with images, and the formality and politeness levels of child characters were uneven. Definitely, there was a serious lack of skills, resulting in animators turning out work contrary to their intentions.

In 1966, filmmakers and animators at the North Korean Film Studio for Children organized a major conference to address these issues. A formula emerged from these deliberations that "emphasized clarity of the main idea, simplicity of the plot, absence of overt moralizing, and appeals of characters and art design" (Mironenko 2014, 224). It was asserted that animators were attempting to promote new values and policies using old language, tropes, and techniques (225). As a result of these discussions, filmmakers applied pressure on screenwriters to come up with better scripts, and there was a turn to different genres, such as science fiction and current events satire (*sisa pungja yeonghwa*). *Return to Your Cave* (*Chegullo torakara*, 1966) was the first current events satire animation film, a strong critique of the US presence in Vietnam.

The directional changes paid off from 1973 to 1984, as studios emphasized personification and good storytelling designed to interest children, and featured nature subjects and values such as virtue and reprisal of vice rather than proselytizing messages for communism (Jang 1995; Yun 2001). The next decade (1985–1994) found North Korea in an economic slump, which the country's leadership attempted to remedy by opening up a bit to the outside world, in the process improving animation technology, huckstering North Korea's animated films globally, and bringing in needed revenue (Kim S-s 2002; Yun 2001). By this time, the animators had accumulated much expertise, and their films became competitive, especially in Europe, because of their high quality and low cost (Kim S-s 2002; Kitchens 2003).

The North Korean animation industry also began to attract offshore production and collaborative contracts from Italy, Spain, and France. Much of this work was carried out by the April 26 Children's Animation Film Studio (later, the SEK), using sophisticated approaches.

The "sunshine policy" initiated by President Kim Dae-jung of South Korea in 1998 stimulated inter-Korean economic cooperation. Animation figured prominently in this process, even being singled out by Kim Jong-il as benefiting both countries when he met with top South Korean press and broadcasting officials in August 2000 (Lee J and Lee 2004; Kim K-t 2003; Lee Y-b 2001). South Korea had been one of the world's leading animation subcontractors for decades until rising labor costs in the 1990s diverted the work elsewhere. It made business sense to cooperate with North Korea, where labor was less expensive; the South would sell animation globally that had been produced by the North. It was apparent that both countries simultaneously in the 1990s recognized the potential of animation while in the throes of economic setbacks. Not only did animation production have the capacity to bring in much-needed foreign currency, but the resultant films, child-friendly as they were, served important indoctrinational and educational purposes. (See Kao 2018 for an overview of North Korean animation through 2000; see also Kim Chunhyo and Lent 2005.)

The first inter-Korean animated film was *Dinga the Lazy Cat*, a 3-D computer work produced by North Korea's Samcholli General Corporation and Hanaro Telecom of the South that gained audiences in Southeast Asia. It also made it to the second round of an international competition in Italy. Two other early joint films were *Empress Chung* (*Wanghu Simcheong*, 2005), North Korea's largest production until then, produced by the SEK's top animator, Kim Kwang-sung, and AKOM's head, Nelson Shin, in South Korea; and *Pororo the Little Penguin* (*Pporong-pporong Ppororo*, 2003–2021), a collaborative product of Iconix and the SEK.

Empress Chung was based on a Korean folk story about a young woman who battled serious adversities in an attempt to help restore her father's eyesight. It was the first film to be released simultaneously in both sectors of the Korean peninsula, and likely the first collaboration between North Korean and US animation because of Shin's work experience with both countries. *Pororo the Little Penguin* related the adventures of an anthropomorphic penguin, produced in a manner that neutralized the character to avoid sensitive issues related to cultural codes, gender, and historical events. *Pororo* became a world phenomenon, exported to at least eighty-two countries, usually with high viewership. The trade-off for the two producing countries was mutually beneficial; the South Korean partner made use of inexpensive North Korean talent, who, in turn, learned IT technology to advance their own industry (Anonymous 2014).

Accounting for the majority of the animation was the SEK, North Korea's largest animation studio, consisting of a main building and a second, sixteen-floor production center. Built in 1996, the studio accommodated more than 1,600 workers at its peak in the early 2000s. The total workforce had dropped to about 900 by 2014. The inner structure of the studio holds two complexes that produce domestic animation, one for the computer stages of 3-D and ten handling subcontracted foreign animation (Lee J and Lee 2004). At one point in the 2000s, the SEK animated up to sixty domestic and foreign films a year and dealt with more than seventy different European companies (Kao 2018).

Two other companies operating into the 2000s were Animation and Film Production, Pyongyang Information Center, which was assigned inter-Korean animation, and Samji Production of the Association of Publication Interchange, in charge of interactions with foreign countries.

Animation aspirants in North Korea received arduous training, starting in middle and high school, where they took an extra curriculum created especially for them. They followed through in one of the country's few universities with a major in art, and after completing

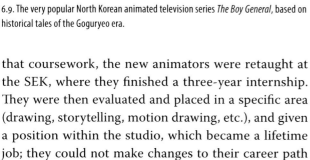

6.9. The very popular North Korean animated television series *The Boy General*, based on historical tales of the Goguryeo era.

6.10. *Clever Raccoon Dog* revolves around a bear, a raccoon dog, and a cat who solve problems they run into by applying education, morality, and ideology.

that coursework, the new animators were retaught at the SEK, where they finished a three-year internship. They were then evaluated and placed in a specific area (drawing, storytelling, motion drawing, etc.), and given a position within the studio, which became a lifetime job; they could not make changes to their career path (Lee J and Lee 2004).

When North Korea's relationships with parts of the international community soured after its nuclear tests in 2007 and 2009, most of the country's foreign animation contracts disappeared. The high point of the SEK's collaboration work was 2007; the only visible foreign animation done at the SEK after 2009 was for the Chinese (Kao 2018). It was then that North Korea increasingly concentrated on domestic animation production. Much of the output consisted of continuing episodes of popular titles started in the 1980s. One example is *The Boy General* (*Sonyeonjangsu*), a television series originating in 1982 with fifty episodes through 1997, and ordered by leader Kim Jong-un in 2015 to be continued in fifty additional segments through 2019. The story, written by Kim Jong-suk of the country's ruling family, relates a very popular Goguryeo period (first century BC to seventh century AD) tale about a boy, Soe Me, who overcomes many obstacles to become a brave general against invading Japanese and Chinese armies. One observer describes *The Boy General* as a story in which "foreign invaders are sent to their maker in droves, sometimes skewered in a row, kebab-like, with swords and spears. The enemies' moral degeneracy is reinforced by their shabby dress, and is even written on their strikingly ugly faces—snaggleteeth and pig noses abound. The Koreans, by contrast, are generally beautiful and well dressed" (Power 2015).

Grouped with *The Boy General* as the most popular North Korean animation series, *Clever Raccoon Dog* (1987–2005) and *Squirrel and Hedgehog* (2012) both came from SEK Studio and feature anthropomorphic animals with innocent names. *Clever Raccoon Dog*, produced in sixty-three episodes, stars a raccoon dog, a bear, and a blue cat engaged in minor adventures and problems, which they solve by putting to use the knowledge they have accumulated about science, safety, morality, and juche ideology. *Squirrel and Hedgehog* is set in the fictional Flower Hill, a community of squirrels, hedgehogs, and ducks on one side and the weasel army (mice and weasels) and wolf den on the other. The two sides often engage in bloody conflicts, interpreted as being a negative allusion to North Korea's international relations, with the attacking weasels and wolves representing Japan and the United States, respectively, and the squirrels, hedgehogs, and ducks as North Korean victims (Kao 2018). SEK staff denied that this was the intended meaning; instead, they maintained that the series was meant to teach love, friendship, and patriotism to children.

The nine sections at the SEK function as if they were separate companies, each assigned a specific project to complete. Painters are rotated from team to team, making it difficult to keep the quality consistent. Nelson Shin, who collaborated with the Pyongyang studio, traveling there at least nineteen times, said in his *Animatoon* magazine (no. 87, 2010) that SEK animators possessed "very high technological" skills. The studio's most distinguished director,

6.11. *Squirrel and Hedgehog* ran infrequently between 1977 and 2012 (only one episode in 1977 and four between 1977 and 1983), but it still ranks among the top animated shows of North Korea.

Kim Kwang-sung, was well known for his technological contributions, especially in the use of lighthearted action scenes full of special effects (see Jang 1995; Kim S-s 2002). Other notable director-writers have been Kim Jun-ok, who administered foreign joint projects at the SEK and directed and wrote more than four hundred animation films (see Lee Y-b 2001; Lee J and Lee 2004; Yun 2001), and Son Jong-kwan, whose career began in 1965. All three worked on the classic *The Boy General*.

Summing up, after a shaky start, North Korean animation, by the twenty-first century, had matured to become an art and industry with well-trained personnel, advanced technological skills, much educational and ideological content, and a precisely executed product worthy of entering the global market either as a subcontractor for foreign studios or as a coproducer. However, as earlier noted, the North Korean animation industry experienced a downturn after political relations with the Western world soured in the wake of North Korea's nuclear testing in 2007. International sanctions are still in effect, hampering coproductions and other collaborations; offshore production is at the mercy of the ability to fill expertise gaps in making tech-heavy 3-D features and catching up in the use of more effective communication techniques (e.g., the internet); and domestic production feels pressure as the number of animated 2-D feature films has declined steeply (Kao 2018).

Conclusion

Despite being labeled the "hermit" country, North Korea has absorbed outside influences during the birth and nourishment of its comics and animation industries. For example, the country's first satire magazine, *Hwalsal*, was modeled after the Soviet Union's *Krokodil*, and at times even copied its contents. In animation, North Korea attempted to counter its economic slump of 1985–1994 by selling its works to the outside world and cooperating with South Korea to produce offshore animation for foreign studios and jointly make domestic film cartoons. The connections to South Korea and other countries were irregular; after the North's nuclear tests in 2007 and 2009, they were mostly terminated.

North Korean comics art follows the mass media pattern of other communist countries, being stringently organized both structurally and functionally, owned and controlled by the government, and mainly used as a propaganda tool. The educational philosophy and ideology by which North Korean comics and animation are governed emanated from founder Kim Il-Sung's juche (self-reliance) thinking and were refined by his son and successor, Kim Jong-il, in his book *On Fine Art*.

In sum, the trajectory of North Korean comics and animation, from the beginning, has been designated, controlled, and financed by the government, solely with the aim to steer society in the direction dictated by the Kim family leaders.

Notes

1. B. G. Muhn, in a 2018 monograph, makes some points about North Korean art generally that are worth sharing. He writes that in the early days of Great Leader Kim Il-sung's regime (1950s–1960s), *chosonhwa* was the dominant art medium, the main channel of ideological expression. The technique is traditional ink wash on rice paper, the latter made of the inner bark of mulberry trees. Muhn praised *chosonhwa*, saying that its "poetic expression and rendition of the human figure" (6) developed an aesthetics that was unique in Northeast Asia (16), with its vibrant use of color, three-dimensional rendering, and expressionistic brush strokes (22). When Kim Il-sung formed his juche ideology (self-reliance, or mastering one's own fate), *chosonhwa* fit in as "art characterized by purely Korean culture" (16).

Claiming that North Korea is the only country supporting social realist art (which *chosonhwa* is), Muhn said that such art has the clear purpose of promoting the ideals of socialism, usually in the context of revolutionary propaganda of the regime and the idolization of leaders (24).

2. Founded in November 1945 as Pyongyang Children's Culture Publisher (Pyongyang Adong Munhwasa), the Kumsong Youth Publishing House went through a number of name changes, settling for five years on Sarochong Publishing House (the League of Socialist Working Youth of Korea Publishing House) in March 1970, before reverting to the Kumsong Youth Publishing House in March 1975. Its major purpose is to educate children and youth into being "dependable heirs of the cause of Juche revolution, who are endlessly loyal to the Party and the Leader" (Petersen 2019, 40).

References

Anonymous. 2014. "Popular Children's Cartoons in North Korea." North Korea Strategy Center (Seoul), August 4.

Cain, Geoffrey. 2010. "The Comic Books That Brainwash North Koreans." *Global Post*, February 26. https://www.minnpost.com/global-post/2010/03/comic-books-brainwash-north-koreans/.

Cheong, Hyeon-ho. 2011. "The Plastic Combination of Image and Text in the Compositional Structure of Artistic Illustrations" [Yesul saphwa kudo jhujigeseo kurimgwa geului chohyeongjeok gyeolhap]. *Joseon Yeseul* 4: 54–55.

Cho, Kyu-seop. 1966. "Uriga geoleo on gil" (The Road We Have Taken). *Joseon Yeonghwa* 6: 21–22.

Eom, Jeong-hui, and Ko Im-hong. 2011. "The Secret of Frequency A: An Incredible Disaster." *Words without Borders*, February 1. https://www.wordswithoutborders.org/graphic-lit/the-secret-of-frequency-a-an-incredible-disaster.

Han, Sang-jeong. 2011. "Nambukhan 'manhwa' yongbeopui chai: Bukhan 'kurimchaek' (Seosan Taesa)" [Differences between North and South Korean Usage of "Manhwa": Focusing on the Hybridity of the North Korean "Kurimchaek" Seosan Taesa (The Great Monk)]. *Hyeondae Bukhan Yeongu* [Review of North Korean Studies] 14, no. 2: 7–34.

Hirsch, Paul S. 2021. *Pulp Empire: The Secret History of Comic Book Imperialism*. Chicago: University of Chicago Press.

James. 2012. "North Korean Comic Books: Propaganda or Propamanga?" KoreaBANG, May 14. https://www.koreabang.com/2012/pictures/north-korean-comic-books-propaganda-or-propamanga.html.

Jang, M.-j. 1995. *A Study of Children's Animation in North Korea*. Seoul: Korea Culture and Tourism Policy Institute.

Kao, Anthony. 2018. "A Short History of North Korea's Animation Industry." *Cinema Escapist*, June 6. https://www.cinemaescapist.com/2018/06/short-history-north-korea-animation-sek/.

Kim, Chunhyo, and John A. Lent. 2005. "The Inside and Outside Worlds of North Korean Animation." *International Journal of Comic Art* 7, no. 2 (Fall): 273–82.

Kim, Jong-il. 1991. *On Fine Art*. Pyongyang: Foreign Languages Publishing House.

Kim, K.-t. 2003. "Filial Shim Chung Animation to Help Rapprochement with NK." *Korea Times*, April 6, 17.

Kim, S.-s. 2002. "The In-Depth Research on Current Trends of Animation in North Korea of the Korea Trade Promotion Corporation." KOTRA.

Kim, Se-jeong. 2010. "North Korea Emerges as Animation Producer." *Korea Times*, November 1. http://www.koreatimes.co.kr/www/news/nation/2010/11/113_75584.html.

Kim, Seong-hun, and Park Sohyeon. 2005. *An Understanding of North Korean Comics* (*Bukhan Manhwaui ihae*). Paju, South Korea: Sallim Press.

Kim, Yong-il, and Ri Chae-il. 2003. *A New Turn in Graphic Arts* [*Chulpan misul eseoui saeroeun cheonhwan*]. Pyongyang: Munhak Yesul Chulpansa.

Kitchens, Susan. 2003. "Axis of Animation." *Forbes*, March 3. https://www.forbes.com/global/2003/0303/014.html?sh=13a66a3b3a60.

Lam, Katherine. 2017. "North Korea Hid Anti-US Propaganda in Children's Cartoons for Decades." Fox News, September 27. https://www.foxnews.com/world/north-korea-hid-anti-us-propaganda-in-childrens-cartoons-for-decades.

Lee, J., and Lee S.-g. 2004. *The White Paper on Interchange between South Korea and North Korea*. Seoul: Korean Film Council.

Lee, Sunny. 2007. "US Cartoons 'Made in North Korea.'" *Asia Times*, March 14. https://www.nkeconwatch.com/2007/03/14/us-cartoons-made-in-north-korea/.

Lee, Wonhee, et al. 2006. "North Korea Quietly Emerges as Major Player in Animation Industry." Radio Free Asia, December 6.

https://www.rfa.org/english/korea/nkorea_cartoon-20061206.html.

Lee, Y.-b. 2001. *A Study about the Status of the North Korean Animation Industry and Intra-Korean Interchange and Cooperation for Animation*. Seoul: published by the author.

Lent, John A. 2012. “Sanmao and Tokai: Popular Street Urchins of Asian Comic Strips.” *International Journal of Comic Art* 14, no. 1 (Spring): 35–50.

Lent, John A. 2015. *Asian Comics*. Jackson: University Press of Mississippi.

Mayorov, Yu. A. 1954. “Spravka ob izdanii gazet, zhurnalov i lietertury v KNDR na i marta 1954 goda” [A Memorandum on the Publication of Newspapers, Journals, and Literature in the DPRK for March 1, 1954].

Mironenko, Dmitry. 2007. “The Role of Animation in the System of Ideological Education in North Korea.” AM thesis, Harvard University.

Mironenko, Dmitry. 2014. “A Jester with Chameleon Faces: Laughter and Comedy in North Korea, 1953–1969.” PhD dissertation, Harvard University.

Muhn, B. G. 2018. *North Korean Art: Paradoxical Realism*. Irvine, CA: Seoul Selection.

Petersen, Martin. 2012a. “The Downfall of a Model Citizen? Family Background in North Korean Graphic Novels.” *Korean Studies* 36, no. 1: 83–122.

Petersen, Martin. 2012b. “A New Deal: Graphic Novel Representations of Food Issues in Post-Famine North Korea.” In *Korea 2012: Politics, Economy and Society*, edited by Frank Rüdiger, James E. Hoare, Patrick Köllner, and Susan Pares, 181–208. Leiden: Brill.

Petersen, Martin. 2012c. “Sleepless in the DPRK: Graphic Negotiations of ‘Family’ in *The True Identity of Pear Blossom*.” *Scandinavian Journal of Comic Art* 1, no. 2 (Autumn): 30–58.

Petersen, Martin. 2013. “Patriots behind Enemy Lines: Hyperreality and the Stories of Self and Other in Recent North Korean War-Theme Graphic Novels.” *Journal of Korean Studies* 18, no. 2 (Fall): 371–402.

Petersen, Martin. 2019. *North Korean Graphic Novels: Seduction of the Innocent?* Abingdon, Oxon., England: Routledge.

Power, John. 2015. “Kim Jong-un Likes Cartoons, So He Remade North Korea’s Favorite One.” *Vice*, October 15. https://www.vice.com/en/article/nn9qnq/kim-jong-un-likes-cartoons-so-he-remade-north-koreas-favorite-one-511.

Ri, Chang-hyeok. 2010a. “Characteristics of Sequential Image Format Illustrations” [Yeosok keurim hyeongshik saphwaui teukjing]. *Joseon Yeseul* 11: 53–54.

Ri, Chang-hyeok. 2010b. “Illustrations of the Sequential Picture Format and Their Types” [Ryeonsok keurim hyeongsikui saphwawa geu ryuhyeong]. *Joseon Yeseul* 7: 62.

Rusling, Matthew. 2006. “Comics Stoke Japan-Korea Tension.” *Asia Times*, April 21.

Sakamoto, Rumi, and Matthew Allen. 2007. “Hating ‘The Korean Wave’ Comic Books: A Sign of New Nationalism in Japan?” *Asia-Pacific Journal* 5, no. 10. https://apjjf.org/-Rumi-SAKAMOTO/2535/article.html.

Sand, Benjamin. 2005. “Cartoons Show North Korea’s Lighter Side.” Voice of America, August 22. https://www.voanews.com/a/a-13-2005-08-22-voa31-66393082/548528.html.

Smith, Hazel. 2015. *North Korea: Markets and Military Rule*. Cambridge: Cambridge University Press.

Stahler, Kevin. 2013. “Comics in North Korea.” Peterson Institute for International Economics, September 29. http://blogs.piie.com/nk/?p=11822.

Strangio, Sebastian. 2011. “‘You Are Followers of the Juche Philosophy, So I Can Put My Trust in You’: Reading North Korea’s Comic Book Propaganda.” *Slate*, June 21. http://www.slate.com/id/2296642/.

Won, Chong-chan. 2012. *North Korean Children’s Literature (Pukhanui adong munhak)*. Paju, South Korea: Cheongdong Koul.

Yun, Y.-b. 2001. *The Yesterday and Today of Animation in North Korea*. Seoul: Seoul International Cartoon and Animation Festival 2001.

Zupančič, Alenka. 2008. *The Odd One In: On Comedy*. Cambridge, MA: MIT Press.

Zwetsloot, Jacco. 2015. “North Korean Comics and Their Visual Language in the Work of Ch’oe Hyŏk.” Master’s thesis, Leiden University.

Chapter 7

Conclusion

By now, it is apparent that the road of Korea's comics art has run into many detours while climbing to the high position it has held in recent years as one of the world's top three animation producers, the "inventor" and leading creator of webcomics, and a heavy exporter of comics and graphic novels, ranking just below US comics, Japanese manga, and Franco-Belgian *bande dessinée.*

Many of Korean manhwa's setbacks have been common among most countries—economic ups and downs, government oppression, and competition from new media forms. More unique to Korea, and by extension to its comics art, were long periods of estrangement from the outside world, decades of foreign occupation, two long wars on its own soil, and a politically motivated split of the country. During these and other times of crisis, for the most part, Korean cartoonists did not flee their country, but stayed put—some sought ingenious ways to cope; others kept a "wait-and-see" attitude.

Comics Art in Korea has aimed to capture the highlights along the winding road of Korean comics art, pausing occasionally to contextualize them within the country's history. I undertook this task by focusing on six topics-cum-questions: (1) threads that run throughout the comics history; (2) sociopolitical-economic factors that may have changed the trajectory of Korean comics art; (3) relations between the Korean governments and comics art; (4) useful dimensions that Korean comics artists have brought to the industry and profession; (5) outside factors that may have played a role in the creation and nourishment of Korean comics art; and (6) the professional standing of Korean comics art.

A theme that runs through the more than a century of Korean comics art is that of survival. Initially, this entailed the subjugation of the Japanese occupation, which for a few decades prescribed what cartoons could and could not do—a bit lenient at first, but increasingly more controlled in the direction of supporting and propagandizing for Japan's militarist ambitions. At other times, Korean cartoonists had to survive an uncaring and unappreciative public, nonsupportive editors, decades of dictatorships, economic downturns, and strong corporate ownership and editorial interference.

Alongside the survival challenges has been the ability of Korean cartoonists to cope—whether by salvaging used cels and fashioning their own equipment, as pioneer animators had to do in the 1960s; enduring imprisonment and torture, as political cartoonist Kim Song-hwan experienced under President Park Chung-hee; layering cartoons with hidden meanings during the dictatorships; forging one of the world's largest animation industries by doing other countries' production work and benefiting from the resultant transfer of skills; or creating new venues to keep comics art alive, such as manhwa magazines, specially designed books of reprints, and webtoons.

The sociopolitical-economic factor that changed the trajectory of Korean comics art most significantly was the country's "economic miracle." It raised Korea to a status where the country and its cultural products were no longer ignored or dismissed but now held center stage. Later embedded in the "economic miracle" was *hallyu* or the Korean Wave, a sociocultural phenomenon that added large doses of pride, international fame, and self-esteem to the Korean collective character. Particularly, South Korea metamorphosed into a trendsetter culture on the heels of *hallyu*.

That South Korea is the world's most highly wired country certainly changed the course of comics art, from print to online manhwa and then to webtoons, receivable on "smart" phones that can be viewed at any time and any place. This has had a profound effect worldwide, changing the way comics are read. Korean society's traditional separation of men and women also had an impact on comics, divided as they were between those for boys and those for girls. For years, the secondary roles of women were reflected in comics authorship (even girls' manhwa were created by men), but this has changed to the extent that a large portion of the pool of comics creators is made up of women.

Other sociocultural traits that have appeared in South Korea are too recent to project their potential impact, for example the tendency toward a "solo society" and the *sampo* generation of young people who are willing to give up relationships, marriage, and children.

The relationship between the Korean government and cartoons, comics, and animation has usually been viewed as sour, which it has been at times—especially during the Japanese occupation, wartime, and the dictatorships of Syngman Rhee, Park Chung-hee, and Chun Doo-hwan. Viewing potential relationships with officialdom as restrictive, regulatory, and faciliatory, South Korean comics art has experienced all three in somewhat equal proportions. This is unusual in that many governments do not facilitate comics and the media that carry them. The South Korean government has and still does. In fact, it does so in plentiful quantities—through large amounts of funding, tax and other benefits, sponsorship of comics, cartoon, and animation centers in Seoul and Bucheon, funding of SICAF and other festivals, building and maintenance of top-of-the-line museums, and generally honoring the profession.

Korean comics art has the distinction of being situated in three government ministries—the Ministry of Culture, Sports, and Tourism, the Ministry of Energy and Resources, and the Ministry of Telecommunications—all of which have some regulatory powers, such as to oversee the professions; represent character content (mostly licensing) through KOCCA; enact quota systems; and handle ethical issues. For years, a government ethics committee existed to detect and censor Japanese manga, which ironically were already banned along with other Japanese cultural products. The regulatory role of government has not been misused, as far as is known.

South Korea's, and certainly North Korea's, restrictive powers have been used with great force against comics art—South Korea during dictatorial regimes, North Korea as state policy. In both countries, cartoonists abide (sometimes unknowingly or subconsciously) by a "guided cartooning" principle, whereby artists are steered by editors, or guide themselves, away from sensitive topics or toward subjects favorable to the government.

Another topic given considerable attention in these pages is the contribution made to the overall comics scene by Korean cartoonists. For a country that existed under political subjugation (foreign and domestic) and economic deprivation for the first eighty years of its comics art history (about 1910–1990), South Korea has added much to the enhancement of comics. Foremost is the already mentioned webtoon. Others are the further development of the factory/rental shop system; the exemplary battles against piracy and the manga invasion; the unique vertical, four-panel political cartoon; a successful program to use manhwa for educational purposes with the *haksup* genre; the creation or support of rather new genres such as *yori*; and the wide opening of the field to women, something that does not exist in many parts of the world.

Outside factors played a role in the history of Korean comics art but not in a direct manner as occurred in a few other Asian countries. For example, China produced its first pictorial magazine, *Ying Huan Pictorial*, in 1877, edited by a Britisher, and its first cartoon/humor periodicals, *China Punch*, started by a British journalist, and *Puck; or, The Shanghai Charivari*, in 1867 and 1871, respectively, both emulating British and American magazines; much of the earliest cartooning in Japan (after *kibyoshi* and the art of Hokusai) emanated from Britisher Charles Wirgman's *Japan Punch* (1862) and Frenchman Georges Bigot's *Tôbaé* (1887); and nineteenth-century India was dotted with an abundance of humor/cartoon magazines, most of which carried *Punch* in their names.

Korea was different. The history to date has not revealed any named westerner as an influence, nor any Western cartoon/humor magazine. Of course, the outsiders who seriously affected Korean manhwa were the Japanese, through their more than four-decades-long colonial occupation followed by their more than fifty-year illegal inundation of the country with manga and anime. Certainly, the offshore animation production brought in workmanship skills and advanced technology to Korea's advantage.

As enunciated at various times in these pages, Korean comics art stands firm and relatively much advanced professionally, largely because of government encouragement and support. All branches of comics art are built around a super-infrastructure of associations and agencies under three ministries of government, which can handle any conceivable issue. Many universities (some say too many) have degree programs in comics and animation, though some of the latter concentrate mainly on technical skills rather than principles of animation such as scriptwriting, timing, and movement. Having visited major cartoon and comics museums worldwide (e.g., in Canada, the United States, Cuba, England, Poland, Slovakia, Iran, China, Japan, Thailand, and Switzerland), I can attest that none compares with the multistory, ultramodern Seoul Cartoon Museum.

Concerning North Korea, one can conclude that its comics art took a different road from that of its southern neighbor: first, because its publishers and studios are not privately owned; second, because its purpose is to support and promote the family dynasty of leaders and the country's juche philosophy; third, because its outside influences early on were from the Soviet Union; and fourth, because of its content, made up to a large degree of stories about spies, wartime patriots, revolutionary heroes, and deprivations said to have been suffered by South Koreans.

Appendix I

Interviews Conducted by John A. Lent

Ahn, Hyun-dong. President, Daiwon Animation. Seoul, July 6, 1992.

Ahn, Hyun-dong. President, Daiwon Animation. Seoul, July 2, 1994.

Cha, Ae-ock. Member, Cartoon Division. Korean Publications Ethics Commission. Seoul, July 2, 1994.

Chang, C.-m. Manager, import, export, and foreign affairs. Motion Picture Promotion Corporation of Korea. Seoul, October 12, 1982.

Cho, Joo-chung. Magazine cartoonist. Seoul, July 3, 1992.

Cho, Kwan-je. Head of center. Bucheon Cartoon Information Center. Bucheon, August 16, 2003.

Choi, Kyu-seok. Graphic novelist. Bucheon, August 11, 2018.

Choi, Peter M. President, Hahn Shin Corporation. Seoul, August 15, 1995.

Choi, Suk-tae. Cartoon critic and curator, Art Center Gallery. Seoul, July 3, 1994.

Chung, Woon-kyung. Political cartoonist, *JoongAng Ilbo*. Character: "Walsun." Seoul, July 7, 1992.

Gendry-Kim, Keum suk. Graphic novelist. Seoul, August 8, 2018.

Han, Chang-wan. Lecturer/reviewer. Seoul, August 15, 1995.

Hong, Sunny. Marketing director and CEO, Universal Contents. Seoul, August 14, 2003.

Hwang, Kyung-tae. Head, Daiwon Publishing Company. Seoul, July 2, 1994.

Im, Kwon-taek. Film director, Tae Hung Films Company. Seoul, August 15, 1995.

Jo, Woon-hak. Master cartoonist and head, JWH Publications. Seoul, August 14, 1995.

Jun, Chang-rok. Executive director, Seoul Movie Company. Seoul, August 14, 1995.

Jung, Joon-young. Cartoon columnist. Seoul, July 3, 1994.

Jung, Wook. Pioneer animator. Seoul, August 14, 1995.

Kim, Byung-heon. Manager, Domestic Support Section 2. Korean Film Commission. Seoul, August 15, 2003.

Kim, Byung-joon. President, Jigyungsa Ltd. Publishing. Seoul, July 7, 1994.

Kim, Chong. Proprietor, Kachei Rental Shop. Seoul, July 2, 1994.

Kim, Hyo-sik. Director, Jigyungsa Ltd. Publishing. Seoul, July 7, 1994.

Kim, Jae-jung. Director, Seoul Animation Center. Seoul, August 15, 2003.

Kim, Mun-hwan. Editor in chief, *Weekly IQ Jump*, *Monthly IQ Jump*. Seoul, July 7, 1994.

Kim, Nak-ho. Researcher, Center for Intercultural Studies of Comics. Chungkang College of Cultural Industries. Seoul, August 17, 2003.

Kim, Pan-kook. Political cartoonist, *Kyunghyang Shinmun*. Character: "Changgaeguli." Seoul, July 2, 1992.

Kim, Seok-ki. President, Hanho Heung-Up. Seoul, August 13, 1995.

Kim, Song-hwan. Political cartoonist, *Chosun Ilbo*. Character: "Gobau." Seoul, July 4, 1992.

Kim, Soo-bak. Graphic novelist. Seoul, August 6, 2018.

Kim, Sung-hee. Graphic novelist. Seoul, August 6, 2018.

Kim, Tayk. President, LUK Studio. Seoul, August 16, 1995.

Lee, Eunice. Assistant, Daiwon Animation. Seoul, July 6, 1992.

Lee, Hee-jae. Manhwa creator, graphic novelist. Seoul, August 19, 2018.

Lee, Jin-keun. President, Motion Picture Promotion Corporation. Seoul, October 12, 1982.

Lee, Won-bok. Researcher, educator. Seoul, July 2, 1992.

Lim, Bum. Critic and fine arts reporter, *Hankyoreh Shinmun*. Seoul, July 8, 1994.

Lim, Cheong-san. Cartoon professor, Kongju National Junior College. Seoul, July 5, 1994.

Park, In-ha. Chair, Center for Intercultural Studies of Comics. Chungkang College of Cultural Industries. Seoul, August 17, 2003.

Park, Jae-dong. Political cartoonist, *Hankyoreh Shinmun*. Columns: "Hankyoreh Canvas" and "Cartoon Story." Seoul, July 7, 1992.

Park, Jae-dong. Political cartoonist, *Hankyoreh Shinmun*. Seoul, July 3, 5, 1994.

Park, Jae-dong. Political cartoonist, *Hankyoreh Shinmun*. Seoul, August 15, 2003.

Park, Jae-dong. Cartoonist, animator. Seoul, August 10, 2018.

Park, Kun-woong. Graphic novelist. Seoul, August 9, 2018.

Park, Se-hyung. Chief, Department of Illustration and Computer Graphics. Kongju National Junior College. Seoul, August 12, 1995.

Park, Se-hyung. Director, SICAF. Seoul, August 14, 2003.

Park, Su-dong. Cartoonist. Character: "Goindol." Seoul, July 7, 1992.

Roh, Byung-sung. Assistant professor of book publishing, Dae Jun Junior College. Seoul, July 2, 6, 1994.

Seon, Jeong-u. Researcher. Seoul, August 17, 2003.

Shin, Dong-hun. Pioneer animator. Seoul, August 13, 15, 1995.

Shin, Dong-hun. Pioneer animator. Seoul, August 17, 2003.

Shin, Nelson. Animation pioneer; founder and president, AKOM Studio. Seoul, August 16, 1995.

Shin, Nelson. Animation pioneer; founder and president, AKOM Studio. Seoul, August 14, 2003.

Song, Dae-ho. Bucheon Cartoon Information Center. Bucheon, August 16, 2003.

Yi, Won-soo. Cartoonist, *Seoul Shinmun*. Seoul, July 6, 1994.

Yoon, Yong-ok. Political cartoonist, *Seoul Shinmun*. Character: "Kkaturi." Seoul, July 3, 1992.

Yu, Hyun-mok. Film director. Seoul, October 7, 1982.

Comic Champ

Appendix II

South Korean Contemporary Comics Magazines

Started in 1991. Biweekly, published by Daiwon. Originally named *Boy Champ* until the 2000s. Series licensed in United States by Tokyopop. Includes a line of twenty-two manga series from *Shōnen* manga magazines. *Comic Champ* stories are listed here sequentially; the others (*Issue, Super Champ, Wink*) alphabetically.

Series in *Comic Champ*

TITLE	CREATOR	YEARS
Eojjeonji . . . Jeonyeok (어쩐지 . . . 저녁, literally "Somehow . . . in the Evening")	Lee Myung-jin (이명진)	1993–1994
Taepungui Gonggyeoksu (태풍의 공격수, literally "Possible Attack of Typhoon")	Lee Yong-tak (이용탁)	1993–1995
Ragnarök (라그나로크)	Lee Myung-jin (이명진)	1995–hiatus
No No Boy (노노 보이)	Jeon Se-hun (전세훈)	1994–1996
Sasinjeon	Art: Pu Reu-moe (푸르뫼); story: Kang Tae-jun (강태준)	1995–1998
Good Morning! Teacher (굿모닝! 티처)	Seo Yeong-ung (서영웅)	1996–1999
Fight Ball (파이트볼)	Park Chul-ho (박철호)	1996–2000
8×8	Seong Jong-hwa (성종화)	1997–1997
Mister Bu (미스터 부)	Jeon Sang-yeong (전상영)	1997–1997
Geomppangmaen (검빵맨, literally "The Very Sword")	Choe Mi-reu (최미르)	1997–1999
Rebirth (리버스 [REBIRTH], literally "Rebirth [REBIRTH]")	Lee Kang-woo	1998–present
Magic Academy Zeus (매직 아카데미 제우스)	Son Hui-jun (손희준)	1998–1998
Yoho!! (야호!!)	Ryu Byeong-min (류병민)	1998–1999
Geomjeong Gomusin (검정 고무신, literally "Black Rubber Shoes")	Art: Doremi (도래미); story: Lee U-yeong (이우영)	1998–2006
Gangho, Paedogi (강호패도기, 江湖覇道記, literally "Veteran Black Pottery")	Choe Mi-reu (최미르)	1998–present
Samgukjanggunjeon (삼국장군전, literally "Before the Three Generals of the Bureau Armies")	Park Su-yeong (박수영)	1998–present
Madojeongi Albion (마도전기 알비온, literally "Defiant Flag in the Rain")	Seong Gyeong-jae (성경재)	1999–1999
Jungle Bell (정글벨)	Lee Ik-seon (이익선)	1999–1999

TITLE	CREATOR	YEARS
Raven (레이븐)	Seo Yeong-ung (서영웅)	1999–2001
Shooting (슈팅)	Jeon Se-hun (전세훈)	1999–2002
Jjang (짱, literally "Boss")	Lim Jae-won (임재원)	1999–present
Yongyeori (용열이, literally "Ten")	Lee Jae-seok (이재석)	2000–2000
Dangsineun Eneonsaege Maja Bon Jeogi Itnayo (당신은 천사에게 맞아 본 적이 있나요, literally "You've Seen the Angel Right There")	Yun Seok (윤석)	2000–2000
Dummy Run (더미런 *Deomireon*)	Bae Seong-hwan (배성환)	2000–2001
Mirimbanjeom Suhoyeoljeon (미림반점 수호열전, literally "Mirin Fierce Guardian Spot")	Lee Hyeon-seok (이현석)	2000–2001
Mutjima Gajok (묻지마 가족, literally "Don't Ask the Family")	Art: Lee Tak (이탁); story: Yeom Jeong-hun (염정훈)	2000–2001
Sallyetap (살례탑)	Noh Mi-yeong (노미영)	2000–2003
Blazin' Barrels (웨스턴 샷건 *Weysu Syasgan*, literally "Western Shotgun")	Park Min-seo (박민서)	2000-present
King of Hell (마제 *Majeh*, literally "Evil Sacrifice")	Art: Ran In-soo (나인수); story: Kim Jae-hwan (김재환)	2001–2016
Baccus (박카스)	Art: Park Jin-seok (박진석); story: Han Hui-jin (한희진)	2001–2001
Peulleosi! (플러시!, literally "Flush!")	Lee Gi-heun (이기훈)	2001–2001
She's Scorer (쉬콜러 *Swikolleo*)	Mun Seong-gi (문성기)	2001–2001
Alien Hunter (에어리언 헌터)	Kim Deok-jin (김덕진)	2001–2002
Bultaneun Orikkwon Bu (불타는 오리꿘 부, literally "Minor Burns")	Mun Hui-seok (문희석)	2001–2002
Gutseeora! Magach-A (굳세어라! 마가크-A, literally "Fighting! Magach-A")	Jeong Dong-su (정동수)	2001–2002
Haebaragi Kkocminam (해바라기 꽃미남, literally "Handsome Sunflower")	Kim Yong-hoe (김용회)	2001–2002
Hong Gil-dong Neo² (홍길동 Neo² *Hong Gil-dong Neosu Squara*, literally "East Path Neo²")	Kim Je-hyeon (김제현)	2001–2002
Wild Teacher (와일드 티처)	Jung Ki-chul (정기철)	2001–2002
Gadirok (가디록)	Hwang Jeong-ho (황정호)	2001–2003
PhD: Phantasy Degree (Korean: 마스터스쿨 올림프스, literally "Master School Olympus")	Son Hui-jun (손희준)	2001–present
Song Chang Ho Jushin (손창호 Jushin, literally "Hand Window Jushin")	Lee Tae-ho (이태호)	2002–2002
America America (아메리카 아메리카)	Art: Jang Sung (장성); story: Son Chang-ho (손창호)	2002–2003
Sarib Yeongung Hagwon Cheon (Ten) (사립영웅학원 천[天], literally "Private School of [Ten] Thousand Heroes")*	Son Byeong-jun (손병준)	2002–2003
Recast (comics) (리캐스트)	Kye Seung-hui (계승희)	2003–2004
A. I. Hunter (에이아이헌터)	Jung Soo-chul (정수철)	2004–2004
Adrenalin (아드레날린)	Lee Jung-hwa (이정화)	2004–2004
Gouneyoseogui Romance (그녀석의 로망, literally "The Kid's Romance")	Son Byeong-jun (손병준)	2004–2005
Pineapple (파인애플)	Ahn Kwang-hyun (안광현)	2004–2005

* The title uses the Japanese character 天 (*ten*).

TITLE	CREATOR	YEARS
Sweety (스위티)	Art: Park Jae-sung (박재성); story: Kim Ju-ri (김주리)	2004–2005
Casting (캐스팅)	Art: Kitt (킷트); story: Park Sang-yong (박상용)	2004–2006
Live (라이브 [LIVE] *Raibu*, literally "Live")	Hwang Jeong-ho (황정호)	2004–2006
Suhoji EX (수호지 EX, literally "Protection EX")	Art: R. S.; story: Kwon Su-yeong (권수영)	2005–2005
G School (G 스쿨)	Art: Kim Byeong-chul (김병철); story: Son Hang-cho (손창호)	2005–present
Chronicles of the Cursed Sword (파검기 *PaGumKi*, literally "Wave Sword")	Art: Yeo Beop-ryong (여법룡); story: Park Hui-jin (박희진)	2006–present
Yeongung Seogi—Solita ui Baram (영웅서기—솔티아의 바람, literally "Heroic Era—Wind of Solita")	Yun Won-shik (윤원식)	2006–2006
Pascal (파스칼)	Art: Lee Jin-u (이진우); story: Kye Seung-hui (계승희)	2006–2006
Battle of Decker (배틀데커)	Son Tae-gyu (손태규)	2006–2007
Injak (인작, literally "Is Work")	Art: Lee Jae-heon (이재헌); story: Hong Ki-u (홍기우)	2007–present
Surado (수라도, literally "Possibility")	Art: Kim Jeong-uk (김정욱); story: Choe Bo-ha (최보하)	2008–present
Tyr Jeongi (티르전기, literally "Tyr Chronicles")	Art: Ra In-soo (나인수); story: Son Chang-ho (손창호)	2008–present
Avatar (아바타르)	Art: Lee Hye-yeong (이혜영)	2009–present

Issue

Started in 1995. Monthly. Published by Daiwon. Individual titles collected into volumes and published under the *Issue Comics* imprint.

TITLE	CREATOR	YEARS
Antikwin Sseupageol (안티퀸 쓰파걸)	Jeon Su-hyeon (전수현)	2007–2008
Aron's Absurd Armada (아론의 무적함대 *Aronui Mujeokhamdae*)	Kim Mi-seon (김미선)	2008–present
Banzi's Dream Bubbling (반지꿈은 방울방울, *Banjikkumeun Bangulbangul*)	Jong-i (종이)	2008–2008
Dear Diary (디어 다이어리)	Yun Lee-hyeon (윤이현)	2006–2007
BL Girl's Diary (동인백서 *Donginbaekseo*)	Art: Jang So-yeong (장소영); story: Park Jim-i (박진아)	2008–2009
Gakko no Ojikan (학교에 가자 *Hakgyoe Gaja*)	Mimi Tajima	2004–2009
Gakuen Prince (학원왕자 *Hagwonwangja*)	Jun Yuzuki	2007–present
Ghost Gate (귀문 [鬼門], *Gwimun*)	Yeondu (연두)	2007–2008
Heaven Like You (하늘과 날다 *Haneulgwa Nalda*)	Kang Hye-jin (강혜진)	2007–2009
Love at One Sight! (한눈에 반하다 *Hannune Banhada*)	Lee Si-yeong (이시영)	2006–present
Perfect Place for Me (이곳은 나의 네잎클로버 *Igoseun Naui Neipkeullobeo*)	Park Mi-suk (박미숙)	2008–present

TITLE	CREATOR	YEARS
Boarding House in Wonderland (이상한 나라의 하숙집 *Isanghan Naraui Hasukjip*)	Ha Seong-hyeon (하성현)	2006–2007
Koucha Ōji no Himegimi (애장판 홍차왕자 *AeJangpan Hongchawangja*)	Nanpei Yamada	2008–present
Welcome to Utopia (무릉도원으로 오세요 *Mureungdowoneuro Oseyo*)	Choe Su-jeong (최수정)	2008–present
My Guardian Chick, Pi (안녕, Pi *Annyoung, Pi*)	Shin Yu-ha (신유하)	2007–2009
Nabi the Prototype (나비, *Nabi*)	Kim Yoon-joo (김연주)	2005–present
One Fine Day (나나이랑 그루's One Fine Day, *Nanairang Geuru's One Fine Day*)	Sirial (시리얼)	2007–2008
Liar Town (라이어 타운)	Lee Ju-ryeong (이주령)	2007–2008
Nocturne (녹턴)	Park Eun-ah (박은아)	2008–present
Office Girl J (오피스 걸 J)	Cider (사이다)	2008–2009
Papillon Hana to Chō (빠삐용 *Ppappiyon*)	Miwa Ueda	2007–present
My Bloody School Life (피바다 학원기 *Pibada Hagwongi*)	Art: Eun-hui (은희); story: Park Yeon-ah (박연아)	2006–2007
Princess (프린세스)	Han Seung-won (한승원)	1999–present
Promise (프라미스)	Lee Eun-young (이은영)	2005–present
Rolling (롤링)	Cha Kyung-hee (신지상)	2004–2006
Ruby Doll (루비돌)	Choi Kyung-ah (최경아)	2006–2008
Saint Marie	Yang Yoo-jin (양여진)	2002–2005
Saver (세이버)	Lee Eun-young (이은영)	2002–present
Shanimuni Go (저스트 고고! *Just Go Go!*)	Marimo Ragawa	1999–present
Spam Mail Hunter (SM 헌터 *SM Heonteo*)	You Na (유나)	2005–present
Sprout (스프라우트 *Seupeurauetu*)	Atsuko Nanba	2006–present
The Serection Record (The 세렉숀 음반사 *The Sareksyon Eumbansa*)	Yun Rin (윤린)	2004–2005
Time between Dog and Wolf (개와 늑대의 시간 *Gaewa Neukdaeui Sigan*)	You Na (유나)	2007–2007

Super Champ

Started in 2006. Monthly. Published by Daiwon. Only online. Individual series were later collected into volumes and published in hard copy.

TITLE	CREATOR	YEARS
Devil Kings Basara (브레이브10 *Brave 10*)	Kairi Shimotsuki	2008–present
Kamisama Kazoku (신족가족 *Sinjok Gajok*)	Art: TaPari; story: Yoshikazu Kuwashima	2006–present
Karma (카르마)	Jo Jun-hui (조준희)	2007–present
Nephilim (네피림존 *Nepirimjon*)	Ryu Kum-chel	2007–present
New Kumiho (신구미호 *Sin Guimho*)	Han Hyeon-dong (한현동)	2002–present
North Aria (노녀의 아리아 *Nonyeokui Aria*)	Art: Kang Ji-min (강지민); story: Kang Gyeong-mi (강경미)	2008–present

TITLE	CREATOR	YEARS
Paradise Murdered (극락도 살인사건 *Geukrakdo Sarinsageon*)	Kim Sun-chul (김순철)	2007–present
Raiders (레이더스)	Park Jin-jun (박진준)	2007–present
Taimashin (퇴마침 아카무시마살기 *Toemachim Akamusimasalgi*)	Art: Shin Yong-gwan (신용관); story: Hideyuki Kikuchi	2008–present
Tenshi no Frypan (천사의 프라이팬 *Cheonsa ui Peuraipaen*)	Etsushi Ogawa	2007–present
Vampire Bund (뱀파이어 번드 *Baempaieo Beondeu*)	Tamaki Nozomu	2007–present
Witch Hunter (위치헌터)	Cho Jung-man (조정만)	2006–present
Zatch Bell (금색의 갓슈!! *Geumsaegui Gatsyu!!*)	Makoto Raiku	2005–present

Wink

Started in 1993. Monthly. Published by Seoul Media Group (Seoul Munhwasa). Moved to digital format in 2012. Magazine series available through monthly online subscription.

TITLE	CREATOR	YEARS
Absolute Witch (절대마녀 *Jeoldae Manyeo*)	Kim Tae-yoon (김태연)	2006–2010
Angel Shop (엔젤 샵)	Hwang Sook-ji (황숙지)	2003–2004
Antique Romance (소녀화첩 *Son Yeohwa Cheob*)	Kim Mi-jung (김미정)	2006–2008
Bride of the Water God (하백의 신부 *Habaek-eui Shinbu*)	Yun Mi-kyung (윤미경)	2006–present
Book Club (독서클럽 *Dogseokeulleob*)	Cho Ju-hee (조주희)	2006–2008
Chronicles of Choon Eng (춘앵전 *Choon Eng Jeon*)	Jun Jin-suk (전진석)	2008–2012
Cool Hot (쿨핫)	Yoo Shi-jin	1997
DIY Girl (디아이와이걸)	Lee Eun (이은)	2008–2010
DoDoRi (도도리)	Lee Eun (이은)	2011–present
Dokebi Bride (도깨비 신부 *Chun-aengjeondokkaebi Shinbu*)	Marley (말리)	2002–2009
Don't Cry Boreum (어화둥둥 내보르미 *Eohwadungdungnae Boreumi*)	Lee Yun-hee (이윤희)	2010–present
DVD	Chon Kye-young (천계영)	2003–2006
Fever	Park Hee-jung (박희정)	2003–2007
Girl in Heels (하이힐을 신은 소녀 *Haihil-eul Sin-eun Sonyeo*)	Chon Kye-young (천계영)	2007–2010
God Is Love (하나님, 연애하다 *Hananim, Yeonaehada*)	Park Hui-hyeol (박희열)	2011–present
The Royal Palace: Goong (궁 *Goong*)	Park So-hee (박소희)	2002–2012
H_2O	Hwang Sook-ji (황숙지)	2005–2007
Hello, I'm Simba (안녕하세요? 세바스찬입니다 *Annyeonghaseyo? Seba-seuchan-ibnida*)	Shim Hye-jin (심혜진)	1997
Hissing (히싱)	Kang Eun-young (강은영)	2004–2006
Kitchen (키친)	Cho Ju-hee (조주희)	2009–2011
Let Dai (렛 다이)	Won Soo-yeon (원수연)	1995–2005
Lingerie (란제리)	Seo Yoon-young (서윤영)	2008–2010

TITLE	CREATOR	YEARS
Mana (마나)	Lee Vin (이빈)	2006–2008
Mani (마니)	Yoo Shi-jin	1995
Martin & John (마틴 & 존)	Park Hee-jung (박희정)	2006–2011
My Mother and the Game-Room Guest (게임방 손님과 어머니 *Geimbang Son-nimgwa Eomeoni*)	Kisun (기선)	2005–2007
Nexio (넥시오)	Jun Euho (신유오)	2012–present
A Night of a Thousand Dreams (천일야화 *Cheon-il-yahwa*)	Han Seung-hee (한승희)	2004–2008
Oh, My Romantic Kumiho (Oh, My 로맨틱 구미호)	Kim Yeong-mi (김영미)	2010–present
Outside (아웃사이드)	Yoo Shi-jin	1994
Railroad (레일로드)	Yun Mi-kyung (윤미경)	2004–2006
Red Moon (레드문)	Hwang Mi-na (황미나)	1993
Romantic Dream (헬프 미 베이베 *Helpeu Mi Beibe*)	Lee Han-ah (이한아)	2008
Royal Love (로열 러브)	Lee Han-ah (이한아)	2009
Running through the City in the Sunset (잿빛 도시숲을 달리다 *Jaesbich Dosisup-eul Dallida*)	Uhm Jung-hyun (엄정현)	2005–2006
Safe Again Today (오늘도 무사히! *Oneuldo Musahi!*)	Art: Park Suhlah (박설아); story: Yuu Jin-soo (유진수)	2006–2007
Shipwrecked (탐나는 도다 *Tamnaneun Doda*)	Jung Hye-na (정혜나)	2007-present
Sugar Addiction (설탕 중독 *Seoltang Jungdog*)	Maria (マリア) and Gong Gu-gu (공구구)	2005–2007
The Summit (절정 *Jeoljeong*)	Lee Young-lee (이영희)	2005–hiatus
Shiwhamong (시화몽)	Lee Jong-eun (이종은)	2002–hiatus
Youthful Animator Sihwa (생기발랄 시화관 *Saeng-giballal Sihwagwan*)	Park Tae-yoon (김태연)	2011–present

Appendix III

Filmography of South Korean Animated Films, 1967–2023

Compiled and edited by Suh HaeLim

This list includes feature-length animated films, described as at least sixty minutes or slightly under, and for the most part designed for and/or released in theaters.

The 1960s

- A Story of Hong Gil-dong / 홍길동 [Hong Gil-dong jeon] (1967, Shin Dong-hun)
- Hopi and Chadol Bawi / 호피와 차돌바위 [Hopewa Chadolbawi] (1967, Shin Dong-hun)
- Heungbu and Nolbu / 흥부와 놀부 [Heungbuwa Nolbu] (1967, Gang Tae-ung)
- The Golden Iron Man / 황금철인 [Hwanggeum choel-in] (1968, Park Yeong-il)
- Sun Wukong / 손오공 [Son Ogong] (1968, Park Yeong-il)
- Treasure Island / 보물섬 [Bomulseon] (1968, Park Yeong-il)
- General Hong Gil-dong / 홍길동 장군 [Honggildong Janggun] (1969, Yong Yu-su)

The 1970s

- Prince Hodong and Princess Nakrang / 호동왕자와 낙랑공주 [Hodongwangjawa nangnanggongju] (1970, Yong Yu-su)
- Lightning Atom/ 번개아텀 [Beongae ateom] (1971, Yong Yu-su)
- The Return of Lightning Atom / 돌아온 번개아톰 [Doraon beongae ateom] (1971, Yong Yu-su)
- The War of Great Monsters / 괴수대전쟁 [Geosudae-jeongjaeng] (1972, Yong Yu-su)
- Iron Man 007 / 철인 007 [Cheorin 007] (1976, Han Ha-rim)
- Robot Taekwon V / 로보트 태권브이 [Roboteu Taekwon V] (1976, Kim Cheong-gi)
- Robot Taekwon V: Space Mission / 로보트 태권 V: 제 2 탄 우주작전 [Roboteu Taekwon V: Je yi tan ujujakjeon] (1976, Kim Cheong-gi)
- Electronic Man 337 / 전자인간 337 [Jeonjaingan 337] (1977, Im Jeong-gyu)

- Robot Taekwon V 3 / 로보트 태권 V: 제 3탄 수중특공대 [Roboteu Taekwon V: Je sam tan sujungteukgongdae] (1977, Kim Cheong-gi)
- Taegwondongja Maruchi Arachi / 태권동자 마루치 아라치 [Taegwondongja mauchi arachi] (1977, Im Jeong-gyu)
- Kongjwi and Patjwi / 콩쥐 팥쥐 [Kongjwi Patjwi] (1977, Gang Tae-ung)

- 77 Group's Secret / 77단의 비밀 [77 Danui bimil] (1978, Park Seung-cheol)
- Robot Taekwon V vs. Gold Wing / 로보트 태권 V 대 황금날개의 대결 [Roboteu taegwonbeuiwa hwanggeum-nalgaeui daegyeol] (1978, Kim Cheong-gi)
- Gold Wing 1, 2, 3 / 무적의 용사 V 황금날개 1, 2, 3 [Mujeongui yongsa V hwanggeumnalgae 1, 2, 3] (1978, Kim Cheong-gi)
- Fly, the Princess of Wonder / 날아라 원더공주 [Narara wondeogongju] (1978, Kim Cheong-gi)
- General Ttori 3 / 똘이장군 제3땅굴편 [Ttolijang-gun je3ddang-gulpyeon] (1979, Kim Cheong-gi)
- Majingga-X / 달려라 마징가 X [Dallyeora majingga X] (1978, Kim Hyeon-yong)
- Star Wars with Sun Wukong / 손오공과 별들의 전쟁 [Sonogonggwa byeoldeurui jeonjang] (1979, Han Heon-myeong)
- The Black Knight of the Universe / 우주 흑기사 [Uju heukgisa] (1979, Park Jong-hui)
- Starland Trio / 별나라 삼총사 [Byeollara samchongsa] (1979, Park Jong-hui)
- Black Star and Golden Bat / 검은별과 황금박쥐 [Keomeunbyoelgwa hwanggeumbakjwi] (1979, Han Heon-myeong)
- General Ttori / 간첩잡는 똘이 장군 [Gancheopjamneun Ttorijanggun] (1979, Kim Cheong-gi)
- Let's Fly! Space Turtle Battle Ship / 날아라! 우주전함 거북선 [Narara ujujeonham geobukseon] (1979, Song Jeong-yul)
- Animal Treasure Island / 동물 보물섬 [Dongmul bomulseom] (1979, Song Jeong-hun)
- Galaxy Fleet Jiguho / 은하함대 지구호 [Eunhahamdae jiguho] (1979, Song Jeong-hun)
- Romance of the Three Kingdoms / 삼국지 [Samgukji] (1979, Kim Cheong-gi)
- White Eagle, The Taegeuk Boy / 태극소년 흰 독수리 [Taegeuksonyeon huin doksuri] (1979, Kim Tae-jong)
- Goblin's Hat / 도깨비 감투 [Dokkaebi gamtu] (1979, Park Seung-cheol)
- Spaceboy Cache / 우주소년 캐시 [Ujusonyeon kaesi] (1979, Park Seung-cheol)

The 1980s

- Fifteen Children Space Adventure / 15소년 우주 표류기 [15 Sonyeon uju pyoryugi] (1980, Jeong Su-yong)
- Boy 007: Galaxy Special Force / 소년 007 은하특공대 [Sonycon 007 eunhateukgongdae] (1980, Im Jeong-gyu, Seo Kyeong-jung)
- Time Machine 001 / 삼총사 타임머신 001 [Samchongsa taimmeosin 001] (1980, Im Jeong-gyu)
- Five Eagle Brothers / 독수리 5형제 [Doksuri oheyongje] (1980, Lee Gyu-hong)
- Cheeky Little Angels / 개구장이 천사들 [Gaegujangi cheonsadeul] (1980, Bae Yeong-rang)
- Space Captain Cyclopean / 우주대장 애꾸눈 [Ujudaejang aekkunun] (1980, Kim Dae-jung)
- Romance of the Three Kingdoms—Breaking Through the Five Gulfs / 삼국지—관우 오관돌파편 (1980)
- Robot King / 로보트킹 [Roboteuking] (1981, Bae Yeong-rang)
- Ddoli, the Royal Secret Inspector / 꼬마어사 똘이 [Kko-maeosa ttori] (1980, Kim Cheong-gi)
- Dinosaur One Million Year Ddoli / 공룡 100만년 똘이 [Gongnyong baengmannyeon ttori] (1981, Kim Cheong-gi)
- Phoenix Robot Phoenix King / 불사조 로보트 피닉스 킹 [Bulsajo roboteu pinkikseu-King] (1981, Jeong Su-yong)
- The Sun of Saving the Country, Great Admiral Lee Sun-shin / 구국의 태양 성웅 이순신 [Gugugui taeyang seongung isunsin] (1981, Kim Seong-chil)
- 30,000 Leagues in Search of Mother / 엄마 찾아 삼천리 [Eomma chaja sammalli] (1981, Jeong Su-yong)

- Boy 007: Underground Empire / 소년 007: 지하제국 [Sonyeon 007: Jihajeguk] (1981, Jeong Su-yong, Kim Cheol-jong)
- Super Majingga 3 / 슈퍼마징가 3 [Syupeo Majingga 3] (1982, Park Seung-cheol)
- Super Titan 15 / 슈퍼 타이탄 15 [Syupeo Taitan 15] (1983, Park Seung-cheol)
- Future Boy Kunta Bermuda 5,000 Years / 미래소년 쿤타 버뮤다 5000년 [Miraesonyeon kunta Beomyuda 5,000 nyeon] (1982, Park Seol-hyeong)
- Super Trio / 슈퍼 삼총사 [Syupeo samchongsa] (1982, Song Jeong-yul)
- Adventure of Haedol / 해돌이 대모험 [Haedori daemoheom] (1982, Kim Hyeon-dong) / (1983)
- Super Metal Robot Solar 1, 2, 3 / 초합금 로보트 쏠라 원투쓰리 [Chohapgeum roboteu ssolla won, tu, deuri] (1982, Kim Cheong-gi)
- Planet Robot Thunder A / 혹성 로보트 썬더 A [Hokseong roboteu Sseondeo A] (1982, Jo Hang-ri, Kim Cheong-gi)
- Super Taekwon V / 슈퍼 태권V [Syupeo Taegwon V] (1982, Kim Cheong-gi)
- King Black Dragon and Young Boy Biho / 흑룡왕과 비호동자 [Heungnyongwanggwa Bihodongja] (1982, Han Heon-myeong)
- David & Goliath / 다윗과 골리앗 [Dawitgwa Golliat] (1983, Kim Cheong-gi)
- Undersea Expedition Marin X / 해저탐험대 마린엑스 [Haejeotamheomdae Marin X] (1983, Kim Hyeon-dong)
- The Arm of Gold / 황금의 팔 [Hwanggeum-ui pal] (1983, Choi Jin-wu)
- Space Champion Hong Gil-dong / 우주전사 홍길동 [Wujujeongsa Honggildong] (1983, Kim Hyeon-dong, Jeong Su-yong)
- Iron Man Trio / 철인 삼총사 [Cheol-in samchongsa] (1983, Park Seung-cheol)
- Dokgotak, Throw It Toward the Sun / 독고탁 태양을 향해 던져라 [Dokgotak, taeyangul hyanghae deonjyeora] (1983, Park Si-ok)
- Golden Pencil and Alien Boy / 황금연필과 개구장이 외계소년 [Hwanggeumnyeonpilgwa gaegujangi oegyesonyeon] (1983, Lee Yeong-su)
- Super Express Majingga 7 / 슈퍼특급 마징가 7 [Syupeo teukgeup majingga 7] (1983, Lee Gyu-hong)
- Galactic Legent Tera / 은하전설 테라 [Eunhajeonseol tera] (1983, Hong Sang-man)
- Alien Prince on a UFO / UFO를 타고 온 외계인 왕자 [UFO reul tagoon oegyein wangja] (1983, Jo Min-cheol)
- Super Titan 15 / 슈퍼 타이탄 15 [Syupeo taitan 15] (1983, Park Seung-cheol)
- Computer Nuclear Battleship Explosion Mission / 컴퓨터 핵전함 폭파대작전 [Computer haekjeonham pokpadaejakjeon] (1983, Jeong Su-yong)
- 84 Taekwon V / 84태권V [84 Taekwon V] (1984, Kim Cheong-gi)
- Little Rascals, Great Inventors / 꾸러기 발명왕 [Ggureogi balmyeongwang] (1984, Kim Cheong-gi)
- My Name is Dokgo Tak / 내 이름은 독고탁 [Nae ireumeun dokgotak] (1984, Hong Sang-man)
- Space Gundam V / 스페이스 간담 브이 [Speis geondam V] (1983, Kim Cheong-gi)
- Dokgo Tak 3—The Mound Taken Back / 독고탁 3—다시 찾은 마운드 [Dokgotak 3 dasi chajeun maundeu] (1985, Mun Deok-seong)
- Robot King Sun Shark / 로보트왕 썬샤크 [Roboteuwang sseon shakeu] (1985, Park Seung-cheol)
- Video Ranger 007 / 비디오 레인저 007 [Vidio reinjeo 007] (1985, Lee Seong-u)
- An Invincible Iron Man Rambot / 무적철인 람보트 [Mujeokcheorin lamboteu] (1985, Mun Deok-seong)
- The Robotic Corps and Meka 3 / 로보트 군단과 메카 3 [Roboteugundangwa Meka 3] (1985, Kim Cheong-gi)
- Ddoli and Zeta Robot / 똘이와 제타 로보트 [Ttoriwa Jeta Roboteu] (1985, Kim Cheong-gi)
- Space Transformer / 마이크로 특공대 다이야 트론 5 [Maikeuro teukgongdae daiya teuron 5] (1985, An Bong-sik, Jeong Su-yong)
- Bridal Mask / 각시탈 [Gaksital] (1986, Lee Hak-bin)
- Goblin's Magic Wand / 도깨비 방망이 [Dokkaebi bang-mang-i] (1986, Park Seung-cheol)
- Hwarang V Trio / 화랑 V 삼총사 [Wharangbeui samchongsa] (1987, Kim Yeong-han)

- A Drifter Kkachi / 떠돌이 까치 [Tteodori Kkachi] (1987, Jo Bong-nam)
- Future Star in Arisubyeon / 아리수변의 꿈나무 [Arisubyeongui kkumnamu] (1987, Kim Ju-in)

The 1990s

- Lotti's Adventure / 로티의 모험 [Lotiui moheom] (1990, Song Jeong-yul)
- Shimg Cheong / 효녀 심청 [Hyonyeo simcheong] (1992, Min Gyeong-ho)
- Jang Dok-dae / 장독대 [Jangdokdae] (1991, Bae Yeong-rang)
- Street Fighter / 거리의 무법자 [Georiui mubeopja] (1993, Shim Sang-il)
- Special Gag Force Robot Twins / 개그특공대 로봇 트윈스 [Gaegeu teukgongdae] (1993, Kim Cheong-gi)
- Super Kid / 슈퍼 차일드 [Syupeochaildeu] (1994, Eom Yi-yong)
- Blue Seagull / 블루시걸 [Beullusigeol] (1994, O Jung-il)
- The Red Hawk / 붉은 매 [Bulgeum mae] (1995, Shim Sang-il, Hwang Jeong-ryeol)
- The Hungry Best 5 / 헝그리 베스트 5 [Heonggeuri beseuteu 5] (1995, Lee Gyu-hong)
- Hong Gil-dong / 돌아온 영웅 홍길동 [Dolaon yeongung Hong Gil-dong] (1995, Shin Dong-hun)
- Armageddon / 아마게돈 [Armagaedon] (1996, Lee Hyeon-sae)
- Fighting Taekwon V / 파이팅 태권 V [Paiting taegwon V] (1996, Kim Cheong-gi)
- A Little Dinosaur Dooly—The Adventure of Ice Planet / 아기공룡 둘리—얼음별 대모험 [Agigongnyong duli—eoreumbyeol daemoheom] (1996, Kim Su-jung, Im Gyeong-won)
- Empress Esther / 왕후 에스더 [Wanghu Eseudeo] (1996, Kim Cheong-gi)
- Lim Kkeok-jeong, Korean Robin Hood / 의적 임꺽정 [Uijeok Im Kkeok-jeong] (1997, Kim Cheong-gi)
- Admiral's Diary / 난중일기 [Nanjung ilgi], (1997, Byeon Gang-mun)
- Rian / 전사 라이안 [Jeonsa Laian] (1997, Im Beyong-seok)
- The King of Kings, Jesus / 예수 [Yesu] (1997, Jeong Su-yong, Yang Seung-hoon, Mun Deok-seong)
- Nudlnude / 누들누드 [Nudeul nudeu] (1998, Park Byeong-san, O Seung-jin, Jeon Chang-rok, Baek Dong-ryeol, Yi Seung-ik, Choi Gi-seok, Jang Hyo-sik)
- Grandma and Her Ghost Friends / 또또와 유령친구들 [Ttottowa yulyeong chingudeul] (1998, Lee Chun-man)
- Black Trio / 블랙 트리오 [Beullaeg teulio] (1998, Park Geon)
- The Steel Force / 철인 사천왕 [Cheolin sacheonwang] (1998, Kim Hyeok, Kim Gang-deok, Kim Hyeon-seok, Park Seung-hyeon)
- 69 Pink Riders / 69 핑크라이더스 [Yukgu pinkeu raideos] (1999, Kim Il-bae)
- Nudlnude 2 / 누들누드 2 [Nudeul nudeu tu] (1999, Park Byeong-san, Jang Hyo-sik, Lasko, Choi Yun-seok, Lee Dal, Jeon Chang-rok, O Seung-jin, Choi Eung-sik, Kenny Hwang, Jeong Mun-gyu, Kim Yeong-ho, released as VHS)
- Goindol / 고인돌 [Goindol] (1999, Lee Chun-baek, released as VHS)
- The Love Story of Juliet / 성춘향뎐 [Seong chunhyang-dyeon] (1999, Andy Kim)

The 2000s

- Happy Day / 해피데이 [Haepidei] (2000, Park Jong-hi)
- Turtle Haero / 별주부 해로 [Byeoljubu Haero] (2001, Kim Deok-ho)
- Run = Dim / 런딤 '네서스의 반란' [Reondim neseoseuui ballan] (2001, Han Ok-rye)
- Ark / 아크 [Arrk] (2001, Hwang Hyo-seon)
- The King / 더 킹 [Deo King] (2001, Lee Chung-yeong)
- My Beautiful Girl, Mari / 마리이야기 [Mari iyagi] (2002, Lee Seong-gang)
- Hurogutz / 후로거츠 [Hurogeotseu] (2002, Je Ji-hye, Yun Ju-yeong, Kim Hye-a)
- Ghost Station / 고스트 스테이션 [Goseuteu steisyeon] (2003, Lee Yeong-un)
- Hammerboy / 망치 [Mangchi] (2003, An Tae-geun)
- Elysium / 엘리시움 [Elisium] (2003, Kwon Jae-wung)

- Oseam / 오세암 [Oseam] (2003, Seong Baek-yeop, Yang Jin-cheol)
- Doggy Poo / 강아지 똥 [Gangajittong] (2003, Kwon Oh-seong, 35-minute TV clay animation)
- Wonderful Days / 원더플 데이즈 [Wondeopeul daeijeu] (2003, Kim Mun-saeng)
- Blade of the Phantom Master / 신 암행어사 [Sin amhaengeosa] (2003, An Tae-geun, Shimura Joji, Kobayasi Takasi, et al.)
- Flying Pig—Pirate Mateo / 날으는 돼지 해적 마테오 [Nareuneun dwaeji—Haejeok Mateo] (2004, Song Geun-sik)
- Pi Story (Shark Bait) / 파이스토리 [Pai seutori] (2006, Lee Gyeong-ho, John Fox, Howard E. Baker)
- Empress Chung / 왕후 심청 [Wanghu Sim-cheong] (2005, Nelson Shin [Shin Neung-kyun])
- If You Were Me: Anima Vision / 별별이야기 [Byeol-byeol iyagi] (2005, Yu Jin-hi, Kwon Oh-seong, Kim Jun, Park Yun-kyeong, Lee Jin-seok, Jang Hyeong-yun, Jeong Yeon-ju, Lee Ae-rim, Lee Seong-gang, Park Jae-dong)
- Aachi & Ssipak / 아치와 씨팍 [Achiwa ssipak] (2006, Jo Beom-jin)
- Colin the Invincible / 무적의 콜린 [Mujeokui Kollin] (2006, Jo Jeong-hye, Kim Dae-jung)
- Adrenalin Drive / 아드레날린 드라이브 [Adrenalin deuraibeu] (2006, Maeng Ju-gong)
- Mug Trave / 빼꼼의 머그잔 여행 [Bbaeggomui meo-geujan yeohaeng] (2007, Im A-ron)
- The Toy Warrior Jinu / 장난감 전사 지누 [Jangnangam jeonsa Jinu] (2007, Im Kyeong-won)
- Yobi, The Five-Tailed Fox / 천년여우 여우비 [Cheon-nyeon yeowoo yeowoobi] (2007, Lee Seong-gang)
- If You Were Me 2: Anima Vision / 별별이야기 2—여섯 빛깔 무지개 [Byeolbyeol iyagi tu—yeoseotbitkkal mujigae], (2007, An Dong-hui, Ryu Jeong-wu, Hong Deok-pyo, Lee Hong-su, Lee Hong-min, Kwon Mi-jeong, Jeong Min-yeong, Park Yong-je)
- The Story of Mr. Sorry / 제불찰씨 이야기 [Jebulchalssi yiyagi] (2008, Kwak In-geun, Kim Il-hyeon, Ryu Ji-na, Lee Eun-mi, Lee Hye-yeong)
- Indie-Anibox: Selma's Protein Coffee / 인디 애니박스: 셀마의 단백질 커피 [Indiaenibakseu: Selmaui danbaekjil keopi] (2008, Kim Un-gi, Yeun Sang-ho, Jang Hyeong-yun)
- Giga Tribe / 기가 트라이브 [Giga traibeu] (2008, Han Mun-jung)
- Life Is Cool / 그녀는 예뻤다 [Geunyeoneun yeppeotda] (2008, Choi Ik-hwan)
- Audition / 오디션 [Odisyeon] (2008, Min Gyeong-ho)
- What Is Not Romance? / 로망은 없다 [Romangeun eopda] (2009, Hong Eun-ji, Park Jae-ok, Su Kyeong)

The 2010s

- Magic Hanja—Stopping the Resurrection of the Great Devil / 마법천자문—대마왕의 부활을 막아라 [Mabeop-cheonjamun—daemawangui buhwareul magara] (2010, Yun Yeong-gi)
- House / 집 [Jip] (2010, Park Mi-seon, Park Eun-yeong, Ban Ju-yeong, Lee Hyeon-jin, Lee Jae-ho)
- The King of Pigs / 돼지의 왕 [Dwaejiui wang] (2010, Yeun Sang-ho)
- Green Days / 소중한 날의 꿈 [Sojunghan nalui ggum] (2011, Han Hye-jin, Ahn Jae-hun)
- Action Boy 2084 / 홍길동 2084 [Honggildong igongpalsa] (2011, Lee Jeong-in)
- Leafie, a Hen into the Wild / 마당을 나온 암탉 [Madangeul naon amtak] (2011, Oh Seong-yun)
- Bolts & Blip / 볼츠와 블립: 달나라리그의 전투 3D [Bol-cheuwa beullip: dallara rigeuui jeontu 3D] (2012, Peter William Lepeniotis)
- Dino Time / 다이노 타임 [Daino taim] (2012, Choi Yun-seok, John Kafka)
- Pororo, the Racing Adventure / 뽀로로 극장판 슈퍼썰매 대모험 [Bbororo syupeosseolmae daemoheom] (2012, Park Yeong-gyun)
- The Three Musketeers / 삼총사: 용감한 친구들 [Sam-chongsa: yonggamhan chingudeul] (2012, Lee Jong-kwan)
- The Outback / 코알라 키드: 영웅의 탄생 [Koalla kideu: yeongungui tansaeng] (2012, Lee Gyeong-ho)
- Padak / 파다파닥 [Padakpadak] (2012, Lee Dae-hui)

- T-pang Rescue: 극장판 뛰뛰빵빵 구조대 미션: 둥둥이를 구하라 [Ttwittwippangppang gujodae] (2013, Bang Hyeong-woo)
- The Fake / 사이비 [Saibi] (2013, Yeun Sang-ho)
- The Satellite Girl and Milk Cow / 우리별 일호와 얼룩소 [Uribyeol ilhowa eolrookso] (2013, Jang Hyeong-yun)
- Change Zoororing / 쥬로링 동물탐정 극장판 [Juroring dongmeultamjeong geukjangpan] (2013, Choi Jeong-guk)
- On the White Planet / 창백한 얼굴들 [Changbaekhan eolguldeul] (2014, Heo Beom-uk)
- Jungle Shuffle / 정글히어로 [Jungle Hero] (2014, Park Tae-dong)
- Ghost Messenger / 고스트 메신저 [Goseuteu maesingeo] (2014, Gu Bong-hoe)
- Timing / 타이밍 [Taiming] (2014, Min Gyeong-ho, Park Dae-yeol)
- The Nut Job / 넛잡: 땅콩 도둑들 [Neot jab: Ttangkong dodukdeul] (2014, Peter William Lepeniotis)
- Shining Modern History / 발광하는 현대사 [Balgwanghaneun hyeondaesa] (2014, Hong Deok-pyo)
- The Road Called Life / 메밀꽃, 운수 좋은 날, 그리고 봄봄 [Memilkkot, unsujoeunnal, geurigo bombom] (2014, Ahn Jae-hun, Han Hye-jin)
- The Squishes / 스퀴시랜드 [Skwisi raendeu] (2014, Kim Tae-ik, Han Kyeong-su)
- The Strong and Mini Special Forces: The Attack of a New Villain / 최강전사 미니특공대: 새로운 악당의 습격 [Choegangjeonsa miniteukgongdae: saeroun akdangui seupgyeok] (2014, Lee Yeong-jun)
- You Are So Yummy—Happy to Be with You / 고녀석 맛나겠다 2: 함께라서 행복해 [Gonyeoseok matnagetda teu: hamkkeraseo haengbokhae] (2014, Choi Gyeong-seok, Nonaka Kazmi)
- Clearer than You Think / 생각보다 맑은 [Saenggakboda malgeun] (2014, Han Ji-won)
- Crimson Whale / 화산고래 [Hwasangorae] (2014, Park Hye-mi)
- Bling / 슈퍼 프렌즈 [Syupeo peurenjeu] (2015, Lee Gyeong-ho, Lee Won-jae)
- Hello, Jeonwoochi! The Robot Armageddon / 안녕, 전우치! 도술로봇 대결전 [Annyeong, jeonuchi! Dosullobotdaegyeoljeon] (2015, Kim Dae-chang)
- Super Race Enzy / 슈퍼레이서 엔지 [Syupeo reiseo enji] (2015, Heo Seon)
- Seoul Station / 서울역 [Seoul yeok] (2015, Yeun Sang-ho)
- Pororo 3: Cyber Space Adventure / 뽀로로 극장판 컴퓨터 왕국 대모험 [Ppororo geukjangpan keompyuteo wang guk daemoheom] (2015, Park Yeong-gyun)
- Kuru Kuru and Friends: The Rainbow Tree Forest / 꾸루꾸루와 친구들: 무지개 나무의 비밀 [Kkurukkuruwa chingudeul: mujigae namuui bimil] (2015, Mun Je-dae)
- Mini Force: New Heroes Rise / 최강전사 미니특공대: 영웅의 탄생 [Choegangjeonsa miniteukgongdae: yeongungui tansaeng] (2015, Lee Yeong-jun)
- Tyon and Taekwon Heroes / 타이온과 태권히어로즈 [Taiongwa taegwonhieorojeu] (2015, Heo Uk-jun)
- My Dogs, Jinjin and Akida / 우리집 멍멍이 진진과 아키다 [Urijip meongmeongi jijigwa akida] (2016, Jo Jong-deok)
- Talking Kungfu Battle / 만담강호 [Mandamgangho] (2015, O In-yong)
- Love Slate / 러브슬레이트 [Reobeu seuleiteu] (2016, Kim Hyeon-su)
- Hello Jadoo / 극장판 안녕 자두야 [Geukjangpan annyeong jaduya] (2016, Son Seok-wu)
- Kai / 카이: 거울 호수의 전설 [Kai: geoul hosuui jeonseol] (2016, Lee Seong-gang)
- Lost in the Moonlight / 달빛 궁궐 [Dalbit gunggwol] (2016, Kim Hyeon-ju)
- Power Battle Watchcar: Blazing Race / 파워배틀 와치카 미니카 배틀리그: 불꽃의 질주 [Pawobaeteul wachika minika baeteul ligeu: bulkkochui jilju] (2016, Lee Yeong-jun)
- Frankie and Friends, the Movie: The Tree of Life / 극장판 프랭키와 친구들: 생명의 나무 [Geukjangpan peuraengkiwa chingudeul: saengmyeongui namu] (2016, Park Jeong-o)
- Vroom! Vroom! Vroomiz / 부릉! 부릉! 브루미즈: 스피더의 모험일기 [Buleung! Buleung! Beulumijeu: Seupideoui moheomilgi] (2016, Lee Yeong-jun)

- The Senior Class / 졸업반 [Joleobban] (2016, Hong Deok-pyo)
- Ulsik, the Clumsy Boy / 을식이는 재수 없어 [Eulsigineun jaesu eopseo] (2016, Kim Dae-chang, Hwang Cheol)
- Pororo, Dinosaur Island Adventure / 뽀로로 극장판 공룡섬 대모험 [Ppororo geukjangpan gongnyongseom daemoheom] (2017, Kim Hyeon-ho, Yun Je-wan)
- Tobot Movie: Attack of Robot Force / 극장판 또봇: 로봇군단의 습격 [Geukjangpan ttobot: Robotgundanui seupgyeok] (2017, Lee Dal, Go Dong-u)
- Drago Village / 드래곤 빌리지: 화이트니스 타운을 구하라 [Deuraegon bilrigi: hwaiteuniseu tauneul guhara] (2017, Min Gyeong-ho)
- Super White Bear: Spy Adventures / 슈퍼 빼꼼: 스파이 대작전 [Syupeo bbaekkom: Seupai daejakjeon] (2017, Im A-ron)
- I'll Just Live in Bando / 반도에 살어리랏다 [Bandoe saleoriratda] (2017, Lee Yong-seon)
- Power Battle Watch-Car: Return of Watch Mast / 파워배틀 와치카: 와치가면의 역습 [Pawobaeteul wachika: Wachigamyeonui yeokseub] (2017, Lee Yeong-jun, Kim Rae-gyeong)
- The Shaman Sorceress / 무녀도 [Muneyodo] (2018, Ahn Jae-hun)
- Super Moon / 슈퍼문 [Syupeomun] (2018, Hong Dae-yeong)
- Hello Carbot, the Movie: The Secret of Omphalos Island / 극장판 헬로카봇: 옴파로스 섬의 비밀 [Geukjangpan hello kabot: omparoseu seomui bimil] (2018, Choi Sin-gyu, Kim Jin-cheol)
- Dinosaur Mecard: Tinysaur Island / 극장판 공룡메카드: 타이니소어의 섬 [Geukjangpan gongnyongmekadeu: tainisoeoui seom] (2018, Choi Sin-gyu, Yu Jae-un)
- Dino King 3D: Journey to Fire Mountain / 점박이 한반도의 공룡 2: 새로운 낙원 [Jeombagi hanbandoui gongnyong 2: Saeroun nagwon] (2018, Han Sang-ho)
- Zak Strom / 해적왕 작스톰 [Haejeokwang jakseutom] (2018, Philippe Guyenne)
- Ireesha, the Daughter of Elf-King / 마왕의 딸 이리샤 [Mawangui Ttal Irisha] (2018, Jang Hyeong-yun)
- Bad Boss / 나쁜 상사 [Nappeun sangsa] (2018, Baek Jong-seok)
- Running Man: Pululu's Counterattack / 런닝맨: 풀룰루의 역습 [Reonningmaen: Pullulluui yeokseup] (2018, Yun Jun-sang)
- Mini Force X / 미니특공대 X [Miniteukgongdae X] (2018, Lee Yeong-jun)
- Hello Carbot, the Movie: The Cretaceous Period / 극장판 헬로카봇: 백악기 시대 [Geukjangpan hellokabot: baekakgi sidae] (2018, Choi Sin-gyu, Kim Jin-cheol)
- The Haunted House: The Secret of the Cave / 신비아파트: 금빛 도깨비와 비밀의 동굴 [Sinbiapateu: geumbit dokkaebiwa bimirui donggul] (2018, Kim Byeong-gap)
- Underdog / 언더독 [Eondeodok] (2018, Oh Seong-yun, Lee Chun-baek)
- Astro Gardener / 별의 정원 [Byeolui jeongwon] (2019, Won Jong-sik)
- Pinkfong Cinema Concert / 핑크퐁 시네마 콘서트: 우주 대탐험 [Pingkeupong sinema konseoteu: ujudaetamheom] (2019, Byeon Hui-seon, Jeong Jin-yeong, Kim Na-yun)
- Princess Aya / 프린세스 아야 [Peurinseseu aya] (2019, Lee Seong-gang)
- Red Shoes / 레드슈즈 [Raedeu syujeu] (2019, Hong Seong-ho, Jang Mu-hyeon, Eom Yeong-sik)
- Miniforce: Deeno, the King of Dinosaurs / 극장판 미니특공대: 공룡왕 디노 [Geukjangpan miniteukgongdae: gongnyuongwang dino] (2019, Lee Yeong-jun)
- The Haunted House: The Sky Goblin vs. Jormungandr / 극장판 신비아파트: 하늘도깨비 대 요르문간드 [Sinbiapateu geukjangpan haneuldokkaebi dae yoreumungandeu] (2019, Byeon Yeong-gyu)
- Banzi's Secret Diary / 극장판 반지의 비밀일기 [Geukjangpan Banjiui bimil ilgi] (2019, Han Seung-u)
- Hello Carbot, the Movie: Save the Moon / 극장판 헬로카봇: 달나라를 구해줘! [Geukjangpan hellokabot: dalnarareul guhaejwo!] (2019, Choi Sin-gyu, Kim Jin-cheol)
- A Big City Adventure / 극장판 엄마 까투리: 도시로 간 까투리 가족 [Geukjangpan eomma kkaturi: dosiro gan kkaturi gajok] (2019, Jeong Gil-hun)

- The Return of Dark Assault / 극장판 타오르지마 버스터—블랙어썰트의 귀환 [Geukjangpan taoreujima beoseuteo—beullaegeosseolteuui gwihwan] (2019, Jo Yeong-kwang)

The 2020s

- Spookiz, the Movie / 스푸키즈 극장판 비밀과외 [Seupukiseu geukjangpan bimilgwaoe] (2020, Kim Bong-ho)
- Running Man: Revengers / 러닝맨: 리벤져스 [Reonningmaen: ribenjeos] (2020, Eom Yeong-sik)
- Magical: Make the Princess Laugh! / 매지컬 공주를 웃겨라 [Maejikeol: gongjureul utgyeora] (2020, Jeong Yun-cheol)
- Climbing / 클라이밍 [Keullaiming] (2020, Kim Hye-mi)
- The Precious Memory of Gogo Brothers / 추억의 검정고무신 [Chueogui geomjeonggomusin] (2020, Song Jeong-yul, Song Yo-han)
- Bungaeman: The Beginning / 번개맨: 더 비기닝 [Beongaemaen: deo biginning] (2020, Han Sang-ho, Park Seong-bae)
- Mini-Force / 극장판 미니특공대: 햄버거 괴물의 습격 [Geukjangpan miniteukgongdae: haembeogeogoemurui seupgyeok] (2020, Lee Yeong-jun)
- Beauty Water / 기기괴괴—성형수 [Gigigeogeo seonghyeongsu] (2020, Jo Kyeong-hun)
- Stress Zero / 스트레스 제로 [Seuteureseu jero] (2020, Lee Dae-hui)
- Kongsuni the Movie: Toy World Adventure / 극장판 콩순이: 장난감나라 대모험 [Geukjangpan kongsuni: jangnangamnara daemoheom] (2020, Lee Seon-myung)
- The Haunted House: The Dimensional Goblin and the Seven Worlds / 신비아파트 극장판 차원도깨비와 7개의 세계 [Sinbiapateu geukjangpan chawondokkaebiwa chilgaeui segye] (2022, Byeon Yeong-gyu)
- Chun Tae-Il / 태일이 [Taeiri] (2021, Hong Jun-pyo)
- Madonna—Sang / 마돈나—상 [Madonna—Sang] (2021, Lee Ji-hoon)
- Hello Jadoo: The Secret of Jeju Island / 극장판 안녕 자두야: 제주도의 비밀 [Jeukjangpan annyeongjaduya jejudoui bimil] (2021, Son Seok-wu)
- Robotcar Poli: A Transportation Safety Course / 로보카 폴리: 안전교실 교통편 [Robokapolli anjeongyosil gyotongpyeon] (2022, Eom Jun-yeong)
- Hello Carbot, the Movie: The Secret of the Suspicious Magic Troupe / 극장판 헬로카봇: 수상한 마술단의 비밀 [Geukjangpan hellokabot: susanghan masuldanui bimil] (2022, Choi Sin-gyu, Lee Seul-gi, Jeong Seung-won)
- Pinkfong Sing-Along Movie 2: Wonderstar Concert / 핑크퐁 시네마 콘서트 2: 원더스타 콘서트 대작전 [Pinkeupong sinema konseoteu 2: wondeoseuta konseoteu daejakjeon] (2022, Kim Su-kyeong)
- Mother Land / 엄마의 땅: 그리샤와 숲의 주인 [Eommaui ttang: Geurisyawa supui juin] (2022, Park Jae-beom)
- Black Rubber Shoes, the Movie: My Happy Home / 극장판 검정고무신: 즐기운 니의 집 [Geukjangpan geomjeonggomusin: jeulgeoun naui jip] (2022, Song Jeong-yul, Song Yo-han)
- Carrie & Superkola / 캐리와 슈퍼콜라 [Kaeriwa syupeokolla] (2022, Oh Seong-yun, Lee Chun-baek)
- Jurassic Cops: Adventure of the Age of the Dinosaurs / 쥬라기캅스 극장판: 공룡시대 대모험 [Jyuragikapseu geukjangpan: gongjyongsidae daemoheon] (2022, Kim Ho-rak)
- Colossus: Child of the Wind / 거신: 바람의 아이 [Geosin: baramui ai] (2022, Shin Chang-seop)
- Super Wings: Maximum Speed / 극장판 슈퍼윙스: 맥시멈 스피드 [Geukjangpan syupeowingseu: maeksimeom seupideu] (2023, Jeong Gil-hun)
- The Summer / 그 여름 [Geu yeoreum] (2023, Han Ji-won)

Appendix IV

List of Early Essay Cartoons (Webcomics), October–December 2004

Compiled by Kwon Jae-woong

This list is likely the earliest and most complete compilation of essay toons, or what were to be called webtoons. It is the result of a survey that Kwon Jae-woong conducted from October to December 2004 and was published in the *International Journal of Comic Art* 7, no. 1 (Spring 2005): 320–50. Kwon provided the English name of the essay cartoons, their website addresses, whether they were diary or other type, and their adaptations (spin-offs). (JAL)

Y = Yes, N = No

TITLE	WEBSITES	DIARY TOON	OTHER TOON	SPIN-OFF BUSINESS
2Nagi Project	http://2nagi.com	Y	Y	N
Angelback	http://angelback.org	Y	N	N
AniVirus	www.anivirus.net	Y	N	N
Art Kiki	www.artkiki.com	Y	N	N
Attack	http://attackstyle.com	N	Y	Book
Babman House 4.5	http://babman98.zo.ly	Y	Y	N
Bad Cartoon	www.toonsoo.net	N	Y	Cellular phone download service
Baribari	http://bari2.made.com	Y	Y	N
Bburn's Net	www.bburn.net	N	Y	Book Diary Goods sales
Bebop Mechanics	www.bebop.co.kr	Y	Y	N
Big Eve	http://knnoon.com	Y	N	N
Blackjelly	www.blackjelly.net	Y	N	Book Internet games Internet item sales
Blue Workshop	www.blueworkshop.com	N	Y	Book Newspaper publishing
Booking Day	www.bookingday.com	N	Y	N
Cartoonis	www.cartoonis.com	Y	Y	N
Cat Trio	www.cattrio.com	Y	Y	N

TITLE	WEBSITES	DIARY TOON	OTHER TOON	SPIN-OFF BUSINESS
Choon Master	www.choonmaster.co.kr	N	Y	N
Chung Sul Mo	www.sulmo.com	N	Y	Serial publishing on the web
Club Onion	www.clubonion.com	Y	Y	N
Coolmorning	www.coolmorning.net	N	Y	N
Comix	www.comix.pe.kr	Y	N	N
Cream Toon	www.creamtoon.com	N	Y	Goods sales Serial publishing on the web Book
Dailykoo	www.dailykoo.com	Y	Y	N
Damagoon	www.damagoon.com	Y	N	N
Dandani + Moorni	www.danmoo.com	N	Y	N
DaengGhiJay	http://user.kacl.co.kr/dmsrb	Y	Y	N
Darl	www.jangdal.com	Y	Y	N
Ddebo	www.jangdal.com	N	Y	N
Ddody, Happy Family	www.ddody.net	Y	Y	Book
Ddurinari	www.ddurinari.net	N	Y	N
Dog and Monkey	www.minymin.com	Y	Y	Serial publishing on the web
Dog Trio	www.dogtrio.com	Y	Y	Goods sales Newspaper publishing
Doguli	www.doguli.com	N	Y	N
Dotori Trio	www.dotoritrio.co.kr	Y	Y	Book
Dwing-Gle	http://user.chollian.net/-tearsofwind	Y	Y	N
Eco Toon	www.ecotoon.com	Y	Y	N
Empty Dream	www.emptydream.net	Y	Y	N
Fafamonkey	www.fafamonkey.com	Y	N	N
Finger Kids	www.fingerkids.com	Y	Y	Book Exhibition
Fish Girl	www.fishfantasy.com	Y	Y	N
Garden of Common Sense	www.1p53.com	Y	Y	N
Goguma Toon	http://gogumagoon.com	Y	Y	Book Serial publishing on the web
Gol-chi Story	www.abyo.co.kr	Y	N	N
Googims	www.googims.com	Y	Y	Book Goods sales
Gorita	www.gorita.net	Y	Y	Book Serial publishing on the web
Great Jangun	www.greatjangun.com	Y	N	N
Gumiccho	http://chkoomi.cafe24.com	N	Y	N

TITLE	WEBSITES	DIARY TOON	OTHER TOON	SPIN-OFF BUSINESS
Gyuu	www.gyuu.com	Y	N	N
Happyddung	www.happyddung.com	Y	Y	N
Happy Report	www.behappy.tv	N	Y	N
Happy Tycoon	www.bju.co.kr	N	Y	N
Hardboard Paper Man	www.hardpaper.net	Y	Y	N
Harogi's Home	www.harogi.net	N	Y	N
Haruillust	www.haruillust.com	Y	N	Book
Haru Talk	www.harutalk.com	Y	N	N
Heheheh	www.heheheh.com.ne.kr	Y	Y	N
Hello Onion	www.helloonion.com	Y	N	N
Hoonys	www.hoonys.com	Y	N	N
Hoya Cartoon	www.hoyacartoon.com	N	Y	Book
Hozo	www.hozo.net	N	Y	N
Hwanee's Happy & Joy	www.hwanee.co.kr	Y	Y	N
Hyoni	www.hyoni.com	Y	N	N
Hyun-Ha	www.hyun-ha.com	Y	N	N
Ilmo Story	www.miskinkr.com	N	Y	N
Imugu	www.imugu.com	Y	Y	N
Indigo Blues	www.indigoblues.net	Y	Y	N
It's Hwi	http://itzhwi.ez.ro	Y	N	N
Jeljoa	www.jeljoa.com	Y	Y	Book
Jonny Taro	www.jonnytaro.com	Y	Y	Book
Kaburin's WebToon	www.kaburin.com	N	Y	N
Kkae-mong's House	http://shrekanddonky.hihome.com	Y	Y	N
Kang Do Yong's Cartoon Story	www.kangfull.com	N	Y	Book Newspaper publishing Serial publishing on the web Others
Keun Young	www.nodotone.com	N	Y	N
Kim Pyung	www.kimpyung.com	Y	N	N
Kkomabi	www.kkomabi.co.kr	Y	Y	N
Koal Gun	www.koalgun.pe.kr	Y	Y	Serial publishing on the web
Koorisu's Sky Story	www.koorisu.com	N	Y	N
Kuya's Story	http://jo9jaeng2.com.ne.kr/index.html	N	Y	N
Kwanpal Sensei	www.kwangpal.com	Y	N	N
Lazy Photo	www.lazyphoto.com	Y	Y	Serial publishing on the web
Life Is Good	http://myhome.naver.com/moonheek	Y	N	N

List of Early Essay Cartoons (Webcomics), October–December 2004

TITLE	WEBSITES	DIARY TOON	OTHER TOON	SPIN-OFF BUSINESS
Love Toon	www.lovetoon.net	N	Y	serial publishing on the web Book
Lulu Pet	www.lulupet.net	Y	N	N
Magic Soup	www.magicsoup.co.kr	N	Y	Goods sales Book
Maldac	www.maldac.net	Y	N	N
Manamana	www.mirinea.net	Y	Y	N
Mandu Nara	www.mandugun.net	Y	N	N
Mapi's Attic	www.mapi.co.kr	Y	N	Serial publishing on the web Cellular phone download service
Marineblues	www.marineblues.net	Y	Y	Book Cellular phone download service Goods sales
Maru Zzang's Essay Cartoon	www.maruzzang.net	Y	Y	N
Master Bbang	http://masterbbang.nacom.net	N	Y	N
Mega Shocking Altari	www.altari.net	N	Y	Book
Mihokitty	www.mihokitty.com	N	N	N
Milkaroo	www.milkaroo.com	Y	Y	Goods sales
Min-A	www.min-a.net	Y	Y	N
Mini Bottary	www.minibottary.com	Y	N	N
Mongsil	www.jujupfamily.com	Y	N	N
Mong Toon	www.mongtoon.com	N	Y	Cellular phone download service
Monob Story	www.monob.com	Y	Y	N
Moons Family	www.moonsfamily.net	N	Y	Book
Mr. Don Ttaeng	http://jin.pe.ne.kr	Y	Y	Newspaper publishing
Munge's Cartoon World	www.munge.co.kr	Y	Y	Book Goods sales
Musiga	www.musiga.com	N	Y	Newspaper publishing
My Nightmare	www.crazylov.x-y.net	Y	N	N
Neverland	www.seriousday.com	Y	N	N
Nineweek	www.nineweek.com	Y	Y	Serial publishing on the web
Nul Toon	www.nultoon.com	Y	Y	N
Nurijo	www.nuirijo.com	Y	Y	N
Oowho	www.oowho.com	Y	Y	N
Orange Boy	www.orangeboy.er.ro	Y	Y	N
Over Kwon	www.overkwon.com	N	Y	N
Oz City	www.ozcity.net	Y	Y	N
Pami World	www.pamiworld.com	Y	Y	N

TITLE	WEBSITES	DIARY TOON	OTHER TOON	SPIN-OFF BUSINESS
Panda Dance	www.panda-dance.com	Y	N	Book
Papepopo	www.papepopo.com	N	Y	Book
Pari's Picture Diary	www.pariya.pe.kr	Y	Y	Serial publishing on the web
Pleasant Hotdog Workroom	www.hotdogworks.com	N	Y	Cellular phone download service Serial publishing on the web Newspaper publishing Book
Poker Face	www.poker-face.net	Y	N	N
Porori	http://porori.new21.net	Y	Y	Serial publishing on the web Book
Psymini	www.psymini.net	Y	Y	Goods sales
Puhut	www.puhut.com	Y	N	Book
Queer Toon	www.queertoon.info	N	Y	N
R2apa	www.r2apa.com	N	Y	Book
Radiopeep	www.pockethead.net	Y	Y	N
Rain Light	www.rainlight.net	Y	N	N
Realbox Diary	www.klaatu.co.kr	Y	N	N
SamBakZa	www.sambakza.net	N	Y	Book Serial publishing in a magazine
Simyeon	www.simyeon.net	Y	Y	N
Sketchbook	http://humaneyes.co.kr	N	Y	Newspaper publishing Book
Snowcat	www.snowcat.co.kr	Y	Y	Book
Sodasoo Free Space	www.sodasoo.net	Y	Y	N
Somatoon	www.somatoon.com	Y	Y	N
Soon9	www.soon9.com	N	Y	Book Serial publishing in a magazine
Strong Berry	www.strongberry.com	Y	N	N
Sunny the Single	www.sunnythesingle.com	Y	Y	N
Sun Toon	www.suntoon.net	N	Y	N
Suya World	www.suyaworld.com	Y	Y	Serial publishing on the web
The Kid of a Snowing Day	www.snowyday.pe.kr	N	Y	N
The Story How Narm Is Living	www.narm.co.kr	Y	Y	N
Toon Book	www.toonbook.com	Y	Y	Serial publishing on the web
Toy Bomb	www.toybomb.net	Y	Y	N
Trueye	www.trueye.net	Y	Y	N
TT Pas	www.ttpas.com	N	Y	Book

List of Early Essay Cartoons (Webcomics), October–December 2004

TITLE	WEBSITES	DIARY TOON	OTHER TOON	SPIN-OFF BUSINESS
Ulzima	www.ulzima.net	Y	Y	N
Unenemy Turtle	www.unenemy.com	Y	Y	Newspaper publishing Serial publishing on the web
Yao House	www.yaohouse.net	Y	N	N
Yichanet	www.2cha.net	Y	Y	N
Yomangzin	http://yomangzin.ye.to	Y	Y	N
Yu Ryung Jak Up Sil	www.sisicculung.net	Y	Y	N
Zem	www.zem.co.kr	N	Y	Newspaper publishing
Zeze Book	www.zezebook.com	Y	Y	N

Appendix V

Pertinent Information from the KOCCA Report

The sales volume of the Korean webtoon market in 2019 was 640 billion won (US$577 million), 173.7 billion won or 37.3 percent higher than the previous year. Of that revenue, 69 percent came from paid content, 16.2 percent from content exported overseas, 4.1 percent from publishing, and 4 percent from advertising. The number of new webtoons saw a slight decrease, going from 2,853 in 2018 to 2,767 in 2019.

Over half of the companies surveyed answered that COVID-19 helped boost sales, especially outside of Korea. A total of 60.5 percent of webtoon companies said their local sales increased, and 71.9 percent said their overseas sales also saw a boost. While 37.2 percent of companies said they were looking forward to increased revenue in 2021, 30.2 percent answered that they didn't think revenue would change. A total of 51.2 percent responded that not being able to work on-site was the biggest difficulty they faced due to the pandemic, while 46.5 percent chose not being able to launch overseas.

KOCCA estimated the damage inflicted by the illegal distribution of webtoons online at 318.3 billion won. According to the agency's interviews with people who have experience using illegal sites, most people were aware that they were accessing content illegally but chose to continue because the payments for legitimate sites are "pricy." Many such users were found to use similar illegal sites for other content consumption, such as films and games, and confessed that they will likely continue to do so in the future.

KOCCA and the Ministry of Culture, Sports, and Tourism have been promoting the "webtoon user awareness campaign" since 2018 to eradicate illegal distribution and consumption of webtoons. The ministry has also worked with a special police force to shut down twenty-five illegal webtoon and comics websites, arresting twenty-two offenders.

Webtoon companies identified 3,438 webtoonists in 2019, of whom 1,692 were exclusively signed to certain companies and 1,746 were not. Of the 635 respondents, 60.8 percent were women and 39.2 percent were men; 48 percent of the total were in their thirties. Two-thirds of webtoonists said they were active on webtoon-only platforms such as Lezhin or Kakao Page, and a third said they were active on the portal sites Naver and Daum. Most, or 80.5 percent, said they had not revealed their work on social media, while 19.5 percent answered that they had.

Over half, or 69.9 percent, said they worked on both their drawings and storylines, while 11.8 percent said they only created the story and 18.3 percent only worked on the drawings. Slightly over half of authors, 52.6 percent, answered that they used assistants. Webtoonists worked 5.8 days a week on average, 10.5 hours every day. Their average annual income was 48.4 million won, but only 30.6 percent earned more than 50 million won.

Respondents were asked to choose the three things that were most difficult about their jobs, and the answers were: deteriorating mental and physical health due to overwork, stated by 84.4 percent; lack of time to rest and pressure to meet deadlines, 84.3 percent; and economic hardship, 74 percent.

With authors coming forward about having been either tricked or forced into signing unfair contracts or not signing contracts at all, 50.4 percent of respondents answered that they had experienced such unfairness in contracts.

Only 9.4 percent said they had signed a contract in the standard form provided by the government. Over half of webtoonists answered that COVID-19 did not pose many problems to their working conditions, but 23.1 percent said they saw fewer opportunities for new contracts or work, while 4.7 percent experienced unexplained cancellations of contracts.

Index

About the Author

Professor John A. Lent taught journalism and mass communications from 1960 to 2011, including stints in the Philippines, where he designed and taught the first mass communications courses at De La Salle College, in 1964–1965; in Malaysia, where he founded, organized, and directed the country's first university-level mass communication school at Universiti Sains Malaysia, from 1972 to 1974; at the University of Western Ontario in Canada, as the first Rogers Distinguished Professor; in China, as a visiting professor at four universities; and similarly at Universiti Kebangsaan in Malaysia. He is professor emeritus at Temple University.

Dr. Lent pioneered in the study of development communication, critical media studies, mass communication and popular culture in Asia (since 1964), mass communication and popular culture in the Caribbean (since 1968), and comic art and animation. Many of the eighty-nine books he has authored or coauthored were the first in their respective fields.

In addition to the books he has authored, Professor Lent has written many dozens of chapters or forewords for other volumes, edited four book series (one each with Westview Press and Hampton Press, and two with Palgrave), and compiled many bibliographies, including the world's largest on comic art. He has given lectures in seventy-two countries, founded and chaired six international organizations on comics, popular culture, animation, and Malaysian/Singaporean/Bruneian studies, and founded and edited the *International Journal of Comic Art* (1999–present), *Asian Cinema* (1994–2012), and *Berita* (1975–2001).

He has been rewarded for his service with awards from groups in the United States, Colombia, China, Cyprus, Peru, and Spain, a festschrift, and prizes in his name with the Popular Culture Association, the International Comics Art Forum, and the Malaysia/Singapore/Brunei Studies Group.

Photo courtesy of the author

Printed in the United States
by Baker & Taylor Publisher Services